Atatürk

Atatürk

An Intellectual Biography

M. Şükrü Hanioğlu

PRINCETON UNIVERSITY PRESS
Princeton & Oxford

Published by Princeton University Press, 41 William Street, Princeton,
New Jersey 08540

In the United Kingdom: Princeton University Press, 6 Oxford Street,
Woodstock, Oxfordshire OX20 1TW

press.princeton.edu

Jacket art: President Mustafa Kemal at Dumlupınar (1924). Courtesy of
http://www.tccb.gov.tr/sayfa/ata_ozel/fotograf/, picture #27.

Library of Congress Cataloging-in-Publication Data

Hanioglu, M. Sükrü.
    Atatürk : an intellectual biography / M. Sükrü Hanioglu.
        p.   cm.
    Includes bibliographical references and index.
    ISBN 978-0-691-15109-0
    1. Atatürk, Kemal, 1881–1938.   2. Atatürk, Kemal, 1881–1938—Political
and social views.   3. Atatürk, Kemal, 1881–1938—Knowledge and
learning.   4. Turkey—Politics and government—1918–1960.   5. Turkey—
Intellectual life—20th century.   6. Turkey—Social conditions—20th
century.   7. Social change—Turkey—History—20th century.   I. Title.
    DR592.K4H36 2011
    956.1'024092—dc22
    [B]   2010043767

British Library Cataloging-in-Publication Data is available

This book has been composed in Garamond Pro

Printed on acid-free paper. ∞

Printed in the United States of America

10 9 8 7 6 5 4 3 2

For Sinan

CONTENTS

FIGURES AND TABLES

FIGURES

TABLES

A NOTE ON TRANSLITERATION AND PERSONAL AND PLACE NAMES

Names and titles in Ottoman Turkish are rendered according to modern Turkish usage rather than strict transliteration. (A pronunciation guide is provided herein to help readers who are not acquainted with the Turkish language). Arabic names and titles are normally transliterated according to a slightly simplified system based on that of the *International Journal of Middle East Studies*. However, Arabic names and titles of non-Arab individuals and institutions are not transliterated, but are rendered according to their pronunciation in the relevant vernacular. Thus we have Rashīd Riḍā, but Reza Pahlavi. Likewise, we have Muḥammad ʿAbduh, but Mahathir bin Muhammad.

Muslim Ottomans and Turks did not have family names until the Surname Law of June 21, 1934. This ruling required all citizens of the Turkish Republic to adopt a family name by January 1, 1935. Thus, the names by which individuals are referred to before and after the implementation of this law are different. For instance, the founder of the Turkish Republic is referred to as Mustafa Kemal before November 24, 1934 and Atatürk after this date.

For those geographical names frequently used in English language material, common English forms are preferred. Thus we have Salonica, Monastir, and Damascus, and not Thessaloniki, Bitola, and Dimashq, respectively. For all others, the current names are used to avoid confusion.

TURKISH PRONUNCIATION GUIDE

a—as English "u" in "but"
â—as English "a" in "far"
b—as in English, or pronounced as "p" at the end of a syllable
c—as English "j" in "jam"
ç—as English "ch" in "charm"
d—as in English, or pronounced as "t" at the end of a syllable
ğ—as English "gh" in "through," or pronounced as English "y" in "saying" after front vowels (e, i, ö, ü), or not pronounced after back vowels (a, ı, o, u).
i—as English "i" in "fit"
ı—as English "i" in "dirt"
î—as English "ee" in "feet"
j—as English "s" in "treasury"
ö—as German "ö" in "östlich" or French "eu" in "deux"
ş—as English "sh" in "shine"
u—as English "oo" in "book"
û—as English "u" in "rule"
ü—as German "ü" in "übung" or French "u" in "tu"

ACKNOWLEDGMENTS

I have been assisted by many who deserve thanks in the research and writing of this book. My greatest debt is to Michael A. Cook and Jesse Ferris, who have read various drafts of the manuscript and came forward with a wide range of fruitful remarks and suggestions. I also owe special gratitude to Senem Aslan, Patricia Crone, András P. Hámori, Hasan Bülent Kahraman, Mete Tunçay, Benjamin T. White, and Muhammad Qasim Zaman who read the final draft and offered valuable advice. Likewise, I am indebted to my colleagues Fatmagül Demirel, Hossein Modarressi, and Michael Reynolds for answering numerous inquiries and providing valuable information. I should be most ungracious if I were to omit expressing my appreciation of the generous permission of Taha Akyol to reproduce some of the tables in his book *Ama Hangi Atatürk*, on the founder of the Turkish republic. I likewise wish to thank Heath W. Lowry for sharing with me two photographs that he uncovered among the papers of Clarence K. Streit at the Library of Congress; and İffet Baytaş, Sabit Baytaş, and Halit Eren for their help in obtaining some of the illustrations.

At the Press, two wise, competent, and hands-on editors, Brigitta van Rheinberg and Sara Lerner, did everything within their power to make this book as perfect as possible. Brian P. Bendlin in copyediting went above and beyond the call of duty to render the text stylistically more consistent. In the same way, Dimitri Karetnikov, the illustrations specialist, masterfully prepared the final photographic figures to make the book more attractive. The indexer, Maria denBoer, handled numerous foreign terms with great skill to make the book more accessible.

Finally, I am beholden to my wife Arsev and my son Sinan, since working on yet another book deprived them of much of my time.

MŞH
Princeton, New Jersey
March 14, 2010

Atatürk

Introduction

In 1954, a young shepherd was leading his flock out to pasture in the remote village of Yukarı Gündeş in the eastern Turkish province of Ardahan. As the sun set, a shadow falling on a nearby hill seemed to trace the exact profile of Mustafa Kemal Atatürk, the founder of the modern Turkish Republic. Convinced that he had been vouchsafed a religious experience, the incredulous shepherd reported his encounter to the local authorities, who wasted no time in publicizing this rare natural phenomenon nationwide as a miracle. Local excitement did not die down with the passage of time and, in 1997, it was finally decided to launch on this spot a festival that drew enormous crowds of spectators eager to witness the phenomenon for themselves. When, at the seventh annual festival in "the footsteps and shadow of Atatürk," a shepherd inadvertently interrupted the spectacle at the critical moment by innocently guiding his flock through the silhouette just as it was becoming visible; the crowd reacted with fury. One parliamentary deputy from among the spectators bellowed, "Grazing animals here is highly disrespectful, an act of treason.... Why has Karadağ where the miracle occurred not been placed under state protection?"[1] This somewhat bizarre episode captures the quasi-religious quality of the personality cult that sprang up around Mustafa Kemal Atatürk during his lifetime and has persisted in many

[1] "Ata'nın Silueti Varken Hayvan Otlatmak İhanet," *Hürriyet*, July 1, 2003.

quarters of Turkey to this day. Obviously this was not the only way Turks regarded the founder of the modern Turkish Republic, but an attitude of veneration continues to suffuse most scholarly and popular writing on the subject.

For many years, the scholar who aspired to portray Atatürk as he really was resembled the premodern historian rash enough to attempt a depiction of the historical Jesus. Not surprisingly, the more scholarly and authoritative biographies of Atatürk have been authored by non-Turkish scholars, and even these long after his death. Today the subject can be dealt with more openly in Turkey, but demythologizing Atatürk is still difficult. For instance, many of the sayings attributed to Atatürk have become national maxims, and yet a good number of them are fabrications that were invented to serve particular interests. In recent years, some scholars have taken to exposing these fabrications with a passion reminiscent of Muḥammad ibn Ismāʿīl al-Bukhārī (d. 870), the great medieval critic of spurious traditions and sayings ascribed to the Prophet Muḥammad. Turkish taxi and trucking associations were not particularly pleased to learn that Atatürk never uttered their organizational motto, "The Turkish driver is a man of the noblest feelings." But broader sectors of society were affected by the revelation that the following quotations were apocryphal: "A society that does not respect its elderly is not a [real] society" (carved on the wall of the Social Security headquarters in Ankara); "The future is in the skies" (engraved on plaques in commercial airplanes); or "If an issue is related to the fatherland the rest should be considered trivial" (the motto of an ultrasecular-nationalist movement in Turkey).[2]

Hundreds of books have been written on different aspects of Atatürk's life and work, their titles ranging from *Atatürk and Med-*

---

[2] Sevilay Yükselir, "O Söz Atatürk'e Ait Değil Ama Atatürk'çe Bir Söz!" February 26, 2008; accessed February 27, 2008 at http://www.gazeteport.com.tr/Yazarlar/News/Gp_162225.

ical Students and *Atatürk and Meteorology* to *Atatürk and Eurasia* or even *Atatürk's Love for Children*.[3] Most of these are in the form of eulogies that depict the founder of modern Turkey as a sagelike dispenser of wisdom endowed with omniscience and insight in a variety of fields, or even as a philosopher-king who strove to lay down laws *de omni scibili*. Only a small number are solid monographs. Essayists have used his alleged views to prove almost any point. Thus we have both *Atatürk Was an Anti-Communist* and *The Socialist Movement, Atatürk, and the Constitution;*[4] or *I Looked for Atatürk in the Qur'ān and Found Him* alongside *Atatürk and Science*.[5] Meanwhile, Turkish official history tends to portray Atatürk as a leader from birth, with attempts to present his world through the prism of the person rather than vice versa. In Turkey, for instance, there are still history professors who consider Mustafa Kemal the architect of the 1908 Young Turk Revolution, even though his actual role was marginal.[6] Similarly, for many years Turkish historiography maintained that Mustafa Kemal had warned American Chief of Staff Douglas MacArthur in 1932 about an imminent general war that would destroy the civilized world. On this basis, Turkish scholars have credited Atatürk with having foreseen the Second World War even before the Nazis ascended to power.[7] Recent research, however, has revealed that

[3] Metin Özata, *Atatürk ve Tıbbiyeliler* (İzmir: Umay Yayınları, 2007); Mithat Atabay, *Atatürk ve Meteroloji* (Ankara: DMİ Yayınları, 2002); Anıl Çeçen, *Atatürk ve Avrasya* (Istanbul: Cumhuriyet Kitapları, 1999); Cemil Sönmez, *Atatürk'te Çocuk Sevgisi* (Ankara: Atatürk Araştırma Merkezi, 2004).

[4] Hasan Fahri, *Atatürk Bir Anti-Koministti* (Istanbul: Su Yayınları, 1978); Remzi Çaybaşı, *Sosyalist Akım, Atatürk ve Anayasa* (Istanbul: Batur Matbaası, 1967).

[5] Haydar Seçkin, *Atatürk'ü Kur'anda Aradım ve Buldum* (İzmit: H. Seçkin Yayınları, 1995); Güneş Kazdağlı, *Atatürk ve Bilim* (Istanbul: Beyaz Yayınları, 1998).

[6] Zeki Arıkan, "1908 Jön Türk Devrimi ve Mustafa Kemal," *Cumhuriyet*, September 11, 2008.

[7] See "Dünyanın Siyasî Durumu, 27/29. IX. 1932," in *Atatürk'ün Söylev ve*

Atatürk told MacArthur exactly the opposite. The minutes of the meeting read, "When the possible dangers of war were discussed, His Excellency the Gazi said that the occurrence of a world war in the next ten years was virtually impossible."[8]

Thus, any scholar seeking to grapple with the historical Atatürk must engage primarily in demythologizing, historicizing, and contextualizing through the use of primary source material. This is no easy task. While many relevant documents have been published, both during his lifetime and afterward, only recently has a publishing house attempted to bring together all his accessible writings, speeches, and correspondence. The resulting collection, whose publication began in 1998, has currently reached volume 26, thus covering the years 1903–34.[9] As for his personal notes, Mustafa Kemal, like many other contemporary Ottoman/Turkish officers, scribbled them in a number of notebooks; some of these are in diary form, and range from 1904 to 1933. His adopted daughter, Âfet İnan, produced a sanitized version of one of these diaries extending over six notebooks.[10] An additional thirty-two are located in the Military Archives, the Presidential Archives, and the Anıtkabir Archives in Ankara, and a decision was taken to publish them in twelve volumes. So far nine have been issued, with the latest appearing in 2008.[11] The rich collection of materials pertaining to Atatürk located in the Presidential Archives at Çankaya is off

---

Demeçleri, vol. 3, ed. Nimet Unan (Ankara: Türk İnkılâp Tarihi Enstitüsü Yayınları, 1954), 92–94; and Şevket Süreyya Aydemir, *İkinci Adam*, vol. 2, *1938–1950* (Istanbul: Remzi Yayınları, 1979), 83–87.

[8] Cemil Koçak, "Atatürk Hakkında Bazı Belgeler: Ali Rıza Bey, Anıtkabir, MacArtur ile Mülakat," *Toplumsal Tarih* 10/119 (2003): 25–26.

[9] *Atatürk'ün Bütün Eserleri*, vols. 1–26 (Istanbul: Kaynak Yayınları, 1998–2009).

[10] *M. Kemal Atatürk'ün Karlsbad Hatıraları*, ed. Ayşe Afetinan (Ankara: Türk Tarih Kurumu Yayınları, 1983), 29–61.

[11] *Atatürk'ün Not Defterleri*, vols. 1–9 (Ankara: Genelkurmay ATASE Yayınları, 2004–2008).

limits to bona fide scholars without special permission. Likewise, all hopes for access to his divorced wife's personal papers, which had been classified for twenty-five years after her death in 1975, were dashed in 2005 when they were placed under lock and key indefinitely at the Archives of the Turkish Historical Association.

Nevertheless, there is no shortage of accessible material with which to work, and the serious historian's task consists mainly of separating strands of fact from the considerable body of fiction that has accumulated since Atatürk's death. I have found Atatürk's own writings, speeches, and correspondence to be immensely helpful. Unfortunately, the editors of his collected writings have rendered the original Ottoman into modern Turkish, sacrificing the subtle nuances of the original text in the process. I have therefore felt it necessary to go back to the original published source whenever possible. In addition, I have relied heavily upon the notes that Atatürk used to scribble in the margins of books that he read. Finally, I have scoured major Turkish journals and dailies for the period 1919–38 in order to collect supplementary information.

Although Atatürk's own speeches and writings are by far the most important source for this essay, I have consulted a vast selection of secondary literature as well. In particular, I have used three well-written, authoritative biographies to place my subject in a larger context. These are the studies of Klaus Kreiser,[12] Andrew Mango,[13] and Şerafettin Turan, all of which provide a wealth of detail concerning various aspects of Atatürk's life. While the first two are written as scholarly biographies, Turan's superbly researched study, the title of which may be rendered into English as *A Sui Generis Life and Personality: Mustafa Kemal Atatürk*, smacks of hagiogra-

---

[12] Klaus Kreiser, *Atatürk: eine Biographie* (Munich: Verlag C. H. Beck, 2008).
[13] Andrew Mango, *Atatürk* (London: John Murray, 1999).

6 INTRODUCTION

phy.[14] In general, however, given the constraints of writing a brief essay in search of the historical Atatürk, I have avoided taking substantial information from the secondary literature.

Obviously this brief essay does not claim to offer a thorough analysis even of Atatürk's major ideas and policies, let alone a comprehensive biography. It has three major objectives. First, it seeks to place the founder of the modern Turkish republic in his historical context. This approach shows Atatürk to be an intellectual and social product of the late nineteenth and early twentieth centuries. The fact that he led an immense endeavor to create a modern nation-state founded on radically new tenets should not force upon us the conclusion that he changed the course of history by thinking the unthinkable or realizing a vision in an otherwise unimaginable manner. Much Turkish historiography tends to view him as a maker of history who was unaffected by the world around him and who singlehandedly wrought a miracle in the form of modern Turkey. But contrary to this approach of mainstream Turkish historiography, Atatürk should not be viewed as a solitary genius impervious to his upbringing, early socialization, education, institutional membership, social milieu, and intellectual environment. While the enormous impact of his leadership on the shape of the republic that sprang from the ruins of the Ottoman Empire is undeniable, it does not diminish Atatürk's contribution to Turkish history to recognize that his ideas and actions were molded by the intellectual, social, and political realities of his time. The fact that he sided with avant-garde approaches that had previously received only limited support in Ottoman and Turkish society should not mislead us into believing that he originated novel ideas.

The second objective of this book is to trace Atatürk's intellectual development, which is the least well-researched aspect of his life and work. Clearly, he was not an intellectual in the strict sense

[14] Şerafettin Turan, *Kendine Özgü Bir Yaşam ve Kişilik: Mustafa Kemal Atatürk* (Istanbul: Bilgi Yayınevi, 2004).

of the word, but the evolution of his ideas strongly influenced his policies. I have felt it appropriate to treat Atatürk's ideas about religion in general and Islam in particular at some length. The role of religion in human society and in his own country was one of Atatürk's major areas of interest, and he presided over the emergence of the first secular republic in a Muslim country.

Third, through analyzing Atatürk's life, ideas, and work, I have tried to explore the uneasy transition from the Late Ottoman imperial order to the modern Turkish nation-state. In so doing I posit an essential continuity as opposed to the sudden rupture often depicted in the historiography on this subject. A by-product of this investigation is a new assessment of the impact of Atatürk's legacy on modern Turkey.

An incidental feature of this quest for the historical Atatürk, with its emphasis on historicizing his experience and contextualizing his ideas, is that I have largely avoided delving into the details of his personal life, which lie beyond the scope of this study.

1

Fin-de-Siècle Salonica

The ancient Macedonian capital of Salonica had seen numerous overbearing rulers come and go. The Ottoman Turks, who swept across the plains of Anatolia and into the Balkans in the fourteenth century, were merely the last in a long and illustrious series that included the Macedonians, Romans, Byzantines, Normans, Lombards, and Venetians. When the Ottomans conquered the city for the second time in 1430, however, they had little patience for the past; at the end of three days of pillaging, only 2,000 souls remained amid the ruins of the ancient city. These survivors were soon joined by 1,000 Turkish nomads, brought from the east, and the social fabric of Salonica was changed forever.[1] Thus was founded what became the most cosmopolitan city in the Ottoman Empire, and it would serve as the seemingly improbable setting for the childhood of the architect of modern Turkey.

A second crucial impetus to the development of the city under Ottoman rule was the expulsion of the Jews from Spain and Portugal at the end of the fifteenth century. As thousands of Jewish immigrants flooded into the Ottoman domains, the authorities decided to direct a large number of them to Salonica, ensuring the city's future as one of the major Jewish centers of Eastern Europe

---

[1] Speros Vryonis Jr., "The Ottoman Conquest of Thessaloniki in 1430," in *Continuity and Change in Late Byzantine and Early Ottoman Society*, ed. Anthony Bryer and Heath Lowry (Washington, DC: Dumbarton Oaks Research Library and Collection, 1986), 281–321.

and the Mediterranean world. Although a small community of Ashkenazi Jews had lived in the city since before the Ottoman conquest, the influx of large numbers of Sephardic Jews turned Salonica into the only sizable town in Europe with a Jewish majority. The Jewish community of Salonica was not only exceptional in size; it was also unique in composition. When in 1666 the Jewish messianic pretender Shabbetai Zevi converted to Islam to avoid execution, a considerable number of his Salonican followers, believing his conversion to be the final step prior to the fulfillment of the messianic prophecy, followed suit.[2] They began to profess their adherence to Islam in public, while surreptitiously continuing the private practice of Jewish rituals. Thus was born the Shabbetaian *Dönme* (in Hebrew *ma'amin*, or believer) community, which was to become a singular feature of Ottoman Salonica. Despised by pious Jews and Muslims alike, the Dönmes were treated as Muslims by the Ottoman authorities for the purposes of administration and taxation.

By the end of the nineteenth century, the city was made up of three major religious groups inhabiting three distinct neighborhoods: the Jews, numbered approximately 49,000; the Muslims, 25,500 (including the Dönmes); and the Greek Orthodox, 11,000.[3] Such simple confessional distinctions, however, obscured a far richer ethnic diversity of Sephardic and Ashkenazi Jews; Turkish, Albanian, Bosnian, Gypsy, and Dönme Muslims; Greek, Bulgarian, Kutzo-Vlach, and Albanian Orthodox; and pockets of Albanian Catholics, Armenians, and Serbs. In addition, Salonica boasted a sizable non-Ottoman European population, comprising some 7,000 British, French, Italian, Russian, and Spanish subjects, and a number of foreign missions, including the American, Danish,

---

[2] Gershom Scholem, *Sabbatai Şevi: The Mystical Messiah, 1626–1676* (Princeton, NJ: Princeton University Press, 1973), 157–59, 633–35.

[3] Meropi Anastassiadou, *Salonique: 1830–1912: Une ville ottomane à l'âge des Réformes* (Leiden, Netherlands: Brill, 1997), 95–97.

Dutch, and Swedish consulates. This latter-day Tower of Babel epitomized Ottoman cosmopolitanism more than any other city in the realm, with the possible exception of the imperial capital Istanbul.

Not surprisingly, Salonica was a fertile ground for the nationalist movements that mushroomed throughout the European provinces of the empire in the nineteenth century. When, in 1821 the Greeks in the Peloponnese launched their war for independence from Ottoman rule, the Salonican Greeks rose up in support of their brethren but were quickly suppressed by the Ottoman administration.[4] Half a century later, in 1870, the Bulgarian intelligentsia of Salonica lent crucial support to the establishment of the autocephalous Bulgarian exarchate, a splinter denomination of Greek Orthodoxy.[5] This religious-nationalist challenge to Greek domination of Orthodox Christianity sparked violent clashes between Greeks and Bulgars in the province.[6] Eight years later, in the aftermath of the Russo-Ottoman War of 1877–78, the Ottomans ceded most of Macedonia—Salonica's hinterland—to the new autonomous principality of Bulgaria. While the Berlin Congress of 1878 restored Macedonia to the Ottomans on condition that they implemented pro-Christian reforms, Salonica, like other towns in the region, turned into a battleground among rival nationalist movements. The Macedo-Bulgarian revolutionary guerrilla organization VMORO (the Vnatrešna makedonsko-odrinska revolucionerna organizacija, or Internal Macedonian-Adrianopolitan Revolutionary Organization) was founded in the city in 1893,[7]

---

[4] Apostolos E. Vacalopoulos, *A History of Thessaloniki*, trans. T. F. Carney (Thessaloniki, Greece: Institute for Balkan Studies, 1972), 100–101.

[5] Iv[an] Snegarov, *Solun v bŭlgarskata dukhovna kultura: istoricheski ocherk i dokumenti* (Sofia, Bulgaria: Pridvorna Petchatnitsa, 1937), 77ff.

[6] Zina Markova, *Bŭlgarskata ekzarhia, 1870–1879* (Sofia, Bulgaria: Bŭlgarska Akademia na Naukite, 1989), 79–83.

[7] Duncan M. Perry, *The Politics of Terror: The Macedonian Liberation Movements, 1893–1903* (Durham, NC: Duke University Press, 1988), 38–39.

while the local Hellenic consulate served as the headquarters of Greek armed activity in the region.[8]

Like the other cities of the empire, Salonica was profoundly affected by the ambitious program of imperial reform launched by the Ottoman government in the mid-nineteenth century. Commonly referred to as the Tanzimat era, the period 1839–76 witnessed a sustained effort to modernize the Ottoman state. Led by a class of professional bureaucrats, the reforms aimed at achieving a wide variety of transformative changes, ranging from the introduction of equality of rights to the overhaul of the bureaucratic machinery of government. The reformers looked primarily to Europe in search of models for change. They sought to replicate the reforms of Peter the Great in Russia, the empire's great adversary to the north; to imitate the genius of Prince Klemens von Metternich's statecraft; to pursue the course of British industrialization; and to follow the path of enlightenment, legal codification, and centralization of government charted by France. Ultimately, they sought to Westernize the Ottoman Empire and enter, as equals, into the post-Napoleonic club of European states. To this end, the reformers built a host of new institutions of government and learning. They introduced new ideas that revolutionized prevailing worldviews, and reshaped the relationships among the various communities of the empire. Taken together, these changes drastically altered the fabric of Ottoman government and society. Yet in order to pave the way for the new order, the reformist statesmen did not find it expedient or possible to confront and destroy the old. Instead, they permitted time-honored institutions to survive alongside the new, in the hope that the former would naturally recede into oblivion in the face of the palpable advantages of progress. For instance, the government established new civil courts governed by new law codes adapted from European sources, yet it

[8] Douglas Dakin, *The Greek Struggle in Macedonia, 1897–1913* (Thessaloniki, Greece: Institute for Balkan Studies, 1966), 199–209.

did not abolish the religious, sharī'a-governed courts. Similarly, the government launched a new system of education based on the French model, but religious and community-based schooling persisted.

In Istanbul and in Balkan cities like Salonica, the reform movement led to the formation of an exceedingly Westernized Muslim upper class. Knowledge of European manners, mores, languages, and sciences—subsumed under the banner of *Alla Franca*—formed the prerequisite for membership in this new elite, and the key to success and upward social mobility. The new elite accordingly embraced the reforms wholeheartedly.[9] Not so the Muslim masses; to them the reforms appeared as European-instigated machinations, designed to rob them of their privileges and bestow advantage upon non-Muslims. Indeed, the reforms split the Muslim community, opening a chasm between the secular elite and the pious masses. As bureaucrats enthusiastically embraced European mores, devout Muslims fretted at the loss of commercial and moral ground to Christians. Thus, in Salonica in 1876, a Muslim mob lynched the French and German consuls while trying to snatch a Greek-Orthodox Bulgarian girl who wished to convert to Islam from a rival mob of Christians.[10] Repeated attempts by Greeks and Bulgarians to replace the despised wooden church bells—historic markers of Christian inferiority—with metal ones precipitated similarly violent clashes.

The policies of the Tanzimat statesmen naturally engendered fierce opposition from Muslim clerics. Less immediately obvious was the reason for the resistance of non-Muslim religious elites. The reformers subtly challenged organized religion of all types by

[9] Şerif Mardin, "Super Westernization in Urban Life in the Ottoman Empire in the Last Quarter of the Nineteenth Century," in *Turkey: Geographic and Social Perspectives*, ed. Peter Benedict, Erol Tümertekin, and Fatma Mansur (Leiden, Netherlands: Brill, 1974), 422ff.

[10] Vacalopoulos, *A History of Thessaloniki*, 115–19.

launching an ambitious effort to restructure the non-Muslim religious communities from within. Rather than wage war on the entrenched clerical establishments, which had managed the day-to-day affairs of their communities for centuries, they adopted a sophisticated, indirect approach. By endorsing laymen from within the community to promote an agenda of secularization and modernization on their behalf, the reformers were in fact mobilizing internal forces in an effort to edge the obscurantist clerics out of positions of power. At the same time, the government applied universal laws to these communities, thereby destroying centuries of communal autonomy. The empowerment of progressive lay elements within the religious communities, combined with administrative efforts to create universal institutions for all Ottoman subjects, drastically altered life in the various communities and in society as a whole. Although one of the major aims of the Tanzimat reforms was to combat ethnic separatism by centralizing imperial administration, the effect of the emergence of secular intelligentsias with power over community affairs was, ironically, to give impetus to burgeoning nationalist movements.[11]

One area in particular on which laymen and clergy clashed was the school curriculum. While the former urged the adoption of secular curricula, the better to prepare the new generation for life in the modern world and to foster nationalist sentiment in the community, the latter fought to preserve the religious foundation of education. The new Regulations for Education, issued in 1869 under the influence of Jean-Victor Duruy's secular reform program in France, laid out a blueprint for a new educational system featuring preparatory, middle, and high schools, as well as colleges with modern curricula that included foreign languages. They also instituted a chain of military schools at middle school, high school,

[11] Roderic H. Davison, *Reform in the Ottoman Empire, 1856–1876* (Princeton, NJ: Princeton University Press, 1963), 131–35.

and college levels and permitted communities and individuals to establish their own schools.[12]

The reform era left a particularly strong imprint upon Salonica, both because of the city's importance to the government—underscored by Sultan Abdülmecid's (r. 1839–61) unusual visit in 1859—and because of its cosmopolitan character, which amplified the force of reforms targeting the empire's non-Muslim communities. In addition, the influx of European (including Jewish) capital into Salonica empowered local reformers who wished to enhance the city's infrastructure, and accelerated the pace of change. The Law of Provinces, issued in 1864, restructured provincial administration, but also established municipal administrations on the French model. The new municipality of Salonica demolished the city's sea walls and drained the surrounding marshes in the 1870s. A British company introduced street gaslighting in 1881, and electricity was installed in 1899. A great fire in 1890 destroyed the poorest Jewish neighborhoods and adjoining areas, providing an opportunity to widen the streets. Horse-drawn trams began operation in 1893—this was the fifth tram line in the entire empire, and the first in the Balkans.[13] A new telegraph line connected the town to the imperial capital and other major centers. So too did the railway: in 1870 a railway line from Salonica to Mitrovitza opened, later extended to link the city to Skopje, Monastir, and Istanbul. Increasing trade with Europe also played a significant role in the expansion of the city. Salonica became the largest seaport for exports in the Balkans and the fourth largest in the empire as a whole (after İzmir, Istanbul, and Beirut). In addi-

---

[12] "Ma'arif-i Umumiye Nizamnâmesidir," in *Düstûr*, I/2 (Istanbul: Matbaa-i Âmire, 1289 [1872]), 184–219.

[13] For the reshaping of Salonica after the Tanzimat, see Anastassiadou, *Salonique*, 89ff., and Alexandra Yerolympos and Vassilis Colonas, "Un urbanisme cosmopolite," in *Salonique, 1850–1918: La "ville des Juifs" et le réveil des Balkans*, ed. Gilles Veinstein (Paris: Autrement, 1993), 158–76.

tion to commercial shipping, Ottoman, Greek, Egyptian, and European naval vessels scheduled regular visits to Salonica. The Imperial Ottoman Bank opened one of its first branches there in 1864. The Banque de Salonique and the Agricultural Bank (the official bank of the state) soon followed suit. The emergence of small factories for the production of construction materials, garments, tobacco, alcohol, beer, and soap turned the city into a major industrial center, as well as the hub of the Ottoman socialist movement. Industrial growth also triggered an influx of rural populations in search of work. Between 1839 and 1897, migration doubled the town's population.

Salonica—famous in ancient times as Cicero's home in exile, and later as the hometown of Cyril, coinventor of the Glagolitic alphabet and cotranslator of the Bible into Old Slavonic—underwent a cultural renaissance during the reform era. This was particularly remarkable in the realm of print. Although the first Hebrew printing house in the Balkans had been founded in the town in 1512, it published principally religious treatises.[14] A Turkish publishing house was set up in 1727 but did not last very long. The reform era witnessed the establishment of numerous multilingual printing houses. Dailies and journals also appeared. Judah Nehama began to publish the daily *El Lunar* (The Month) in 1864, followed in 1869 by the official provincial gazette *Selânik* (Salonica) in Turkish, Bulgarian, Greek, and Ladino. An independent Turkish daily, *Zaman* (The Times), hosted intellectual debates from 1880 onward. In 1895, one of the major Ottoman provincial newspapers, *Asır* (The Century), started publication.[15] Salonica's first Greek newspaper, *Hermes*, came out in 1875. Muslim intel-

---

[14] Yaron Ben Na'eh, "Hebrew Printing Houses in the Ottoman Empire," in *Jewish Journalism and Printing Houses in the Ottoman Empire and Modern Turkey*, ed. Gad Nassi (Istanbul: Isis Press, 2001), 86.

[15] Türkmen Parlak, *Yeni Asır'ın Selânik Yılları: Evlâd-ı Fatihan Diyarları* (İzmir: Yeni Asır, 1986), 113ff.

lectuals produced many journals such as *Gonce-i Edeb* (Bud of Learning), *Mecelle-i Mu'allimîn* (Teachers' Journal), *Mezra'a-i Maarif* (Field of Education), and *Tuhfetü'l-Edebiye li-Evlâdi'l-Vataniye* (The Gift of Literature to the Children of Patriotism).

The school system in the city also underwent major change, as new institutions emerged to provide a modern education that traditional ones refused to adopt. The old sixteenth-century schools, like the Yakub Pasha Medresesi, the Talmud Torah Seminary, or the Greek Grammar School, had persisted in ignoring the challenges posed by modernity. When Sultan Abdülmecid granted a personal audience "only to those Jewish notables with whom he could converse in French, leaving the rabbinate out in the cold" during his visit, the state sent a strong signal that it was time for a change.[16] Subsequently, the Jewish Alliance Israélite Universelle founded its Salonican branch in 1864, and after protracted debates with local rabbis who vehemently opposed nonreligious education, established a semisecular high school for boys in 1873.[17] A year later the Jewish community instituted a similar school for girls; this was made possible by the generous help of the Baron Maurice de Hirsch, who had funded the construction of the Salonica-Mitrovitza railway (a more grandiose project of his, the construction of a 1,600-mile railway network across European Turkey, did not reach fruition).[18] The Bulgarian community established the first semisecular Christian school in 1869.[19] In 1875, the challenges posed by the onset of modernity proved irresistible even for the old Greek Grammar School, which submitted to the

---

[16] Mark Mazower, *Salonica, City of Ghosts: Christians, Muslims, and Jews, 1430–1950* (London: HarperCollins, 2004), 219.

[17] Ibid., 220.

[18] Kurt Grunwald, *Türkenhirsch; A Study of Baron Maurice de Hirsch, Entrepreneur and Philanthropist* (Jerusalem: Israel Program for Scientific Translations, 1966), 28ff.

[19] Snegarov, *Solun v bŭlgarskata duhovna kultura*, 60–61.

forces of change and became a modern gymnasium.[20] In 1888 the German school opened its doors, primarily to the children of foreign workers. Nevertheless, many Ottoman Muslims and non-Muslims, hoping for a better education for their children, took to sending them there. In the wake of the 1869 reform in education, the central government opened a middle school for boys followed by one for girls; it also established a military middle school in Salonica.

Despite these impressive developments, the ruling establishment of the Muslim community—in Salonica as elsewhere—kept firm control over primary education. The Muslim religious authorities resisted any attempt to reform the elementary schools in which children received their first schooling. Primary schools thus continued to represent tradition, and rejected modern methodologies, curricula, and even equipment, such as blackboards, desks, and maps. While lay elements in non-Muslim communities succeeded in establishing private primary schools that provided a modern education, for most Muslims the only option was the traditional primary school system. It was left to enterprising pedagogues of the Salonican Donme community to found the first private Muslim elementary schools with more modern curricula and less emphasis on religion.

This, then, was the apparently unlikely setting into which the future founder of the Turkish Republic was born one winter, either in 1880 or in 1881. Ali Rıza and Zübeyde named their fourth child Mustafa, one of the titles of the Prophet Muḥammad, meaning "the chosen one." Their first three children had died in infancy or childhood, and only one of the two daughters born after Mustafa survived into adulthood. Zübeyde had grown up in the small village of Sarıyar not far from Salonica. Her father, one Sofuzâde

[20] Sidiroula Ziogou-Karastergiou, "Education in Thessaloniki: The Ottoman Period, 1430–1912," in *Queen of the Worthy: Thessaloniki: History and Culture*, ed. I. K. Hassiotis (Thessaloniki, Greece: Paratiritis, 1997), 354–55.

Feyzullah, worked for Muslim landowners. The family was said to have migrated from Vodina (present-day Edessa), and claimed descent from an old Turcoman family. Zübeyde had received some basic traditional education and could apparently recite the Qurʾān by heart. She was also literate, a rarity among Muslim women at the time.[21]

Mustafa's paternal grandfather, Hafız Ahmed, was the scion of a local Turkish family. Religiously educated, he served as a minor government official until his participation in the infamous riots of 1876—which culminated in the assassination of the French and German consuls—had the effect of putting an end to his career. In response to the murders, several European powers intervened, sending their men-of-war to Salonica and compelling the Ottoman authorities to punish many of the Muslims involved. Hafız Ahmed fled to the mountains, where he ended his days in voluntary exile.[22] His son, Ali Rıza, also a petty official with some education, worked for the Ottoman Administration of Pious Foundations, and subsequently found employment at the Customs Administration. Turkish historians, bent on establishing a military pedigree for Atatürk, allege that his father had joined the Salonican reserves in response to the threat of war with Russia in 1876,[23] but this is unproven.[24] His last official position was that of customs enforcement official, in charge of preventing the smuggling of timber between the Greek kingdom and the Ottoman Empire. In theory, this job came with a decent salary. In practice,

[21] Şerafettin Turan, *Kendine Özgü Bir Yaşam ve Kişilik: Mustafa Kemal Atatürk* (Istanbul: Bilgi Yayınevi, 2004), 19–20; Andrew Mango, *Atatürk* (London: John Murray, 1999), 26–30.
[22] Şevket Süreyya Aydemir, *Tek Adam: Mustafa Kemal*, vol. 1, *1881–1919* (Istanbul: Remzi Kitabevi, 1981), 31.
[23] İhsan Sungu, "Atatürk'ün Babası Ali Efendi ve Mensup Olduğu Selânikli Asâkiri Milliye Taburu," *Belleten* 3/10 (April 1, 1939): 289–348.
[24] Falih Rıfkı Atay, *Çankaya: Atatürk'ün Doğumundan Ölümüne Kadar* (Istanbul: Sena Matbaası, 1960), 17.

however, after 1878 the impoverished state paid salaries only a few months out of the year. To supplement his meager earnings, Ali Rıza used his experience and connections to establish a partnership with a Salonican timber merchant. At first successful, he soon fell out with the Greek brigands who made a living by extorting bribes from timber merchants. The partnership disintegrated and, after a brief spell in the salt trade, Ali Rıza sank into bankruptcy. His desperation triggered illness and death at the age of forty-seven. Mustafa was thus left fatherless at the age of seven, while Zübeyde became a widow at twenty-seven.[25]

Until his father's death, Mustafa had enjoyed relative prosperity as a member of the middle class. The family lived in a three-story building in the Ahmed Subaşı neighborhood, one of the more desirable neighborhoods of Salonica's Muslim quarter, and could afford a black servant and a wet nurse for young Mustafa. His upbringing was more liberal than that of most lower-class Muslims. No one in his family's circle of friends and relatives, for instance, practiced polygamy. Likewise, his father reportedly drank alcohol, which was abhorred by conservatives.

The confusing dualism produced in Ottoman society by the reforms of the nineteenth century had its first imprint on Mustafa when his parents entered into a heated argument about his education. In most urban families of the period, the debate between proponents of "Alla Franca" and "Alla Turca" took on a generational aspect, pitting children against parents. The tension in Mustafa's family, by contrast, split the parents. Ali Rıza, who as a petty bureaucrat appreciated the advantages of a modern education for social mobility, aspired to send his son to a Dönme institution, the Şemsi Efendi School, which strongly encouraged critical thinking instead of rote learning and recitation. This was the choice of many middle- and upper-class Muslims (as well as Dönmes); they were

[25] Mango, *Atatürk*, 29.

drawn to the French aspects of this modern school with its desks, colored maps, and strong focus on mathematics and science (though religious subjects were also taught). Mustafa's pious mother, on the other hand, preferred to send her only surviving son to a traditional primary school, in which clerics taught a curriculum centered on religion and Arabic. The dispute ended in a peculiar compromise. In order to please his mother, Mustafa first went to the religious school (wearing a bound fascicule of the Qur'ān strapped to his chest). He remained there, however, only a few days, in the course of which he managed to learn a few hymns. Then Ali Rıza, considering his pledge to Zübeyde fulfilled, whisked young Mustafa away to Şemsi Efendi School.[26]

There is little doubt that Mustafa Kemal's deep-seated predilection for new institutions and practices owed much to his years as one of a handful of students in the empire who had their primary education at a private elementary school devoid of a strong religious focus. The school's avant-garde practices—such as gymnastics classes—drew the ire of conservatives, prompting occasional closures and even attacks by vandalistic mobs.[27] Young Mustafa appears to have thoroughly enjoyed his days at Şemsi Efendi School. The death of his father, however, cut short those happy days.

His mother's exiguous widow's pension of 40 piasters per month (equivalent to approximately US$28 in 2010) compelled her to move back to Langaza, adjacent to her native Vodina. There she could live under the protection of her step-uncle, Langazalı Hüseyin Ağa, who was a steward at a sizable Muslim farm. The move from the comforts of middle-class life in the city to near

---

[26] "Hayatına Ait Hatıralar, January 1922," in *Atatürk'ün Söylev ve Demeçleri Tamim ve Telgrafları*, vol. 5, ed. Sadi Borak and Utkan Kocatürk (Ankara: Türk İnkılâp Tarihi Enstitüsü Yayınları, 1972), 84.

[27] Marc David Baer, *The Dönme: Jewish Converts, Muslim Revolutionaries, and Secular Turks* (Stanford, CA: Stanford University Press, 2010), 48–49.

poverty in the countryside was a painful one. Like the other members of the family, Mustafa attempted to adjust to rural life, but without success. He found little to challenge him in the simple tasks given him by Hüseyin Ağa, such as chasing crows off the horsebean fields.[28] The disruption of his education distressed his mother immensely. Mustafa briefly attended a Greek school at a nearby church. Subsequently, an Albanian steward at the farm taught him some basic subjects. But it was not enough. Finally, Zübeyde decided to send him back to the city for schooling.[29]

Mustafa returned to Salonica to live with his paternal aunt Hatice. Shortly afterward, an unpleasant incident cut short his studies at the town's civilian preparatory school: one of Mustafa's teachers beat him severely in a fit of rage for his participation in a brawl among students. Bloodied and humiliated, he left the school, never to return.[30] The following year, at age thirteen, Mustafa made one of the most important decisions of his life: ignoring his mother's objections, he applied in secret to the military preparatory school in Salonica. In his reminiscences, Mustafa Kemal described how impressed he had been with the uniforms worn by military cadets and officers.[31] He lived next door to an army major whose son attended the school; upon hearing of his acceptance, Zübeyde reluctantly gave in to the fait accompli. It was in this way that Mustafa embarked upon his military career.

The military preparatory schools, like their civilian counterparts, were products of the reform era. All Ottoman subjects, regardless of religious affiliation, were eligible to attend. However,

[28] "Hayatına Ait Hatıralar, January 1922," in *Atatürk'ün Söylev ve Demeçleri*, vol. 5, 85.

[29] Aydemir, *Tek Adam*, vol. 1, 48–49.

[30] "Hayatına Ait Hatıralar, January 1922," in *Atatürk'ün Söylev ve Demeçleri*, vol. 5, 85.

[31] Ibid.

government advertisements encouraging non-Muslims to apply reveal that non-Muslim Ottomans needed some persuasion.[32] Most did not consider these institutions a serious alternative for the education of their children. The military preparatory schools had a curriculum that was modern, though not radically so. They taught French, but also Arabic and Persian. They emphasized mathematics, drawing, and gymnastics, but also some religious subjects. In a sense, they represented a hybrid of classical Ottoman education and modern French schooling. Still, the founders of these schools clearly intended to prepare their pupils for modern life, and the concessions to religion were made primarily to avoid controversy. The foremost difference between the civilian and military schools was the strictness of military discipline. All pupils wore uniforms, saluted their teachers (most of whom were low-ranking officers), and adhered to a strict hierarchy. These schools ardently encouraged competition through an elaborate ranking system. Despite their marked military flavor, their graduates usually went on to nonmilitary high schools. Many had no intention of becoming officers.

Mustafa was an industrious student who excelled in mathematics, an attribute that won him his first leadership position. With the consent of both teachers and pupils, he was appointed class sergeant, serving as a liaison between the students in his class and the school administration. In the strict hierarchical system of the Ottoman military schools, this was a significant position. In fact, many years later his mother cited it as a major accomplishment.[33] Another portentous occurrence left a more lasting imprint on Mustafa. His mathematics teacher, also named Mustafa, asked his assiduous student to add a second name in order to avoid confu-

[32] Osman Ergin, *Türkiye Maarif Tarihi*, vol. 2, *Tanzimat Devri Mektepleri* (Istanbul: Osmanbey Matbaası, 1940), 423.

[33] Aydemir, *Tek Adam*, vol. 1, 63–64.

sion. Such problems were quite common in Ottoman society, since Muslim Ottomans did not possess family names—a novelty that Mustafa himself was to introduce in 1934. The teacher proposed Kemal, meaning "maturity" or "perfection." It was also the name of the most prominent Ottoman patriotic poet, Namık Kemal, who was revered by young Ottomans as the champion and martyr of the struggle against the absolutist regimes of sultans Abdülaziz (r. 1861–76) and Abdülhamid II (r. 1876–1909). Mustafa gladly accepted.[34]

The only cloud over Mustafa Kemal's sunny experience at the military preparatory school was his mother's second marriage. Living as a widow in Ottoman Muslim society was not easy. Zübeyde ran into major financial difficulties and opted to marry a petty enforcement officer at the Régie Ottomane des Tabacs—a monopoly over Ottoman tobacco production and sales established in the wake of the Ottoman declaration of bankruptcy in 1881. Enraged by his mother's decision, and by the fact that she had given him no advance notice, Mustafa Kemal left home and moved in with a distant relative.[35] Upon graduation, and with the encouragement of his teachers, he applied to the military high school in Monastir (modern-day Bitola, in the Republic of Macedonia). Not surprisingly, he passed the exams for this prestigious, state-funded boarding school, and left the city of his youth for another major city of Ottoman Europe.

Mustafa Kemal's seemingly humble Salonican background amounted to a distinguished pedigree in Ottoman terms. To understand why this was so, one must recall that the Ottoman Empire, as opposed to the modern Republic of Turkey, was as much a

[34] "Hayatına Ait Hatıralar, January 1922," in *Atatürk'ün Söylev ve Demeçleri*, vol. 5, 85.
[35] Ali Fuat Cebesoy, *Sınıf Arkadaşım Atatürk: Okul ve Genç Subaylık Hâtıraları* (Istanbul: İnkılâp ve Aka, 1967), 7.

European domain as it was Asiatic. Rumelia (European Turkey) and Anatolia (Asia Minor) formed the two central pillars of the state, with Istanbul, the keystone in the arch, sandwiched in between. Rumelia and Anatolia had constituted the core of the empire even before Constantinople was taken in 1453, and the subsequent conquest of the Arab lands did not alter this conception in the minds of the Turkish-speaking people of the empire. Rumelians and Anatolians nevertheless spoke Turkish with distinct accents marked by local flavors. The Rumelian dialect incorporated numerous Albanian, Greek, and Slavic words, and was considered closer to the dialect of Istanbul whose prestige was similar to that of the Queen's English in Britain. A stranger visiting a new town would first face the question, Are you from Anatolia or Rumelia? Ottoman popular culture attributed sophisticated characteristics to the Rumelians, such as wisdom, charm, and gentlemanly behavior. Anatolians, by contrast, were stereotyped as courageous, honest, and straightforward.

To a certain extent, upper-class Turkish Rumelians substituted for the missing aristocracy as the empire's ruling elite. Salonica, as the major urban center of Rumelia, formed the hub of this Turkish elite. To Rumelians, the fact that they provided more high-ranking officials to the empire than their Anatolian counterparts was no coincidence; nor was it a surprise that in 1808 it was notables from Rumelia who spearheaded the movement that forced the sultan to promulgate a document commonly but mistakenly referred to as the Ottoman Magna Carta, and thus to share his power with local notables. Almost all Rumelian Muslims of Turkish extraction underscored their sense of superiority by proudly identifying themselves as "children of the conquerors" (*evlâd-ı fatihân*). This was an old and prestigious title granted in 1691 to the descendants of the Turkish pioneers who had first settled in the European provinces, and it was associated with extensive fiscal and military privileges.[36] These "children of the conquerors" had traditionally served in battalions of their own and enjoyed preferential treatment over other Muslims, until the Tanzimat reformers, who sought to abolish special statuses throughout the empire, abrogated their privileges in 1845.[37] The prestige associated with the title, however, remained. The appeal of this ethnic designation is suggestive, especially when contrasted with the most prestigious title in Anatolia, *seyyid*; this latter implied a lineage going back to the Prophet Muḥammad. Mustafa Kemal, whose claim to Turkish nomadic ancestry was strengthened by his mother's origins in Langaza, a major center of "children of the conquerors," saw himself, and was seen by others, as a sophisticated member of this privileged caste.

His westward orientation as an adult was thus intimately bound up with his experience as a child growing up in the European provinces of the empire. In fact, Salonica was one of the most conspicuous examples of the uncomfortable juxtaposition of old and new in the Ottoman Empire of the reform era. In this context, *old* meant primarily traditional and religious, while *new* signified European and secular. Many Ottomans of this period viewed life as a perennial tug-of-war between modernity and tradition. In several important ways, Salonica tilted toward the former. The city sported bustling Western-style cafés serving Viennese beer; literary clubs hosting philosophical debates; theaters staging dramas, comedies, and operettas; numerous institutions of learning; and a sizable and vibrant European community. Altogether, Salonica had undergone a major transformation during the reform era and had begun to look like a Western European city. The Muslim com-

[36] M. Tayyib Gökbilgin, *Rumeli'de Yürükler, Tatarlar ve Evlâd-ı Fâtihan* (Istanbul: Edebiyat Fakültesi Yayınları, 1957), 255–56.

[37] Mehmet Zeki Pakalın, "Evlâd-ı Fatihân," *Osmanlı Tarih Deyimleri ve Terimleri Sözlüğü*, vol. 1 (Istanbul: Millî Eğitim Basımevi, 1983), 572.

Figure 1. Fin-de-siècle Salonica. Source: IRCICA Fotoğraf Arşivi
Merkez Derleme Koleksiyonu, no. 251.

munity, and especially its progressive Dönme component, had established the most advanced schools in the empire. Young Mustafa, who had ample opportunity to contrast the old and the new, chose to embrace modernity wholeheartedly.

Mustafa Kemal's cosmopolitan background also enabled him to comprehend the failure of the reforms to arrest the increasingly rancorous rivalries plaguing the empire's major ethnic and religious groups. In the decades prior to his birth, the Tanzimat statesmen sought to overcome communitarian strife, ethnic separatism, and religious obscurantism by constructing a new, supranational Ottoman identity. They asked all subjects to subsume their ethnic and sectarian affiliations under a new identity as Ottoman citizens. But the deep religious and nationalist fractures of the empire simply would not heal. The nationalist revolts in Herzegovina and then Bosnia, followed by the violent clashes between Muslims and Christians in Bulgaria that culminated in the Russo-Ottoman War of 1877–78, dealt crippling blows to the concept of Otto-

manism. And as the empire shrank, shedding its Rumelian prov-
inces to European conquerors and newly independent nation-
states, the proportion of Muslims left within its boundaries grew.
This was one of the factors that prompted Sultan Abdülhamid II
to try to reconstruct Ottomanism as a supranational identity for
Muslims. This new policy of pan-Islamism, which ignored non-
Muslims, naturally exacerbated tensions between Muslims and
Christians within the empire.

The restoration of Macedonia to the empire at the Berlin Congress of 1878, conditional as it was upon the implementation of
pro-Christian reforms, turned it into a hotbed of ethnic strife. The
newly autonomous principality of Bulgaria, which was forced to
cede Macedonia back to the Ottomans, encouraged Macedo-Bul-
garians to launch widespread guerrilla activity against the Ottoman authorities and Muslim citizenry. Macedonian Greeks soon
followed suit. Both groups coveted the port city of Salonica. The
Greeks, who in terms of population came in a distant third after
Jews and Turks, laid claim to the city based on its ancient and Byzantine history. The Bulgarians, who had even less of a demographic
claim, named Macedonia "Western Bulgaria," and coveted the
pearl of the region along with the rest. In the event, the Greeks
were to have their way.

Mustafa Kemal had witnessed the Bulgarian and Greek guerrilla warfare in Macedonia as a child and teenager. As an adult, he
experienced the pain and humiliation of the Greek occupation
and eventual annexation of Salonica in the First Balkan War of
1912. He later recalled, "One day when I was rushing from the
field of operations in Cyrenaica to the fire of the Balkan [Wars], I
observed that all the routes connecting . . . the shores of Africa to
my fatherland were blocked. One day I heard that Salonica, the
land of my father had been ceded to the enemy together with my
mother, sister, and all my relatives. . . . One day I heard that a bell
had been installed in the minaret of the Hortacı Süleyman Mosque

and that the remains of my father there had been trampled upon by the filthy boots of the Greeks."[38] From this point on Mustafa Kemal was a man who could never go home. These events exposed the cosmopolitan pipe dream that Ottomanism had become. They also underscored the importance of military strength, and provided a sharp lesson in the importance of history as a legitimizing force potentially far more powerful than demographic reality in determining the fate of cities, regions, and even entire countries. These lessons played a significant role in Mustafa Kemal's later attempts, as founder of the Turkish republic, to consolidate indisputable Turkish rule over Anatolia. They explain why he did not stop at victory on the battlefield in the ferocious war to destroy Greek irredentism but instead went on to launch a pseudoscientific campaign to prove the Hittite and Sumerian origins of the Turks so as to outsmart anyone who might make historical claims on Anatolia. Moreover, he completely abandoned the old cosmopolitan notion of Ottomanism—with its attempt to bridge the irreconcilable contradiction between empire and nationalism—and set out to build a new state that was as homogeneous, and as un-Balkan, as possible.

There was another important formative process to which Mustafa Kemal bore witness as a child and young adult in Rumelia: the transfer of economic power from Muslims to non-Muslims within Ottoman society. Traditionally Ottoman Muslims had shown no lack of interest in manufacture, business, and commerce; encouraged by substantial tax privileges, they had dominated Ottoman economic life for centuries. However, increasing European trade with the Ottoman Empire in the nineteenth century, and the abolition of Ottoman protective tariffs, resulted in a flood of Western goods and the decline of the Muslim-dominated

[38] "Subay ve Kumandan ile Konuşmalar," in *Atatürk'ün Bütün Eserleri*, vol. 1, *1903–1915* (Istanbul: Kaynak Yayınları, 1998), 165.

manufacturing sector. In an economy powered by imports rather than domestic production, trade naturally came to be central. And it was in the mercantile sector that Muslims suffered the greatest disadvantages.

There were a number of aspects to this. First, European merchants benefited enormously from new liberal trade policies, and through partnerships with non-Muslim Ottomans came to control a sizable portion of Ottoman commerce. Second, a significant number of these non-Muslims obtained foreign citizenship to evade Ottoman taxes and acquire foreign protection, while intervention by European consuls on their behalf became a daily occurrence in the cities of Ottoman Europe. These phenomena gave rise to considerable bitterness among Muslims, who coined the popular adage, "Non-Muslims have European protectors; we have no protector but God."[39] Third, the Ottoman government granted particular privileges to certain Christian groups, such as its Greek Orthodox subjects, who were given the right to sail under the Russian flag. As a result of these factors, non-Muslims profited tremendously from the reform era. Many incidents construed as "Muslim fanaticism" had deep socioeconomic roots in the resentment felt by Muslims who bore the brunt of discrimination in an ostensibly Islamic empire. As we have seen, Mustafa Kemal's own grandfather ended his days as a fugitive in the Macedonian mountains on account of his role in an incident of just such a character. Similarly, his father blamed the failure of his import business on an administration powerless to stop Greek brigands working for non-Muslim merchants[40]—a common complaint of Muslims in the large Ottoman cities of Europe. Finally, his stepfather worked for a foreign-owned company that entrusted decision-making posi-

[39] This saying was frequently used by the press. See, for example, "Londra'dan," *Mizan* 27 (July 5, 1897): 1.

[40] Aydemir, *Tek Adam*, 1, 39.

tions to foreigners and non-Muslims and relegated Muslims to roles as guards or low-level clerks. These childhood impressions help explain another peculiar aspect of Mustafa Kemal's philosophy: although a dedicated, lifelong champion of Westernization, he remained a stalwart opponent of Western economic penetration and political intervention throughout his adult life.

2

Das Volk in Waffen: The Formation of an Ottoman Officer

In January 1896, upon graduating from the military preparatory school in Salonica, Mustafa Kemal enrolled in the military high school in Monastir, then the capital of the Ottoman province of the same name. Seven such military high schools had been established all around the empire as part of a reform effort following the foundation of the Royal Military Academy in 1834.[1] In addition to the one in the capital there were six such schools in Baghdad, Bursa, Damascus, Edirne (Adrianople), Erzurum, and Monastir.[2] For Muslim pupils, in particular, these boarding schools provided the best opportunity for upward mobility in Late Ottoman society, accepting the most qualified students in the provinces. The school in Monastir, established in 1847, took in an average of 75 students per year from a province with a sizable Muslim population of approximately 225,000. Admission was extremely difficult because of competition among the many children of officers and bureaucrats serving in the province. In 1899, at age eighteen, Mustafa Kemal graduated from this high school with flying colors. He was second in his class.[3]

[1] Mehmed Es'ad, *Mir'at-ı Mekteb-i Harbiye* (Istanbul: Artin Asadoryan, 1310 [1892–93]), 166–67.

[2] Ibid.

[3] Şerafettin Turan, *Kendine Özgü Bir Yaşam ve Kişilik: Mustafa Kemal Atatürk* (Istanbul: Bilgi Yayınevi, 2004), 44.

Mustafa Kemal then moved to Istanbul, where he enrolled in one of the most prestigious schools in the empire, the Royal Military Academy. Although several military engineering schools had been established in the eighteenth century as part of the effort to improve the Ottoman armed forces, it was not until 1834 that Sultan Mahmud II overcame conservative resistance and succeeded in founding the first military academy to produce officers for the new European-style Ottoman army corps.[4] While the curriculum was initially quite different from that of European military academies, by the late-1840s the difference had decreased considerably, and instruction came to focus on professional education at the expense of religious subjects, Arabic, and Persian. A group of professors educated in Europe took over the administration of the academy, and French and Prussian instructors taught many of the technical subjects. By the time Mustafa Kemal enrolled at the school, the curriculum, which focused on military subjects, mathematics, science, and European languages, had the reputation of being daunting. Once there, he worked relentlessly to gain admission to the Staff Officer College—a highly competitive elite institution within the academy widely regarded as the pinnacle of military education in the empire. In 1902, he graduated from the academy as the eighth in his class of 459 cadets, and entered the college for two more years of special education.[5] In 1905, he joined the army as a staff officer captain.[6]

Mustafa Kemal's studies at the Royal Military Academy exposed him to a radically new set of ideas. The academy was a product of the Ottoman bureaucratic and military reforms of the early nineteenth century. Like other similar institutions founded at the time, its primary goal was to furnish the empire with professional military men, not to provide ordinary citizens with a broad uni-

[4] Mehmed Es'ad, *Mir'at-ı Mekteb-i Harbiye*, 8–12.
[5] Turan, *Kendine Özgü Bir Yaşam*, 46.
[6] Ibid., 49.

Figure 2. The Royal Military Academy in the last years of the nineteenth century. Source: İ.Ü. Nadir Eserler Kütüphanesi, Yıldız Albümleri, no. 91011/0004.

versity education. Its curriculum accordingly revolved around military topics. Although the original program of study reflected strong French influence (it resembled that of the École Spéciale Militaire de Saint-Cyr), the French defeat at the hands of Prussia in 1870–71 led to an increased interest in German military instruction. In 1883–84, at the sultan's invitation, the celebrated German theorist Colmar von der Goltz led a restructuring of the Ottoman Royal Military Academy on the model of his home institution, the Kriegsakademie of Berlin. Goltz reinforced the teaching of algebra, mathematics, and related technical subjects, and instilled a new ethic of service and discipline. He also promoted an enhanced role for the military in society.[7]

Goltz had written his book *Das Volk in Waffen* (The Nation in Arms, a phrase originally coined by Kaiser Wilhelm I in 1860) under the influence of social Darwinism. In it, he argued that war was an inevitability. And since war in the modern age meant a struggle between entire nations, not merely their armies, it was incumbent upon the military elite to go beyond its traditional role in society and help guide the ship of state. Military commanders, Goltz believed, ought to be more than loyal servants of the state; in fact, a "superior position in the state" was "of necessity the natural due of officers as a class. *Noblesse oblige*."[8] In Goltz's opinion, "born rulers are also great soldiers; and it is easy to conceive that the greatest military leaders must be looked for among the occupants of thrones."[9]

Not without some justice, Goltz thought that his ideas were particularly applicable to the Ottoman Empire, where an "honourable, proud, brave and religious people . . . deprived of the leadership of the upper classes" cried out for the guidance of a new officer class.[10] For centuries the Muslim component of the Ottoman Empire had lived a life on the edge, ready to march into battle at a moment's notice. Moreover, a strict distinction between civil and military spheres did not exist in an empire in which the reality of incessant warfare made military commanders the natural leaders of society. And yet, though army and navy commanders served as cabinet ministers and could become grand viziers, the military as an institution was sidelined in the formulation of policy—until, as

[7] Colmar von der Goltz, *Denkwürdigkeiten* (Berlin: E. S. Mittler und sohn, 1929), 112ff.

[8] [Colmar] von der Goltz, *The Nation in Arms: A Treatise on Modern Military Systems and the Conduct of War*, trans. Philip A. Ashworth (London: Hodder and Stoughton, 1914), 23–24.

[9] Ibid., 30.

[10] Ibid., 22.

a result of the 1908 revolution, the paramilitary Committee of Union and Progress (CUP) swept many officers into power. The Young Turk Revolution thus provided an unexpected opportunity for the fulfillment of Goltz's vision of a militarized nation guided by army officers. It was therefore ironic, but wholly understandable, that Goltz's ideas gained more currency in the Ottoman Empire than they did in his native Germany.[11] He shaped the worldview of several generations of Ottoman officers who studied the Turkish rendition of *Das Volk in Waffen* at the Royal Military Academy from 1886 onward.[12] By 1908, virtually the entire senior Ottoman officer corps had come around to the opinion that it was their duty to transform the empire into a nation in arms.[13]

By the time Mustafa Kemal matriculated, the academy was consciously striving to produce not merely capable officers but "a new class" that would guide the nation. In this sense, the reform of the academy under Goltz served to institutionalize a process of social differentiation that had been taking place for several decades. Although the Tanzimat reforms of the mid-nineteenth century sought to promote equality among Ottoman subjects of various religions, and to reduce the chasm between the ruling class and the masses, the creation of a new Western-style army drove a wedge between the new military elite and the rest of society. For instance, the abolition of discriminatory sartorial laws and the adoption of the universal fez (in place of a plethora of occupation-specific turbans) tended to make the bureaucrat indistinguishable from the average person. Against this background the new European-style uniforms of the armed forces stood out in sharp relief. But the difference went deeper than appearances. The traditional military

[11] Klaus Kreiser, *Atatürk: eine Biographie* (Munich: Verlag C. H. Beck, 2008), 43.

[12] [Colmar] von der Goltz, *Millet-i Müsellaha: Asrımızın Usûl ve Ahvâl-i Askeriyesi,* trans. Mehmed Tahir (Istanbul: Matbaa-i Ebüzziya, 1301 [1886]).

[13] Ali Fu'ad, "Ordu ve Millet," *Asker* 1/1 (September 3, 1908): 16.

Figure 3. Freiherr Colmar von der Goltz and Mustafa Kemal on military maneuvers in Monastir (1909): (1) Freiherr Colmar von der Goltz; (2) Adjutant Major Mustafa Kemal. Source: Pertev Demirhan, *Generalfeldmarschall Colmar Freiherr von der Goltz: das Lebensbild eines großen Soldaten: aus meinen persönlichen Erinnerungen* (Göttingen, Germany: Göttingen Verlagsanstalt, 1960), 112–13.

elite—most notably, the Janissaries—had constituted an integral part of the cultural, religious, and social fabric of the broader Ottoman society. The new military, by contrast, appeared as a cloistered elite; it stood apart from the masses—pretentious, Westernized, and overweeningly ambitious. Although Mustafa Kemal may well have been attracted to the uniforms worn by his peers, a far greater benefit was the potential for upward mobility through membership in this privileged group. His education at the Royal Military Academy made him a respected member of this class, and a potential guide for Goltz's nation in arms.

Although increasingly sympathetic to Goltz's ideas, the new Ottoman officer class had one major reservation about them: his model was Germany, an archetypal nation-state. The Ottoman state, by contrast, was a polyethnic empire coming apart at the seams. How then was the nonexistent nation to be summoned to arms? The forging of a nation in arms required an ideological framework that would cement the bond between the new rulers and the masses. But how could such a framework possibly appeal to the empire's diverse population groups? Clearly a nationalist ideology would have much greater chances of success were the population ethnically homogenous. This line of reasoning contributed to the rising popularity of Turkism among Ottoman officers in the last quarter of the nineteenth century.

Mustafa Kemal embraced some bold ideas in this regard. As early as 1907, he proposed that the Ottoman Empire should voluntarily dissolve itself in order to pave the way for population exchanges that would give rise to a Turkish state.[14] Only a state undergirded by a robust national identity, he reasoned, would be capable of fielding a strong army. What he imagined was a "Turkish nation in arms"—not an Ottoman one. Although the idea was

[14] Ali Fuat Cebesoy, *Sınıf Arkadaşım Atatürk: Okul ve Genç Subaylık Hâtıraları* (Istanbul: İnkılâp ve Aka, 1967), 108, 114–17.

not novel, it was held to be impractical by many of his colleagues who, however sympathetic, insisted on saving what they could of the decaying empire. By 1914, Mustafa Kemal was nevertheless arguing that the fighting spirit of the army depended on the inculcation of a sound Turkish national consciousness. Soldiers not acquainted with "Hulagu, Timur, Genghiz, and Attila, who had reached the city walls of Paris with a Turkish army composed of men and women" would prove useless in combat. Turkish women who "had lived free of the veil for 5,000 years, and had been covered only in the last 600 years" were duty-bound to raise their children to become soldiers.[15] At the same time, like Heinrich von Treitschke, who considered the Prussian military establishment the ideal spawning ground for national consciousness, Mustafa Kemal believed that the process of constructing a Turkish military would promote awareness of the Turkish national identity in society.

Mustafa Kemal's Turkist sympathies also prompted him to stake out a contrarian position on the Westernization of the army. Although otherwise an ardent supporter of thoroughgoing Westernization, he was a fervent opponent of the growing foreign—and especially German—influence on the Ottoman army. He praised Goltz's contribution to the development of the Ottoman military,[16] but he promoted the idea of a purely Turkish officer corps, and was decidedly critical of the German reform mission dispatched to Istanbul on the eve of the Great War under the leadership of Otto Liman von Sanders.[17] To some extent this xenophobic approach to military reform reflected Mustafa Kemal's pro-

---

[15] "Subay ve Kumandan ile Konuşmalar," in *Atatürk'ün Bütün Eserleri*, vol. 1, *1903–1915* (Istanbul: Kaynak Yayınları, 1998), 169.

[16] Ibid., 163; and Afetinan [Âfet İnan], "Atatürk'ü Dinledim," *Belleten* 14/56 (October 1950): 508.

[17] *Atatürk'ün Anıları: "Büyük Gazimizin Büyük Hayatından Hatıralar,"* ed. İsmet Görgülü (Ankara: Bilgi Yayınevi, 1997), 28–29.

found admiration for the Japanese, whose victory over Russia was perceived at the time as the triumph of indigenous modernization over the West.

Mustafa Kemal also stood out as an irreducible opponent of the personality cult surrounding Sultan Abdülhamid II. Along with other officers of his generation, he considered the ritualized veneration of the sultan a betrayal of the ideal of a nation in arms, which stood above any flesh-and-blood ruler. In a sign of growing opposition to the sultan, many students at the imperial colleges demonstrated an increasing aversion to any expression of loyalty to him. One well-known prank during official ceremonies was to shout "The sultan is upside down!" which, in Turkish, could easily be confused with "Long live the sultan!"[18] Mustafa Kemal is said to have outdone his peers in rejecting imperial traditions through such antics.[19]

There was something ironic about the young officers' antagonism toward the regime of Abdülhamid II. After all, it was he who had established or reformed many of the new colleges and schools in an effort to modernize the Ottoman educational system. Thus, many of the officers and bureaucrats who most resented Hamidian rule owed their education and social position to its reforms. The source of much of their resentment was the neopatrimonial aspect of Abdülhamid II's regime. The sultan's insistence on absolute loyalty on the part of appointed cronies contradicted his emphasis on the rationalization of government begun under the Tanzimat.[20] This was true for the bureaucracy as well as the military, but it was in the officer corps that the phenomenon had its most significant implications.

[18] Hikmet Bayur, "İkinci Meşrutiyet Dönemi Üzerine Bazı Düşünceler," *Belleten* 23/90 (April 1959): 269; Kreiser, *Atatürk*, 42.

[19] Cebesoy, *Sınıf Arkadaşım Atatürk*, 12.

[20] See M. Şükrü Hanioğlu, *The Young Turks in Opposition* (New York: Oxford University Press, 1995), 23–28.

At the end of the nineteenth century, the Ottoman army contained a large number of officers who had risen through the ranks, in addition to those educated at the Royal Military Academy. These unschooled officers, some of whom were illiterate, had been drafted as privates and subsequently promoted. Abdülhamid II accorded them favorable treatment, making many of them high-ranking officers and even generals. Key appointees owed their positions solely to the sultan, and in return for their unadulterated loyalty they received lucrative imperial favors such as money, mansions, and a plethora of new ranks and decorations. Not surprisingly, the Hamidian appointees tended to exhibit sycophantic devotion to the sultan, revering him as their august benefactor. For them, a return to the meritocracy of the Tanzimat would spell disaster. But those educated officers whose lot it was to serve under unschooled pashas understandably resented the situation. The abuse of promotions and decorations particularly rankled the graduates of the Royal Military Academy; they were often forced to serve under incompetent men. As a result, fierce tensions developed within the officer corps in the years leading up to 1909. In the aftermath of the Young Turk Revolution of 1908, the newly empowered class of educated officers acted swiftly to annul the additional ranks and decorations, in some cases demoting Hamidian generals to captain or second lieutenant.[21] The unsuccessful counterrevolution of April 1909, in turn, was led by unschooled officers who sought to sideline their educated comrades. The failure of this attempt to restore the old order ended the role of the Hamidian cronies in the Ottoman military.

The educated Ottoman officer corps that emerged in the years after the 1883 reforms, and especially the staff officers, formed the backbone of the CUP's military wing and provided the leadership

---

[21] "Tasfiye-i Rüteb-i Askeriye Kanunu," in *Düstûr*, II/1 (Istanbul: Matbaa-i Osmaniye, 1329 [1911]), 421–23.

of the Young Turk Revolution on the ground. Not surprisingly, the political revolution of 1908 heralded an internal revolution within the army itself. The officers who came to power immediately set about reshaping the military under the inspiration of Goltz. But there was only so much they could do, since most of the revolutionary leadership consisted of officers between the ranks of second lieutenant and lieutenant colonel; they were not equipped to take full charge of the colossal Ottoman army. Numerous opponents of reform were eliminated in the purge of 1909, but some inevitably remained, particularly in the higher ranks. Many of the Ottoman top brass viewed the younger generation of CUP officers with disdain, as naughty children to be tolerated but not feared. To prove that they were in fact ready to take over military affairs, the CUP dispatched a handful of its most talented staff officers to organize the Ottoman resistance to the Italians in Tripoli of Barbary in 1911–12. Mustafa Kemal was one of those smuggled into Cyrenaica through Egypt for the purpose of organizing a local militia that was to fight against the Italian invaders under the leadership of the military hero of the Young Turk Revolution, Staff Major Enver Bey.[22] These men scored an impressive series of victories, preventing the Italians from penetrating the interior of the country; but although their successes won them considerable fame at home, this small-scale guerrilla war was not a sufficient basis for capturing the leadership of the army. For that, an event of far greater magnitude was necessary.

The catastrophe of the Balkan Wars of 1912–13 provided the pretext for revolutionary change within the Ottoman armed forces. A series of ignominious defeats followed by panicked retreats ended in the loss of practically all of Ottoman Europe, and brought the Balkan armies to the gates of Istanbul. Some of the

---

[22] [Hamdi Ertuna], *1911–1912 Osmanlı-İtalyan Harbi ve Kolağası Mustafa Kemal* (Ankara: Kültür ve Turizm Bakanlığı Yayınları, 1985), 101ff.

younger officers had long complained, to little effect, about the ignorance and lack of professionalism of the officers of the old school. Mustafa Kemal himself had submitted a critical report to his superior, General Hasan Tahsin, concerning the poor performances of officers during maneuvers in European Turkey in 1911.[23] The general, who disregarded the report, went on the very next year to commit one of the greatest blunders in Ottoman military history, surrendering Mustafa Kemal's hometown of Salonica to the Greeks without a fight. There were reports of other senior officers who turned to random verses of the Qur'ān in search of guidance during the retreat.[24] The commander on the Ottoman eastern flank, Marshal Abdullah Pasha, was saved from starvation by a war correspondent of the *Daily Telegraph* who agreed to share his food with him.[25] The deficiencies in planning and execution on the part of high-ranking officials were so obvious that Enver Pasha was able to push through an ambitious reform program.

In late 1913, in response to the military deficiencies exposed by the Balkan Wars, the Ottoman government, now totally under the control of the CUP, invited Lieutenant General Otto Liman von Sanders to rebuild the Ottoman army from scratch. The invitation triggered a serious diplomatic crisis with Russia, which regarded the potential German domination of Istanbul as a direct threat to its southern flank.[26] But the CUP was determined to carry out the reform. Enver Pasha oversaw the process, which resulted in the miraculous rebirth of the Ottoman army within a remarkably short

[23] "Subay ve Kumandan ile Konuşmalar," in *Atatürk'ün Bütün Eserleri*, vol. 1, 162–65.

[24] Rahmi Apak, *Yetmişlik Bir Subayın Hatıraları* (Ankara: Türk Tarih Kurumu Yayınları, 1988), 80–81.

[25] Ellis Ashmead Bartlett, *With the Turks in Thrace* (New York: G. H. Doran, 1913), 169.

[26] A[ndrei] S[ergeevich] Avetian, *Germaniskii imperialism na blizhnem vostoke: kolonial'naia politika germanskogo imperializma i missia Limana fon Sandersa* (Moscow: Mezhdunarodnye otnosheniia, 1966), 66ff.

period. Nevertheless, during the German-Ottoman negotiations on the eve of the Great War, Liman von Sanders was initially against an alliance, arguing that the Ottoman army was still worthless.[27] This opinion, however, was not to be borne out by the experience of the First World War, in which Ottoman forces fought surprisingly well against formidable foes on multiple fronts. This superior performance was undoubtedly due to the reforms of 1913–14 and to the new generation of officers commanding the Ottoman armies in battle.

In 1914 it was members of Mustafa Kemal's generation, men who could not have imagined serving in any decision-making capacity as little as two years previously, that now stood in charge of the Ottoman army. This had implications not only for military performance but also for political decision making, since the disciples of Goltz felt entitled to bring the weight of the army as an institution to bear on political questions of the highest order. Enver Bey was hurriedly promoted and became the youngest minister of war in Late Ottoman history. The other prominent military figure in the CUP, Ahmed Cemal Pasha, became minister of the navy early in 1914. Others were not so lucky, but they, too, benefited from the liquidation of the high-ranking generals of the old regime, which opened up many important positions. In 1915, Lieutenant Colonel Mustafa Kemal took charge of a division slated for command by a major general.

Mustafa Kemal's opinions in the years leading up to the Young Turk Revolution reflected the proclivities and dilemmas of the new Ottoman officer corps. Many members of this corps joined the ranks of the opposition out of moral disgust for the regime. Their initial aims were not revolutionary or destructive, however. Unlike other contemporary revolutionaries, such as the Bolshe-

---

[27] Mustafa Aksakal, *The Ottoman Road to War in 1914: The Ottoman Empire and the First World War* (Cambridge: Cambridge University Press, 2008), 94.

viks, they felt an uncompromising loyalty to the state. Their main goal was to revive an ailing empire and save it from collapse. In contrast to many Russian officers of revolutionary bent, populist notions of Narodnism did not appeal to this generation of Ottoman officers. Although it paid lip service to the idea of serving the masses, the new officer corps was elitist at heart. In many ways, its position more closely resembled that of the military establishments in the developing countries after the Second World War. As members of a privileged group, the officers viewed themselves as being above the rest of society, which it was their natural right to lead. Like other members of the Ottoman intellectual elite at this time, and many military men since, they were profoundly attracted to Gustave Le Bon's notions of crowd psychology, in which the military held pride of place as an indispensable part of the ruling elite. They did not aim to empower disenfranchised social elements to overthrow the established order; on the contrary, they sought to strengthen the existing order the better to exercise their leadership over the feckless masses.

This influence of Le Bon on the senior leadership of the CUP cannot be overstated. Enver Pasha justified his opposition to representative government on the basis of Le Bon's criticism of parliaments as gathering places for motley crowds to which the future of a nation should by no means be entrusted.[28] Another leading staff officer with CUP affiliations maintained that the Ottoman defeats in the Balkan Wars could best be understood in light of Le Bon's theories.[29] Mustafa Kemal, too, found Le Bon's ideas compelling. Like Charles de Gaulle's *Le fil de l'épée*,[30] Mustafa Kemal's

[28] *Kendi Mektuplarında Enver Paşa*, ed. M. Şükrü Hanioğlu (Istanbul: Der Yayınları, 1989), 174–75.

[29] [İsmail] Hakkı Hafız, *Bozgun* (Istanbul: Matbaa-i Hayriye ve Şürekâsı, 1334 [1914]), 20–21, 51.

[30] Catherine Rouvier, *Les idées politiques de Gustave Le Bon* (Paris: Presses Universitaires de France, 1986), 255–57.

writings provide vague echoes of Le Bon's theses without direct quotations or references. We know that he read Le Bon's magnum opus *Lois psychologiques de l'évolution des peuples* and later Turkish renditions of Le Bon's *Enseignements psychologiques de la guerre européenne, Le déséquilibre du monde,* and *Hier et demain* with unflagging interest.[31] Many of his marginal comments and underlinings emphasize the crucial role of the elite, as do his personal papers. One passage from his diary entry for July 6, 1918, for example, deals with the necessity of "raising the people to the level of the elite instead of reducing the elite to the level of people."[32] Later, when he was in power, he asseverated, "I don't act for public opinion; I act for the nation and for my own satisfaction."[33] The Turkish republican elitism crafted by Mustafa Kemal and encapsulated in these remarks betrayed the glaring influence of Le Bon, who in his later essays praised the founder of modern Turkey as a "general of genius."[34]

Mustafa Kemal nevertheless differed from many of his peers on one key issue: the role of the military in society. Though he approved of Goltz's theory in general, he did not consider the para-

[31] *Atatürk'ün Okuduğu Kitaplar,* ed. Recep Cengiz, vol. 20, 279–94; and vol. 7, 483–84. Mustafa Kemal's personal library also included Le Bon's books *L'évolution de la matière* (1905) and *L'évolution des forces* (1912). See *Atatürk'ün Özel Kütüphanesinin Kataloğu: Anıtkabir ve Çankaya Bölümleri* (Ankara: Başbakanlık Kültür Müsteşarlığı, 1973), 43.

[32] *M. Kemal Atatürk'ün Karlsbad Hatıraları,* ed. Ayşe Afetinan (Ankara: Türk Tarih Kurumu Yayınları, 1983), 43. This statement calls to mind Le Bon's remark, "Le véritable progrès démocratique n'est pas d'abaisser l'élite au niveau de la foule, mais d'élever la foule vers l'élite," which Mustafa Kemal underlined when he read a Turkish rendition of *Hier et demain.* See *Atatürk'ün Okuduğu Kitaplar,* ed. Recep Cengiz, vol. 7, 484; Gustave Le Bon, *Hier et demain: pensées brèves* (Paris: Ernest Flammarion, 1918), 155.

[33] Lord [Patrick] Kinross, *Ataturk: A Biography of Mustafa Kemal, Father of Modern Turkey* (New York: William Morrow, 1978), 4.

[34] Gustave Le Bon, *Les incertitudes de l'heure présente* (Paris: Ernest Flammarion, 1923), 128.

military organizational model of the CUP suitable for the creation of an Ottoman/Turkish nation in arms. He believed that the crude intervention of the military in politics, through routine coup d'états and the extreme politicization of the military, would prove detrimental to the army as an institution, preventing it from focusing on its genuine military and social roles.[35] Though he was not entirely opposed to military interference in politics, Mustafa Kemal wanted the armed forces to become an *imperium in imperio*, with a position similar to that of the German military between 1871 and 1914. Such views rendered him unfit to become a policy maker within the CUP, and drove the rapid decline of his fortunes in the organization.

Mustafa Kemal first emerged as a critic of the official party line at the 1909 CUP Congress, which he attended as a delegate from Tripoli of Barbary.[36] In February 1913, he condemned the CUP's coup d'état and immediately fell out of favor.[37] In any case, it was difficult for him to advance as long as Enver Pasha was in power. For one thing, Enver Pasha detested Mustafa Kemal's impetuous amour propre and suspected his vaulting ambition and lust for power. Second, it was difficult to compete with the "military hero of the Great Ottoman Revolution," the commander of the "heroic Ottoman resistance" in Cyrenaica, and the "second conqueror of Edirne" in 1913, who, in addition, was betrothed to an Ottoman princess and enjoyed strong ties with the royal family. Under these circumstances, there was little choice for Mustafa Kemal but voluntary exile. His protector, Ahmed Cemal Bey, helped him se-

---

[35] Yusuf Hikmet Bayur, *Atatürk: Hayatı ve Eseri*, vol. 1, *Doğumundan Samsun'a Çıkışına Kadar* (Ankara: Güven Basımevi, 1963), 43–46; Celâl Bayar, *Ben de Yazdım: Millî Mücadeleye Giriş*, vol. 2 (Istanbul : Baha Matbaası, Istanbul, 1966), 506–508.

[36] Turan, *Kendine Özgü Bir Yaşam*, 91–93.

[37] Mithat Sertoğlu, "Balkan Savaşı Sonlarında Edirne'nin Kurtarılması Hususunda Hemen Teşebbüse Geçilmesi İçin Atatürk'ün Harbiye Nezaretini Uyarışına Dair Bilinmeyen Bir Belge," *Belleten* 32/128 (October 1968): 467.

cure an appointment as Ottoman military attaché in Sofia in November 1913.

Mustafa Kemal never forgot the CUP's experience in power, and when he himself seized power he imposed a strict separation of the military and civilian spheres of authority. It took a statesman of his charisma to enforce such a policy after the military had dominated politics for fifteen years. Indeed, once he had left the scene, the Turkish military's unquestioning subordination lasted only until the end of the term of his trusted subordinate and successor, İsmet İnönü, in 1950. Since 1960, the military has noisily reasserted its Goltzian role as guide and guardian of the state.

The Ottoman reforms of the late eighteenth century commenced in the army because their primary objective was to address the military challenge from Europe. For this reason, the Ottoman military embraced modernity long before other social strata. Over time, the reform process replaced a traditional army corps (the Janissaries) and local forces in the provinces with a centralized, Westernized, and modern army. At first, the professionalization of the armed forces sidelined the military as an institutional player in politics. But in a state constantly at war or suppressing rebellion, it was impossible to keep the military at bay for very long. The reforms that created a professional officer corps fed the demand for a greater role for the military in politics. It was these young officers who formed the backbone of the organization that carried out the 1908 revolution; it was they who began to weigh in on policy thereafter. This same generation of officers went on to organize the Turkish nationalist resistance after 1918 and launched a new republic in 1923. Mustafa Kemal's trajectory to power places him squarely within the ideological and political context of this generation. Indeed, his life story traces the contours of the history of the Ottoman military from the late nineteenth century to the 1930s—from insignificance to preponderance to uneasy subordination.

3

The Scientism of the Young Turks

On February 13, 1878, Sultan Abdülhamid II prorogued the Ottoman Chamber of Deputies after it had been in existence for scarcely a year.[1] Although ostensibly a temporary move, the dissolution of the assembly was not reversed for more than three decades, giving birth to one of the most important and sustained opposition movements in modern history. Adversaries of the regime instituted by Abdülhamid II after 1878 are generally referred to as "Young Turks." The dissidents were diverse, ranging from Muslim clerics to ethnic nationalists, Freemasons, and former statesmen who joined the ranks of the Young Turks at various stages. But the core group that led the movement was made up of cadets, students, and graduates of the major royal colleges, institutions upgraded and reformed for the most part by the sultan himself. Mustafa Kemal's attitudes and policies were to be shaped to an extraordinary degree by the ideas he encountered and the experiences he underwent as an activist in the Young Turk movement.

An overwhelming number of these young men were disciples of a peculiar mid-nineteenth-century German philosophy known as *Vulgärmaterialismus*. This was a vulgarized version of the doctrine of materialism, fusing popular notions of materialism, scientism, and Darwinism into a simplistic creed that upheld the role

[1] Hakkı Tarık Us, *Meclis-i Mebusan, 1293 =1877*, vol. 2 (Istanbul: Vakit Kütüphanesi, 1954), 407.

of science in society.[2] The Late Ottoman version of this materialism was a further simplification of the German original and a medley of highly disparate ideas, the common denominator of which was the rejection of religion. The Young Turks were oblivious to the irony inherent in their own uninhibited worship of prominent German materialists. Their chief idol was the German physiologist Ludwig Büchner, whose magnum opus, *Kraft und Stoff* (Force and Matter), was regarded by them as a sort of holy book. Their self-contradictory iconoclasm recalls Fyodor Mikhaylovich Dostoyevsky's novel *Besy* (*The Possessed*), in which the protagonist assaults his landowner's Christian icons with an axe, only to replace them with candle-bedecked lecterns bearing books by Ludwig Büchner, Jacob Moleschott, and Karl Vogt.[3] In its German birthplace, the movement had negligible philosophical and political impact. In the Ottoman Empire, however, it struck root among a particularly influential circle of disciples. Although they were an extremely marginal group at the turn of the century, the Young Turks were destined to rule the Islamic caliphate for almost a decade, and then to go on to craft a secular nation-state out of its remains. It was thus by a bizarre twist of fate that the German doctrine of *Vulgärmaterialismus* came to bear its most significant fruits in a context entirely alien to its original environment, and that a further vulgarized version of its central tenets would in time form one of the ideological pillars of the modern Turkish nation-state.[4]

It is impossible to understand the policies of Mustafa Kemal

[2] For more information, see Frederic Gregory, *Scientific Materialism in Nineteenth Century Germany* (Dordrecht, Netherlands: D. Reidel, 1977); and Dieter Wittich, *Vogt, Moleschott, Büchner; Schriften zum kleinbürgerlichen Materialismus in Deutschland*, vols. 1–2 (Berlin: Akademie-Verlag, 1971).

[3] M. Şükrü Hanioğlu, "Blueprints for a Future Society: Late Ottoman Materialists on Science, Religion, and Art," in *Late Ottoman Society: The Intellectual Legacy*, ed. Elisabeth Özdalga (London: RoutledgeCurzon, 2005), 32, 90.

[4] Ibid., 86–89.

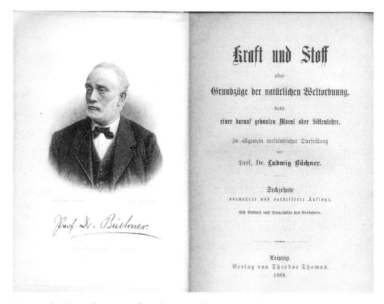

Figure 4. The title page of Ludwig Büchner's *Kraft und Stoff.*

without recognizing that he belonged to the educated class of a generation that embraced a crude conception of science as a panacea for the ills of the empire, and saw in the doctrine of vulgar materialism an indispensable manual for constructing a prosperous, rational, and irreligious modern society. These individuals avidly read such Ottoman journals as *Musavver Cihan* (Illustrated World), which offered "Chemistry Lessons for Everybody,"[5] provided scientific explanations for "supernatural" events, and conveyed the essence of Darwinism by means of simple illustrations.[6] Unlike their popular counterparts in Europe, such as *Die Gegenwart, Die Natur,* or *Science pour tous,* Ottoman materialist publications were treated as serious scientific journals, and their punctum

[5] A[bdullah] Cevdet, "Herkes İçün Kimya," *Musavver Cihan* 4 (September 23, 1891): 30–3, and 34 (April 27, 1892): 266–68.

[6] See, for example, *Musavver Cihan* 43 (August 30, 1892): 344.

saliens—"science reigns supreme"—became the motto of a generation. Consequently, a substantial proportion of that generation's educated class espoused a view of history that revolved around the notion of an epic struggle between religion and science, one that would inevitably end with the triumph of science and its coronation as the new and definitive belief system. Like most millenarians, they tended to believe that the victory of their cause would take place in their own lifetimes. It was not a coincidence that John William Draper's *Conflict between Religion and Science* became a best-seller in the Ottoman Empire upon its translation into Turkish in the closing years of the nineteenth century.[7]

In 1889, a political society with strong scientistic leanings called the Ottoman Union Committee was established at the Royal Medical Academy in Istanbul. One of its first members, Dr. Şerafeddin Mağmumî, became famous for proposing that poetry be abolished on account of its unscientific character.[8] In 1895, in a reflection of the growing influence of positivism on the movement's leadership, its name was changed to the Ottoman Committee of Union and Progress. Although the subsequent transformation of the Committee of Union and Progress (CUP) from a student club into a revolutionary conspiracy tended to conceal the scientistic agenda of the movement in later years, scientism remained a focal tenet of Young Turk ideology. For a long time its disciples were inhibited from expressing it too openly by the awkward requirements of staging a revolution and consolidating power in a multinational realm held together under the banner of Islam, but this constraint disappeared along with the Ottoman Empire itself in 1922, and the devotees of scientism were free once more to make public profession of their beliefs.

[7] Mustafa Kemal later read a French translation of Draper's *A History of the Intellectual Development of Europe*. See *Atatürk 'ün Okuduğu Kitaplar*, ed. Recep Cengiz, vol. 12 (Ankara: Anıtkabir Derneği Yayınları, 2001), 469–74.

[8] Hanioğlu, "Blueprints," 44–45.

Mustafa Kemal belonged to the second generation of Young Turks, born in the early 1880s. His upbringing in Salonica and his education at secular institutions undoubtedly made him more receptive to criticism directed against the religious establishment. Although the Royal Military Academy was not a hotbed of Ottoman materialist activism, one of its prominent graduates, Beşir Fu'ad, committed suicide in 1887 just to prove that life was an experimental "scientific" phenomenon.[9] Like many of his peers, Mustafa Kemal gained his exposure to the movement through popular journals and pamphlets. He later read parts of Ludwig Büchner's *Kraft und Stoff*, and seemed particularly struck by the suggestion that human thinking had a material basis, as evidenced by the centrality of phosphorus in brain processes.[10] Another study of Büchner on the origins and the prospects of the human race influenced him even more deeply.[11] Like many others in his generation, Mustafa Kemal confused the vulgar materialism popularized by the likes of Büchner with the materialist tradition of the Baron d'Holbach and Voltaire.[12] A similar pattern of oversimp-

[9] See Orhan Okay, *Beşir Fuad: İlk Türk Pozitivist ve Natüralisti* (Istanbul: Dergâh Yayınları, 2008), 68–71.

[10] *Atatürk'ün Okuduğu Kitaplar*, ed. Recep Cengiz, vol. 8, 439–40; *Kraft und Stoff oder Grundzüge der natürlichen Weltordnung*, 16th ed. (Leipzig, Germany: Verlag von Theodor Thomas, 1888), 267–69. Mustafa Kemal's personal library included a copy of the French translation of *Kraft und Stoff*. See *Atatürk'ün Özel Kütüphanesinin Kataloğu: Anıtkabir ve Çankaya Bölümleri* (Ankara: Başbakanlık Kültür Müsteşarlığı, 1973), 41.

[11] This study was *Der mensch und seine stellung in der natur in vergangenheit, gegenwart und zukunft, oder Woher kommen wir? Wer sind wir? Wohin gehen wir?* See *Atatürk'ün Okuduğu Kitaplar*, ed. Recep Cengiz, vol. 22, pp.125–224. Mustafa Kemal read the French translation titled *L'homme selon la science: son passé, son présent, son avenir ou, d'où venons-nous? Qui sommes-nous? Où allons-nous? Exposé très simple suivi d'un grand nombre d'éclaircissements et remarques scientifiques* (Paris: C. Reinwald, 1885).

[12] See *Atatürk'ün Okuduğu Kitaplar*, ed. Recep Cengiz, vol. 8, 396–407; and [Paul-Henri Dietrich d'Holbach], *Le bon sens du curé Meslier, suivi de son testa-*

lification plagued his vigorous espousal of evolutionary theory, derived primarily from H. G. Wells. For instance, Mustafa Kemal once commented that "since humans came from the seas like all other reptiles, our forefathers were fish."[13] More generally, his frequent references to life as a natural struggle for survival reveal strong social Darwinist convictions.[14]

Although he skimmed the major works of popular materialism and was profoundly influenced by them, Mustafa Kemal never became an original scientistic thinker in his own right. The simple insight he seems to have derived from what he read was that science promoted progress while religion retarded it. One of his most well-known aphorisms, "The most truthful guide in life is science," reveals a one-dimensional worldview that ascribed an overarching role to science in every aspect of human life. "Seeking any guide other than science," he averred, making an oblique allusion to religion, "is thoughtlessness, prevarication, and ignorance."[15] For him, "nothing which could not be explained by everyday intelligence was worth considering."[16] Similarly, religions were manufactured phenomena, created by their respective prophets in concrete his-

---

ment (Paris: Au Palais des Thermes de Julien, 1802), 175, 178, 181–83, 287–89, 291, 300–302.

[13] Ruşen Eşref Ünaydın, *Atatürk: Tarih ve Dil Kurumları Hâtıralar; VII. Türk Dil Kurultayında Söylenmiştir* (Ankara: T.D.K., 1954), 53; H. G. Wells, *The Outline of History: Being a Plain History of Life and Mankind*, vol. 1 (New York: Review of Reviews, 1924), 23ff. Mustafa Kemal also read the French translation of Ernst Haeckel's *Ewigkeit: Weltkriegsgedanken über Leben und Tod, Religion und Entwicklungslehre*. See *Atatürk'ün Okuduğu Kitaplar*, ed. Recep Cengiz, vol. 20, 263–77.

[14] See, for example, "Tarsus'da Gençlerle Konuşma, 21.III. 1923," in *Atatürk'ün Söylev ve Demeçleri*, vol. 2, *1906–1938*, ed. Nimet Unan (Ankara: Türk İnkılâp Tarihi Enstitüsü Yayımları, 1952), 133.

[15] "Samsun Öğretmenleriyle Konuşma, 22.XI. 1924," ibid., 197.

[16] [Halide Edib], *The Turkish Ordeal: Being the Further Memoirs of Halidé Edib* (New York: Century, 1928), 170.

torical circumstances: "Moses was a man who strove for the emancipation of the Jews, who had been groaning under the lashes of the Egyptians;"[17] "Jesus was a person who comprehended the absolute destitution of his time and turned the reaction against the pains of his age into a religion of love."[18] As for Islam, he agreed that it had not "arisen as a result of the national evolution of the Arabs, but as a consequence of the emergence of Muḥammad,"[19] a remark that closely echoed Thomas Carlyle's judgment on the Prophet of Islam.[20]

Such opinions were quite common during the last decades of the empire, and some went as far as the espousal of the Dutch orientalist Reinhart Dozy's assertion that the emergence of Islam resulted from the Prophet Muḥammad's alleged muscular hysteria, a claim originally put forward by Aloys Sprenger.[21] A Young Turk journal published initially in Geneva and Cairo later propagated these theses in the Ottoman capital.[22] This journal, ironically named *İctihad* (*Ijtihād*; a term used in Islamic jurisprudence for original legal thinking on the part of qualified jurists), attempted to

---

[17] "Subay ve Kumandan ile Konuşmalar," in *Atatürk'ün Bütün Eserleri*, vol. 1, *1903–1915* (Istanbul: Kaynak Yayınları, 1998), 168.

[18] Ibid.

[19] Şerafettin Turan, *Atatürk'ün Düşünce Yapısını Etkileyen Olaylar, Düşünürler, Kitaplar* (Ankara: Türk Tarih Kurumu Yayınları, 1982), 23.

[20] Mustafa Kemal carefully read the French translation of Carlyle's *On Heroes, Hero-worship and the Heroic in History*, and found the account of Muḥammad persuasive. See *Atatürk'ün Okuduğu Kitaplar*, ed. Recep Cengiz, vol. 23, 149ff; *Les héros, le culte des héros et l'héroïque dans l'histoire*, trans. J.-B.-J. Izoulet-Loubatières (Paris, n.d. [1916]), 71ff.

[21] It is most interesting to note that when Mustafa Kemal read a French translation of Dozy's study (*Het Islamisme*) with fascination, he underlined those parts elaborating on this claim. See *Atatürk'ün Okuduğu Kitaplar*, ed. Recep Cengiz, vol. 19, 84–88; *Essai sur l'histoire de l'Islamisme*, trans. Victor Chauvin (Paris: Maisonneuve, 1879), 22ff.

[22] M. Şükrü Hanioğlu, *Bir Siyasal Düşünür Olarak Doktor Abdullah Cevdet ve Dönemi* (Istanbul: Üçdal Neşriyat, 1981), 325ff.

reconstitute Islam as a materialist philosophy that would serve as a cultural resource to build the religion-free society of the future. The idea of a new religion, one free of dogma, myth, ritual, and supernatural commands, was taken from the French philosopher-poet Jean-Marie Guyau and became a tenet of the Late Ottoman scientistic vision. In Arabia, Sharīf Ḥusayn of Mecca listed the attacks on Islam published in the pages of this journal as one of the leading causes of the Arab Revolt of 1916.[23] In Ankara, a decade later, these criticisms became the basis of policy. In 1925, Mustafa Kemal is said to have remarked to the editor of *İctihad*, whom he was considering for a parliamentary appointment, "Doctor, until now you have written about many things. Now we may bring them to realization."[24] In fact, he selected two other leading contributors to the journal as deputies in the Turkish Grand National Assembly.

Although he was later idealized as a mythic harbinger of change, it is imperative to realize that Mustafa Kemal emerged from within a specific social milieu, one that limited the range of options open to any prospective revolutionary leader. The crucial point in the present context is that many of the radical ideas destined to become central planks in his reform program were widely held in intellectual circles at the turn of the century, and were expressed with increasing explicitness after the Young Turk Revolution. Indeed, many former Young Turks of a scientistic orientation later described Mustafa Kemal as the "authoritarian savior" who had brought *their* ideas to fruition.[25]

[23] Sulaymān Mūsā, *al-Ḥusayn ibn ʿAlī waʾl-thawra al-ʿArabīya al-kubrā* (Amman, Jordan: Lajnat Tārīkh al-Urdunn, 1992), 134.

[24] M. Şükrü Hanioğlu, "Garbcılar: Their Attitudes toward Religion and Their Impact on the Official Ideology of the Turkish Republic," *Studia Islamica* 86/2 (August 1997): 147. For a detailed account of this meeting, see Abdullah Cevdet, "Gazi Paşaʾnın Köşkünde," *İctihad* 194 (December 15, 1925): 3813–16.

[25] İbrahim Temo, *Atatürkü Nʾiçin Severim?* (Medgidia, Romania: n.p., 1937), 8.

Like many Ottoman literati, Mustafa Kemal realized that Islam was so profoundly embedded in Ottoman culture that it could not be made to vanish with the wave of a wand. Accordingly, he adopted a much more malleable approach to religion than his contemporaries in the Soviet Union. His attitude can be summed up in a famous maxim of the Late Ottoman devotees of scientism: "Religion is the science of the masses, whereas science is the religion of the elite."[26] According to this line of thought, an all-out attack on Islam in a predominately Muslim society was injudicious. Instead, a reconfigured version of Islam could be co-opted to serve as a vehicle for progress and enlightenment. Some secular intellectuals, and even certain reform-minded Muslim thinkers, thus accepted the view, especially as expressed in François Guizot's *Histoire de la civilisation en Europe*, that social progress in Europe had followed the Protestant reformation.[27] But while some reformist Muslims concluded from the Lutheran experience that the reform of Islam was imperative,[28] Westernist thinkers like Abdullah Cevdet and Kılıçzâde İsmail Hakkı (İsmail Hakkı Kılıçoğlu) took their inspiration rather from the subsequent marginalization of religion in European societies. To them, a reformed religion had only a temporary role to play as an instrument for the modernization of society, after which it would be cast aside.

Another obsession common to the Young Turks and other Ottoman intellectuals was the position of the empire vis-à-vis the West (primarily taken to mean Christian Europe). Although many

---

[26] Abdullah Cevdet, "Şehzâde Mecid Efendi Ḥazretleri'yle Mülâkat," *İctihad* 57 (March 20, 1913): 1257.

[27] Bryan S. Turner, "Islam, Capitalism and the Weber Theses," *British Journal of Sociology* 25/2 (June 1974): 241. See also Felicitas Opwis, "Changes in Modern Islamic Theory: Reform or Reformation?" in *An Islamic Reformation?* ed. Michaelle Browers and Charles Kurzman (Lanham, MD: Lexington Books, 2004), 39ff.

[28] Şeyh ʿUbayd Allāh [al]-Afghānī, *Kavm-i Cedîd: Kitabüʾl-Mevâiz* (Istanbul: Şems Matbaası, 1331 [1913]), 5–6.

literate men of this generation were products of a Western-style education, with an intellectual agenda closely resembling that of their European contemporaries, they developed what can best be described as a love-hate attitude toward the West. On the one hand, the West symbolized intellectual and scientific ascendancy, and provided the blueprint for the ideal society of the future; yet on the other hand, it was a predatory monster that fed on Ottoman wealth and territory. Nevertheless, the Ottoman adherents of scientism fervently advocated Westernization precisely because they believed that the origins of Europe's threatening wealth and technology lay in the wholesale adoption of science along the lines prescribed by scientistic ideology.

Mustafa Kemal adopted a similar approach to the West. He also viewed European civilization as the zenith of progress and the epitome of modernity, yet at the same time was wary of Europe's power and designs on the Ottoman Empire, especially after the Balkan Wars of 1912–13— the most ignominious defeat in Ottoman history, and one that almost instantaneously transformed a multicontinental empire into an Asiatic country. As he confessed to an interviewer in 1923, the West was "an entity that, seeing us as an inferior society, has exerted its best efforts to encompass our destruction."[29]

The proponents of the Ottoman offshoot of scientism split over the way to Westernize society. The so-called "Partial Westernizers" supported a large degree of Westernization of Ottoman society while attempting to guard against the threat of Western imperialism. "The West," in other words, was cast as both model and enemy. With the victorious Japanese in mind, such thinkers advanced the idea of scientific, technological, and industrial transfers

[29] "Türkiye'de Cumhuriyet ve Şarklılık, Garplılık Meselesi, 27. IX. 1923," in *Atatürk'ün Söylev ve Demeçleri*, vol. 3, *1918–1937*, ed. Nimet Unan (Ankara: Türk İnkılâp Tarihi Enstitüsü Yayımları, 1954), 64.

Figure 5. Partition of the European Provinces of the empire after the Balkan Wars of 1912–13.

from Europe.[30] Their opponents, the so-called Comprehensive Westernizers, advocated the wholesale acceptance of Western civilization "with its roses and its thorns" and took the view that Europe, the "peak of superiority," ought to be emulated, not feared

[30] Celâl Nuri, "Şime-i Husumet," *İctihad* 88 (January 22, 1914): 1949–51.

(let alone antagonized).[31] Although Mustafa Kemal's deep-seated suspicions of the West tended to place him in the former camp, his support for wholesale Westernization placed him more properly in the latter. In time, his adoption of an extravagantly flamboyant theory of a universal civilization originating in Turkic culture rendered the entire debate irrelevant.

Like many disciples of scientism, Mustafa Kemal saw no problem in importing the culture and way of life of Europe. He even supported the adoption of European good manners, so that they would eventually displace obsolescent Muslim and Ottoman customs. Writers in post-1908 Ottoman scientistic journals asked people to dress and act like Europeans, featuring helpful illustrations taken from European (especially French) books of etiquette.[32] At the same time, they called upon their compatriots to abandon anachronistic customs that could not be reconciled with the modern way of life. They decried Islamic precepts and conventions such as almsgiving and hospitality as "rules and regulations made in the desert 1,300 years ago" that were no longer practical in the present.[33] Some thinkers went so far as to attack the fundamental Muslim ritual of worship (*namaz/salat*) on the grounds that a modern person could not waste his precious time performing a religious rite five times a day.[34] Although illustrated instructions on how to kiss a lady's hand or help her to dismount from a horse influenced only a handful of secular readers, they infuriated devout ones. Likewise commentary on the social life of couples of mixed faith sparked a fierce outcry from the ʿulamāʾ. To the Westernizers, such protests seemed pointless in the face of the irrefut-

[31] Abdullah Cevdet, "Şime-i Muhabbet," *İctihad* 89 (January 29, 1914): 1979–84.

[32] "Muʿaşeret Edeblerinden," *Yirminci Asırda Zekâ* 1 (March 18, 1912): 13ff.

[33] Keçecizâde İzzet Fuʾad, "Meclis-i Mebʿusan Reʾisi Ahmed Rıza Beyefendiʾye," *İştihad* 132 (November 28, 1918): 2827.

[34] Abdullah Cevdet, "Yara ve Tuz," *İştihad* 132 (November 28, 1918): 2826.

able verdict of "science." As Abdullah Cevdet put it, they were like a struggle between a "pumpkin and a Krupp shell." The pumpkin that dreamed of shattering a Krupp shell would be utterly destroyed.[35] Mustafa Kemal agreed. In promoting European attire (including the compulsory hat introduced for Turkish bureaucrats in 1925), he maintained that "he who says he is civilized should demonstrate it in his way of dressing." To oppose Western dress was to choose to "live with superstitions and ideas of the middle ages, instead of embracing the civilization that could dig holes in mountains, fly in the skies, and observe things ranging from molecules, which could not be seen with the naked eye, to stars."[36]

Like others of his generation, Mustafa Kemal perceived Westernization as a prerequisite for creating a society founded on science. As early as 1913, a leading Westernist, Kılıçzâde Hakkı, whom Mustafa Kemal later made a parliamentary deputy, issued a blueprint for transformation that bore a remarkable resemblance to the reforms subsequently implemented in the early Republican era. Kılıçzâde Hakkı envisaged a future society in which the madrasahs were abolished, the hat took the place of the fez, women participated in social life, dervish lodges were closed down, the state took control of religion, and sweeping legal reforms were enacted.[37]

Yet despite the fact that the Westernist movement strongly influenced Mustafa Kemal, he was no average sympathizer, nor can it be said that he merely implemented a preexisting program. The republican reforms bear the uncompromising and idiosyncratic imprint of Mustafa Kemal himself. Though he was no ideologue, he infused the execution of the reforms with a radicalism that con-

[35] A[bdullah] C[evdet], "[Cevab]," İctihad 96 (March 19, 1914): 2827.
[36] "İnebolu'da Bir Konuşma, 28. VIII. 1925," in Atatürk'ün Söylev ve Demeçleri, vol. 2, 214.
[37] [Kılıçzâde Hakkı], "Pek Uyanık Bir Uyku," İctihad 55 (March 6, 1913): 1226–28, and 57 (March 20, 1913): 1261–64.

siderably exceeded the expectations of the Ottoman Westernizers. Most important, unlike reformers of the Late Ottoman era, he refused to tolerate the survival of time-honored customs and institutions alongside the new ones that emerged through the process of reform; instead, he insisted on abolishing the old and replacing it with a radically new set of norms, structures, and values. Rather than reform the existing alphabet, for example, he banned the use of the Arabo-Persian Ottoman script and replaced it with a modified Latin one. In place of the *Majalla*—the hybrid Ottoman legal code produced in the nineteenth century—he imported the Swiss Civil Code (with minor modifications), banishing Islamic law from every aspect of social life. There was a certain ruthless pragmatism to the implementation process, and this, too, may be attributed to the character of the individual who directed it. Mustafa Kemal was, above all, a practitioner, not a theoretician. He did not split hairs over the interpretation of theory. He eschewed dogma and ploughed ahead. In this sense, he was perhaps the truest adherent of *Vulgärmaterialismus*, shunning all philosophies in an unrelenting drive to build a society governed by science.

As early as 1903, the Young Turk journal *Türk*, with its passionate Turkist proclivities, had maintained that pre-Islamic Turkish customs were more liberal and progressive than those adopted by the Turks after their conversion to Islam.[38] The journal also engaged in an acrimonious debate with the leading Muslim reformist Rashīd Riḍā over its claim of Turkish superiority over other Muslim ethnic groups.[39] Once in power, the CUP initially adopted a more conciliatory stance, and after its establishment of a virtual single-party regime in 1913 it leaned toward a reconciliation of Turkism and religion. Between 1913 and 1918 the CUP provided

[38] See, for example, "Şecaât Nedir?" *Türk* 163 (May 23, 1907): 2.

[39] [Şerafeddin Mağmumî], "Düşündüm ki," *Türk* 7 (December 17, 1903): 1; "Daʿwā al-khilāfa: taʿrīb maqālat nushirat fī jarīdat (Turk) al-gharrāʾ," *al-Manār* 6/24 (March 3, 1904): 954–58.

strong support to an intellectual trend aiming to construct a Turkified Islam that would respond appropriately to the challenges of
modernity. This initiative was led by Ziya Gökalp, a soi-disant so-
ciologist, a devout follower of Émile Durkheim, and the leading
ideologue of the CUP; in one of his poems he set out "Religion
According to a Turk."[40] This movement maintained that many Islamic practices that contradicted modernity, such as polygamy,
could be eliminated through liberal interpretation of Islamic
sources.[41] Mustafa Kemal, though deeply influenced by Ziya
Gökalp's ideas on nationalism,[42] later decided not to draw extensively on Islam for modernization. He did not follow the CUP,
which had embraced Ziya Gökalp's thesis and attempted to use the
Temporary Family Law to curb polygamy through a liberal interpretation of Ḥanbalī law, and to grant a limited right of divorce to
Muslim women.[43] (There were four traditional Sunnī schools of
legal doctrine; the Ottomans normally followed the Ḥanafī, not
the Ḥanbalī school). Instead Mustafa Kemal opted for more
straightforward policies, such as adopting the slightly modified
Swiss Civil Code and a strict ban on polygamy. His recourse to
Islam in such cases did not go beyond superficially presenting the
changes as reforms in perfect accordance with religion.

Although he was reluctant to employ Islam extensively in the
service of modernization, he was sympathetic to the notion that a
Turkified version of Islam could serve as a useful vehicle for advancing Turkish nationalism. Thus, for example, in the early years
of the Republic, *Tanrı*, an old Turkish word also used for pagan
Turkic deities, replaced the customary *Allāh*. Similarly, a Turkish

[40] Ziya Gökalp, "Türk'e Göre Din," *İslâm Mecmuası* 2/22 (February 25,
[1915]), 552.
[41] Mansurizâde Sa'id, "İslâm Kadını: Ta'addüd-i Zevcât İslâmiyetde Men'
Olunabilir," *İslâm Mecmuası* 1/8 (1914): 233–38.
[42] Cavit Orhan Tütengil, "Atatürk ve Ziya Gökalp Bağlantıları," *Türk Dili*
27/302 (November 1, 1976): 579–84.
[43] *Düstûr*, II/9 (Istanbul: Evkaf Matbaası, 1928), 762–81.

call to prayer replaced the traditional Arabic summons used throughout the Muslim world. Nevertheless, the early Republican press often referred to Islam as an "Arab religion." As the examples given demonstrate, efforts toward the Turkification of religion gained considerable momentum during the initial years of the Republic; they eventually culminated in an appeal by pundits closely associated with the regime to replace religion with nationalism, and religious sentiment with ethnic identification. Mustafa Kemal acclaimed the treatise *Din Yok Milliyet Var: Benim Dinim, Benim Türklüğümdür* (There Is No Religion, Just Nationality: My Turkishness Is My Religion), which was prepared for his personal perusal.[44] He seemed especially keen on comments such as, "The Oriental nations have become religious buffoons more than others; this is why since ancient times they have developed traditions such as lying and supporting their words with oaths. Today, Arabs and especially Persians lie all the time." He scribbled in the margins, "with the exception of Turkey."[45] Yet despite his apparent nationalist and scientistic proclivities, Mustafa Kemal did not confront Islam openly. He paid lip service to religion while putting it under strict state control and seeking to redefine it in narrowly scientistic and nationalistic terms.

As a Turk who grew up in the turbulent ethnic mélange of Macedonia, Mustafa Kemal was susceptible to the Turkism that became a pillar of the Young Turk ideology after 1905. But Turkism arose in Macedonia not only as a hostile reaction to the separatist inclinations of Greeks, Macedonians, Serbians, and Bulgarians but also as also the imitative product of genuine admiration for the solidarity of these groups. Service in Macedonia inspired Ottoman officers to seek a Turkish equivalent to the separatist nationalisms of the groups they were confronting in the

---

[44] Ruşenî [Barkın], *Din Yok Milliyet Var: Benim Dinim, Benim Türklüğümdür.*

[45] *Atatürk'ün Okuduğu Kitaplar*, ed. Recep Cengiz, vol. 8, 466.

field. When, for instance, at train stations throughout Macedonia, Ottoman officers witnessed crowds of Bulgarians chanting the Bulgarian national anthem *Shumi Maritsa* in an emotional gesture of farewell to members of nationalist bands being whisked away into captivity, they asked why their empire lacked an anthem, and why the only songs sung in the Ottoman army were marches composed in honor of individual sultans.[46] Macedonia thus served as a school of nationalism for Ottoman officers. Mustafa Kemal in fact attempted to found an underground movement motivated by a proto-Turkist agenda: this was the four-man Fatherland and Freedom organization, formed in Damascus in 1905.[47] The following year, in Salonica, he played a minor role in the formation of the secret Ottoman Freedom Society, which later merged with the CUP to become the standard-bearer of revolution and of the Turkist movement.[48]

After the Young Turk Revolution, the CUP had to shelve its Turkist principles in order to administer a polyethnic empire. But Turkist ideas continued to flourish in the Second Constitutional Period (1908–18). The CUP toned down the prerevolutionary rhetoric of political Turkism, and made some effort to reconcile this revolutionary doctrine with the supranational ideology of Ottomanism. At the same time, the CUP encouraged the spread of this ideology at the cultural level. Subsequent developments, especially the loss of most of European Turkey and the outbreak of the Great War, revived the political fortunes of Turkism by providing an apparent opportunity to transform the Ottoman state into a Turanian empire. Ziya Gökalp encapsulated this vision in his famed poem "Turan": "Neither Turkey nor Turkistan is a fatherland for the Turks / The fatherland is an enormous and eternal

---

[46] M. Şükrü Hanioğlu, *Preparation for a Revolution: The Young Turks, 1902–1908* (New York: Oxford University Press, 2001), 341.

[47] Ibid., 211.

[48] Ibid., 211–12.

country: Turan."[49] Although this sounded like an intellectual fantasy when it was written in 1911, Turan swiftly became the catchword of an ascendant ideology.

Like many other members of the CUP, Mustafa Kemal followed the Turkist fashion with enthusiasm. As a cadet, he read Süleyman Pasha's *Tarih-i Âlem* (World History; 1878), a landmark in Ottoman historiography because of its focus on the pre-Seljuk Turkic states of Central Asia. Similarly, he was deeply influenced by Léon Cahun's *Introduction à l'histoire de l'Asie: Turcs et Mongols; des origins à 1405*, which provided a window onto the pre-Ottoman history of the Turks.[50] Mustafa Kemal also owed much to Ziya Gökalp, a fact that is evident from his speeches and writings. At the same time, he opposed Gökalp's distinction between culture and civilization and ignored the importance Gökalp attributed to Islam in molding the new Turkish ideology.

Among Mustafa Kemal's intimate circle of friends were a number of important Turkists of the prerevolutionary era. One of them, Ömer Naci, was an officer who fled the empire to join the CUP central committee in Paris; he had worked with Mustafa Kemal at the Royal Military Academy to produce a clandestine handwritten journal and circulate it among the cadets.[51] Ömer Naci later became the chief orator of the CUP, and was known for his ability to incite crowds with his strong Turkist rhetoric. Mustafa Kemal later related that a leading Turkist literary figure, Mehmed Emin (Yurdakul), played a significant role in shaping and awakening his national consciousness.[52] Mehmed Emin was to become known as the "national poet" for his early poetry, which

[49] Tevfik Sedad [Ziya Gökalp], "Turan," *Genc Kalemler* 6 (March 1911): 167.
[50] *Atatürk'ün Okuduğu Kitaplar*, ed. Recep Cengiz, vol. 12, 475–84.
[51] Fethi Tevetoğlu, *Ömer Naci* (Ankara: Kültür ve Turizm Bakanlığı Yayınları, 1987), 33.
[52] Faik Reşit Unat, "Ne Mutlu, Türküm Diyene!" *Türk Dili* 13/146 (November 1963): 77.

included such lines as "I am a Turk / Great are my religion and race."[53]

Early Turkism had placed a low priority on race because Turks, along with other Asiatic peoples, lay toward the bottom of the racial hierarchies that were commonplaces at that time. But race became a central theme of Turkism after the Russo-Japanese war of 1904–5, which Mustafa Kemal followed with excitement and enthusiasm.[54] Japan's victories gave impetus to a renewed interest in racial theory and the Turkic past among the Young Turks and Ottoman intellectuals. It is in this context that we find reports of an argument that took place in 1906 between Mustafa Kemal, an Albanian captain, and a Turkish sergeant, in which the former rejected the traditional noble status ascribed to the Arabs and touted instead the "noble qualities of the Turkish race."[55] Later in his career, in the course of constructing the Turkish History Thesis, Mustafa Kemal denounced Eurocentric claims that the Turks belonged to the secondary (*secondaire*) yellow race. (He apparently instructed his adopted daughter, a budding historian, to research the topic.)[56]

As a member of the second generation of the Young Turks, Mustafa Kemal embraced the major characteristics of a weltanschauung shared by many educated young Ottomans. The first commandment of this worldview was reverence for science and its quasi-religious role in modern society. To borrow a phrase

[53] Mehmed Emin, *Türkçe Şiirler* (Istanbul: Matbaa-i Ahmed İhsan ve Şürekâsı, 1334 [1916]), 41–2. Mustafa Kemal read this edition in 1916. See *Atatürk'ün Hatıra Defteri*, ed. Şükrü Tezer (Ankara: Türk Tarih Kurumu Yayınları, 1972), 86.

[54] *Atatürk'ün Not Defterleri*, vol. 2, *Harp Akademisi Öğrencisi Mustafa Kemal'in Not Defteri* (Ankara: Genelkurmay ATASE Yayınları, 2004), 26ff.

[55] Ali Fuat Cebesoy, *Sınıf Arkadaşım Atatürk: Okul ve Genç Subaylık Hâtıraları* (Istanbul: İnkılâp ve Aka, 1967), 99–100; Unat, "Ne Mutlu, Türküm Diyene!" 77–78.

[56] Afet İnan, "Atatürk ve Tarih Tezi," *Belleten* 3/10 (April 1, 1939): 244.

coined by Carlton Hayes, Mustafa Kemal was first and foremost a member of "a generation of materialism."[57] He viewed everything from nationalism to modernism through the prism of scientism. In any European country, Mustafa Kemal would have been considered uncompromisingly scientistic. His assumption of power in a predominantly conservative Muslim society was astoundingly revolutionary.

[57] Carlton J. H. Hayes, *A Generation of Materialism, 1871–1900* (New York: Harper, 1941).

4

From Wars to the Great War: A Hero Is Born

The catastrophic war with Russia in 1877–78 significantly weakened the Ottoman position in the Balkans. Thereafter, Sultan Abdülhamid II made every possible effort to avoid military defeat by minimizing foreign adventure. In the three decades leading up to the Young Turk Revolution of 1908, the empire fought only one brief war, against Greece in 1897, and this produced the first Ottoman military victory since the Crimean War of 1853–56. Yet despite the relative tranquility of the period, territorial losses continued and borders shrank. In 1881, the French established a de facto protectorate over Tunis. The next year, the British occupied Egypt. In 1885, the Italians landed in Massawa and within five years had declared Eritrea an Italian colony. The same year, Bulgaria, ostensibly an Ottoman principality, annexed Eastern Rumelia, an autonomous Ottoman province. Many Arabian leaders, such as the sheikh of Kuwait, signed agreements with the British and broke loose from Istanbul's grip. Still, these losses occurred on the periphery, large parts of which had long been considered effectively lost by successive Ottoman administrations. The Ottoman heartlands, by contrast, enjoyed a period of relative peace and prosperity. In spite of the great economic depression of 1873–96, which shook Europe and enveloped the world, the Ottoman economy enjoyed modest but steady growth for the duration of the Hamidian era.

In an era in which the army was primarily used to suppress domestic uprisings, no major military heroes emerged. In fact, the sultan, fearing a coup or a diminution of his own stature, took care to clip the wings of his top brass. He even prevented rigorous training, thereby impairing Ottoman fighting capacity. İbrahim Edhem Pasha, commander of the Ottoman forces against the Greeks in 1897, gained fame and the title of Gazi (from the Arabic *Ghāzī*, meaning "holy warrior"), but never became a prominent public figure. The two popular heroes of the Russo-Ottoman War—Gazi Osman Pasha and Gazi Ahmed Muhtar Pasha—were placed under close scrutiny by the palace.

The Young Turk Revolution of 1908 brought two young commanders to the fore: Major Enver Bey and Adjutant Major Niyazi Bey, the principal leaders of the military insurrection in Macedonia during the later stages of the Revolution. Musicians and poets composed marches and poems in honor of their heroism, while public figures organized subscriptions to purchase new dreadnoughts to be named after the two revolutionary idols. Parents throughout the Muslim world named their sons after these officers; famous namesakes of Enver Bey include the Albanian Communist leader Enver Hoxha and the Egyptian president Muḥammad Anwar al-Sādāt. The other revolutionary icon, Niyazi Bey, a pious officer of Albanian descent, quickly became disillusioned with the Committee of Union and Progress's (CUP's) secularist and Turkist tendencies, and was killed by Albanian nationalists in 1913. This left Enver Bey, who had led the gallant Ottoman resistance to the Italians in Cyrenaica and who went on to recapture Edirne from the Bulgarians, as the preeminent military hero in the empire.

Meanwhile, Mustafa Kemal spared no effort or sacrifice in his quest for heroism. As he expressed it in a personal letter to a female friend, he had "grand desires" to render extraordinary services to

Figure 6. Staff Major Enver Bey (1908). Source: *Resimli Kitab* 4/22 (June 10 [23], 1326 [1910]): 817.

his homeland.[1] Circumstances, however, were not yet favorable to the realization of that ambition. Up until the Great War, he remained an obscure figure little known outside the circle of young CUP officers.

The German-inspired reorganization of the Ottoman military on the eve of the Great War paved the way for Mustafa Kemal's ascendance. Like many of his colleagues, he agreed with Colmar von der Goltz's opinion that "to make war means to attack."[2] In one of his military essays he wrote, "The army must be the army of offense. Our weapons are good not for defending ourselves from the enemy but for making the enemy shield himself against us."[3] Many military strategists of the period certainly endorsed these views; however, for the Ottomans the application of these principles in combat was still almost impossible at the time. With the exception of the Crimean War of 1853–56, in which the Ottoman military played a secondary role, and the Ottoman-Greek War of 1897, a small-scale struggle against a weak third-tier power, the Ottoman armies had not fought a major offensive war for more than a century and they would remain on the defensive during most of the Great War. The Ottoman-German joint command had indeed developed plans for significant offensives in the Caucasus and in the Suez Canal area, but it was assumed that the two military leaders of the CUP, Enver and Cemal Pashas, would lead those operations.

Mustafa Kemal maintained that only nations inspired by the Japanese attack code of "kōgeki seishin" (aggressive spirit) could

[1] "Madam Corinne'e Mektup, Sofia, January 12, 1914," in *Atatürk'ün Bütün Eserleri*, vol. 1, *1903–1915* (Istanbul: Kaynak Yayınları, 1998), 179.

[2] [Colmar] von der Goltz, *The Nation in Arms: A Treatise on Modern Military Systems and the Conduct of War*, trans. Philip A. Ashworth (London: Hodder and Stoughton, 1914), 156.

[3] "Subay ve Kumandan ile Konuşmalar," in *Atatürk'ün Bütün Eserleri*, vol. 1, 169.

carry out successful offensive wars.[4] In 1914, however, it was difficult to speak of any kind of fighting spirit in the Ottoman military. The Ottoman military reorganization had been underway less than a year, and morale was extremely low following the Balkan Wars of 1912–13, in which the Ottomans had suffered the most humiliating military defeats of their history. Nevertheless, especially during the first two years of the Great War, the Ottoman armies did succeed in mustering the will to fight—to the point where a commander like Mustafa Kemal could expect his men to charge the enemy unflinchingly even when this meant almost certain death.[5]

He was in Sofia when the July Crisis erupted. Promoted to lieutenant colonel, he was serving as the Ottoman military attaché to Bulgaria, Serbia, and Montenegro. His position became more important after the beginning of hostilities since the Ottoman government, which had signed a treaty of alliance with Germany immediately prior to the outbreak of war, did not actually wish to enter the struggle until Bulgaria and possibly Romania joined the alliance.[6] As he negotiated with the Bulgarian authorities in order to persuade them to do so, Mustafa Kemal's mind turned to the possibility of obtaining a combat duty post. After the Ottoman declaration of war in November 1914, he appealed to Enver Pasha for an immediate transfer to active duty.[7] However, his critique of the Ottoman-German alliance and his strained relations with the CUP leadership precluded such an appointment until 1915.

---

[4] Ibid.

[5] Ruşen Eşref [Ünaydın], *Anafartalar Kumandanı Mustafa Kemal ile Mülâkat* (Istanbul: Hamit Matbaası, 1930), 30–31.

[6] See Mustafa Kemal's reports in *Sofya Askerî Ataşesi Mustafa Kemal'in Raporları, Kasım 1913–Kasım 1914*, ed. Ahmet Tetik (Ankara: ATASE Yayınları, 2007), 403ff.

[7] Salih Bozok and Cemil S. Bozok, *Hep Atatürk'ün Yanında: Baba Oğul Bozok'lardan Anılar* (Istanbul: Çağdaş Yayınları, 1985), 175.

On January 20, 1915, Mustafa Kemal finally left Sofia to take command of an Ottoman division that as yet existed only on paper. By this point, the Ottoman military outlook was dismal. A premature Ottoman offensive led by Enver Pasha on the Caucasian front had rapidly turned into a disaster, and most of the troops, ill-equipped for a winter campaign, had frozen to death even before they could confront the Russians. Three days prior to Mustafa Kemal's departure for Istanbul, the Russians mopped up the panic-stricken remnants of the Ottoman Third Army. Having lost approximately 30,000 men, and with thousands more suffering frostbite and combat wounds, this force was reduced to a rabble of no combat value.[8] The gates of Anatolia thus lay wide open to the advancing Russians. Even greater was the threat looming on the horizon. In January 1915, the British war planners, led by First Lord of the Admiralty Winston Churchill, were being hard pressed by their Russian allies, who were desperate for supplies. Russia, with most of its land borders in Europe sealed off by Germany and Austria-Hungary and its Baltic Sea outlet blockaded by the German navy, urgently needed access to the Mediterranean, which the Ottomans denied. Accordingly, the British decided on a campaign to break through the Dardanelles with a naval force, push open an ice-free supply route for the Russian army, and knock the Ottomans out of the war. More than a century before, in 1807, a British naval squadron under Vice Admiral Sir John Thomas Duckworth had forced the Dardanelles and reached the Ottoman capital, though the veteran British naval officer had prognosticated that "without the co-operation of a body of land forces, it would be a wanton sacrifice of the squadrons . . . to at-

[8] Yavuz Özdemir, *Bir Savaşın Bilinmeyen Öyküsü: Sarıkamış Harekâtı* (Erzurum: Erzurum Kalkınma Vakfı Yayınları, 2003), 47–51, 71 ff; N[ikolai]. G[eorgievich] Korsun, *Kavkazskii front Pervoi mirovoi voiny* (Moscow: Izdatel'stvo Tranzitkniga, 2004), 7–432.

tempt to force the passage."[9] Since then the Ottomans had taken the defense of the straits more seriously. But the British, too, had been making preparations for such an operation for nearly a decade, and in 1906, at the height of the Ṭābāh crisis between the Ottoman and British governments, they judged that a squadron of "His Majesty's least valuable ships" would be able to "rush the Straights and reach Constantinople."[10]

Mustafa Kemal had just begun forming his new regiment in Thrace in February 1915 when the British bombardment of Ottoman fortifications in the Dardanelles area compelled the Ministry of War to dispatch his unit there at once. Seated at an embassy desk scarcely one month before, he now found himself in the midst of one of the greatest battles of modern times. At last he would have the chance to command an offensive operation within the context of a defensive campaign and win thereby a place in history.

The Ottoman high command realized that for the six-century-old empire the battle for the Dardanelles was a life-and-death struggle. Prime Minister Herbert Asquith had declared upon the Ottoman Empire's entry into the war that the British were determined to ring the death knell of Ottoman dominion, not only in Europe but in Asia as well.[11] The Ottoman government accordingly started preparing for the worst. Plans were made to move the capital to a town in Anatolia, and special trains began to transfer palace valuables to safe cities in the heartland. But it was generally accepted that the capture of Istanbul would mark the end of the empire. Under these dire circumstances the German General Otto Liman von Sanders, who had tenaciously opposed an alliance with

[9] E. Keble Chatterton, *Dardanelles Dilemma: The Story of the Naval Operations* (London: Rich and Cowan, 1935), 114.

[10] *Military Operations: Gallipoli*, vol. 1, *Inception of the Campaign to May 1915*, ed. C. F. Aspinall-Oglander (London: William Heinemann, 1929), 28.

[11] "The Prime Minister," *Times*, November 10, 1914.

the Ottoman Empire on the grounds that it would become an encumbrance in a serious military conflict, assumed command of the Ottoman forces in the Dardanelles. The Ottoman general staff expended enormous effort in transferring artillery pieces from the Caucasus and dispatched all available troops to the Dardanelles for the decisive battle.

On March 18, 1915, following a series of bombardments, a formidable allied armada appeared at the entrance to the Dardanelles. Comprised of British, French, and Russian ships, the force stood poised to take Istanbul and put an end to the Ottoman Empire. Instead, it suffered one of the most decisive naval defeats in history, as the allied ships fell prey to the Ottoman coastal batteries and to the mines laid immediately prior to the attack.[12] Having lost three major battleships and seen three additional men-of-war severely damaged in a one-day engagement, the Allies decided to abandon the naval campaign.[13] The Royal Navy in particular had not sustained such losses in a single day since the Battle of Trafalgar.

The Allied command did not, however, abandon the idea of forcing the Dardanelles. Instead it established an expeditionary force, composed mainly of British divisions from the homeland together with units from Australia and New Zealand, and carried out the greatest amphibious landing of the Great War. In April the Allies landed five divisions of the newly established Mediterranean Expeditionary Force on the shores of the Gallipoli Peninsula.[14] Over the course of the campaign, this force tripled in size. Although the Ottoman command had fully anticipated an amphibious landing, to be followed by a major ground offensive, the strength of the Allied attack, backed by punishing naval fire, ini-

[12] Victor Rudenno, *Gallipoli: Attack from the Sea* (New Haven, CT: Yale University Press, 2008), 47–56.

[13] *Military Operations: Gallipoli*, vol. 1, 98–100.

[14] Ibid., 162ff.

Figure 7. Colonel Mustafa Kemal at the Dardanelles (1915). Source: http://www.tccb.gov.tr/sayfa/ata_ozel/fotograf/, picture no. 3.

tially overwhelmed the Ottoman defenders. It was on the first day of this assault, at one of the most critical points in the battle, that Mustafa Kemal took matters into his own hands. When a disorderly Ottoman retreat began, he personally rushed to the spot, which was outside his command zone; once there he regrouped the panicked soldiers, ordering them to mount a bold bayonet attack against the Allied troops as a line of defense until reserve forces could arrive. He then launched a series of valiant counter-offensives.[15]

The halt of the initial Allied offensive prompted a bitter trench

---

[15] [Mustafa Kemal], *Arıburnu Muharebeleri Raporu,* ed. Uluğ İğdemir (Ankara: Türk Tarih Kurumu Yayınları, 1968), 22ff.

war that sometimes turned into brutal hand-to-hand combat; some opposing trenches were less than nine yards apart. Four months later, Mustafa Kemal halted another major Allied offensive in his sector and proceeded to carry out a successful all-out counteroffensive.[16] But trench warfare soon resumed and lasted until the final withdrawal of the invading forces in December 1915. There were extensive casualties on both sides, reaching an appalling total of 340,000.

Mustafa Kemal emerged from this life-and-death struggle a hero. Over the course of the battles, he rose to command an entire sector of the front. The magnitude of the victory was unmatched by any other triumph in the late history of the empire, and government propaganda made it appear even greater. The failure of the Gallipoli campaign denied a quick victory to the Allies and weakened Russia, thus indirectly helping the Bolsheviks to instigate their revolution. It also raised national consciousness in Australia and New Zealand, and cost Churchill his job at the admiralty. For the empire it marked the zenith of the Ottoman military in the twentieth century. According to a saying common at that time, they had fought the "seven nations" and taught them a memorable and well-deserved lesson. The fact that the Allied expeditionary force was composed of Britons, Irishmen, Scots, Australians, New Zealanders, Indians, Egyptians, Gurkhas, Frenchmen, and Senegalese helped Ottoman wartime propaganda present the victory as one against almost the entire world.

Following the victory, the title of Gazi was bestowed upon the sultan, who penned a poem commemorating the event:

Together the two strong enemies of Islam,
Attacked the Dardanelles from sea and land

[16] [Mustafa Kemal], *Anafartalar Muharebatı'na Ait Tarihçe*, ed. Uluğ İğdemir (Ankara: Türk Tarih Kurumu Yayınları, 1962), 31ff.

But the divine help of God reached our army,
Each private of which became an iron fortress.
Before the determination of my soldier sons
Finally the enemy comprehended his hopeless plight
And fled, soiling his dignity and honor,
Though he had come to penetrate the heart of Islam.[17]

Most of the credit for the military triumph went to the Ottoman senior officers, however. The CUP now adopted a strong version of Turkism and presented the victory as "the miracle of the Turk against all odds." It did not wish to give much credit to the German commanders. Colmar von der Goltz, who had pursued and besieged the British forces in Mesopotamia, received almost no recognition for his role in bringing about their eventual surrender six months after his death.[18] Likewise, Liman von Sanders garnered scant glory for his contribution to the victory at the Dardanelles.

Mustafa Kemal in fact maintained that the Allied Expeditionary Force would have been driven into the sea at the outset had Liman von Sanders heeded his warnings.[19] He further complained that "the heart of a German like Liman von Sanders does not beat as ours does in defense of our fatherland."[20] In any event, he received a considerable portion of the military credit. He had come to Gallipoli a little-known lieutenant colonel and left a highly decorated colonel. His name appeared in poetry written to celebrate the victory, and streets in remote corners of the empire were

[17] *Harb Mecmuası* 1/11 (July 1332 [1916]): 162.

[18] Pertev Demirhan, *Generalfeldmarschall Colmar Freiherr von der Goltz: das Lebensbild eines großen Soldaten: aus meinen persönlichen Erinnerungen* ([Göttingen, Germany:] Göttingen Verlagsanstalt, 1960), 232.

[19] "Başkumandan Vekili Enver Paşa'ya Mektup, May 3, 1915," in *Atatürk'ün Bütün Eserleri*, vol. 1, 218.

[20] Ibid.

named after him.[21] To honor his noteworthy service, the Ottoman command named the place where he had planned and executed one of his counteroffensives Kemal Yeri (Kemal's Spot).[22] Even the semiofficial *Harb Mecmuası* (War Journal) considered featuring his picture on the cover of an issue. Though Enver Pasha found this excessive and thwarted its publication, a smaller picture did appear inside the journal.[23]

However, Mustafa Kemal's disagreements with high-ranking German officers in general, and with Liman von Sanders in particular, compelled him to go on leave several days before the final Allied withdrawal from the Dardanelles. He then spent some time in Istanbul and Sofia, enjoying his fame as the commander who had performed miracles and "saved the imperial capital," as he himself put it.[24] In this new, self-anointed capacity, he decided to warn the government regarding the war situation. Without an appointment, he went to the Ministry of Foreign Affairs, where he demanded to see the minister, one of the leading members of the CUP's inner circle. At the meeting Mustafa Kemal lambasted the German command and denigrated the Ottoman military leadership, complaining that there was no "national general staff" in the empire. He even expressed serious doubts about the prospects for an eventual German victory. The minister unceremoniously dismissed the audacious colonel, instructing him to report to the

[21] Şerafettin Turan, *Kendine Özgü Bir Yaşam ve Kişilik: Mustafa Kemal Atatürk* (Istanbul: Bilgi Yayınevi, 2004), 139.

[22] Ibid., 132.

[23] "Anafartalar Grubu Kumandanı Miralay Mustafa Kemal Bey," *Harb Mecmuası* 1/2 (December 1331 [1915]): 22. In addition to this photograph he appears anonymously in a picture paying homage to fallen Ottoman soldiers. See "Çanak Kal'a'da Kireç Tepe'de,"*Harb Mecmuası*, 1/4 (January 1331 [1916]): [49].

[24] *Atatürk'ün Anıları: "Büyük Gazimizin Büyük Hayatından Hatıralar,"* ed. İsmet Görgülü (Ankara: Bilgi Yayınevi, 1997), 32.

Ministry of War, and then asked the government to reprimand
Mustafa Kemal for his improper behavior.[25]

The government and the CUP leaders nonetheless opted to
cash in on Mustafa Kemal's exceptional services as a commander.
The Ministry of War first appointed him to the command of an
army corps in Edirne, where he received a hero's welcome, and
then to one in Diyar-ı Bekir to counter the new Russian offensive
that had commenced in January 1916. The Russians attacked in
the north and south simultaneously. In the north, they swiftly captured the key cities of Erzurum and Trabzon; in the south, supported by Armenian volunteers, they seized Muş and Bitlis. This
meant the total collapse of the eastern front, which had been particularly vulnerable since the catastrophic Ottoman defeat at the
outset of the war; it also implied the threat of a Russian advance on
Mesopotamia from the north. Mustafa Kemal, who was now a
brigadier general (pasha), initially halted the Russian advance and
then retook Muş and Bitlis in a daring surprise offensive in August
1916. Although the Russians quickly responded by launching a
counterattack and recapturing Muş, they were compelled to sus-
pend their offensive over the winter. Meanwhile, the Russian Revolution of February 1917 marked the beginning of imperial Russia's internal collapse, which was accompanied by disengagement
from the Ottoman eastern front. Once again Mustafa Kemal received tremendous credit for arresting the enemy advance and
bringing the Ottoman Empire to the verge of victory over Russia.
He garnered new decorations and a reputation as a commander
without a defeat to his name. His prestige was so great that when a
group of officers from the CUP's special forces, the so-called Self-
sacrificing Volunteers, attempted a coup against the CUP-con-
trolled government in order to force the conclusion of a separate
peace with the Allies in the fall of 1916, they insisted that only

[25] Ibid., 32–39.

Mustafa Kemal was fit to serve as minister of war in the postcoup government; this was despite the fact that he had expressed no desire to work with these adventurers, whose leader now faced a brevi manu execution.[26]

In July 1917, the calm on the Ottoman eastern front prompted the Ministry of War to appoint Mustafa Kemal Pasha, who was by now commander of the Second Army, to lead the Ḥijāzī Expeditionary Force—troops to be assembled to quell the Arab Revolt that had erupted in Arabia in June 1916.[27] But the Ottoman command soon abandoned this endeavor and decided to defend Arabia with the forces already there. Instead, Mustafa Kemal was charged with forming a new Ottoman Army, the Seventh, which was to build a line of defense in Palestine to block the ongoing British offensive based on Egypt. This assignment was short-lived, for immediately after his arrival in Aleppo to assume his new command, Mustafa Kemal once again provoked confrontations with the German commanders, especially Marshal Erich von Falkenhayn, who had served as the chief of the German general staff between September 1914 and August 1916.[28] In a lengthy, erudite memorandum submitted to the grand vizier, Mustafa Kemal not only cautioned against German domination of the Ottoman command but went so far as to warn that the Ottoman Empire risked becoming a German colony if the present situation continued and the Central Powers won the war.[29] He demanded sole command of the Ottoman forces in Syria and Palestine; when this was refused, he resigned from his position, took the liberty of appointing a commander in his place, and left abruptly for the capital in Octo-

[26] Ibid., 40–43, 168.

[27] Turan, *Kendine Özgü Bir Yaşam*, 142.

[28] Hikmet Bayur, "Mustafa Kemal'in Falkenhayn'la Çatışmasiyle İlgili Henüz Yayınlanmamış Bir Raporu," *Belleten* 20/80 (October 1956): 619–32.

[29] "Rapor, September 20, 1917," in *Atatürk'ün Bütün Eserleri*, vol. 2, *1915–1919* (Istanbul: Kaynak Yayınları, 1999), 120–25.

ber 1917. In Istanbul, the Ministry of War, by now accustomed to his recalcitrance, chose an easy way out, asking him to accompany the crown prince, Vahdeddin Efendi, on his trip to Berlin in December 1917. During the journey, the two established a relationship that would influence both of their careers when Vahdeddin Efendi became sultan and the war ended the following year. The heir apparent's praise for Mustafa Kemal Pasha's military achievements helped him start a dialogue with the prince; he encouraged Vahdeddin Efendi to assume the command of the Fifth Army, which had its headquarters in the capital, and appoint Mustafa Kemal as his chief of staff. The outspoken pasha further informed the prince in the strongest terms that the war had long been lost.[30]

Upon his return to the empire in January 1918, Mustafa Kemal remained mostly in Istanbul until, in May, he went to Vienna for medical treatment and then to Karlsbad in Bohemia for convalescence. Following the accession of Vahdeddin Efendi to the Ottoman throne as Sultan Mehmed VI, he was ordered to return to Istanbul.[31] The new sultan granted him three audiences in twelve days. At the final meeting, the sovereign personally told him that he had been reappointed as the commander of the Seventh Army in Syria. When Mustafa Kemal arrived at his headquarters in Nablus on September 1, he cautioned that the front was as thin as a "cotton thread" and could not be held much longer.[32] As he had anticipated, the new British operation launched on September 19—a combination of ground and air forces foreshadowing the blitzkrieg of the Second World War—outwitted Ottoman and German war planners and devastated the defenders, who were out-

[30] *Atatürk'ün Anıları: "Büyük Gazimizin Büyük Hayatından Hatıralar,"* 74, 81–82, 94.

[31] Ibid., 96.

[32] Hikmet Bayur, "Mustafa Kemal'in Üç Mektubu," *Belleten* 24/93 (January 1960): 136–37.

numbered two to one.[33] Supported by the Palestine Brigade of the Royal Air Force raining death from the sky, the British Expeditionary Force completely routed three Ottoman armies in twelve days.[34] Utter chaos ensued. Ottoman troops were surrendering en masse, deserting in thousands, and retreating in total disorder. Meanwhile, local Arab populations were rising against the central government. Mustafa Kemal, who had been made an honorary aide-de-camp of the sultan on September 21,[35] desperately attempted to withdraw his beleaguered troops to Aleppo in order to form a final defensive line, but an Anglo-Indian force accompanied by Arab rebels from the Ḥijāz captured the city on October 26, forcing him to retreat yet farther north.[36] On October 30, the Ottoman government signed the Armistice of Mudros and withdrew from the war. This also meant the end of the German military mission in the Ottoman Empire. The next day, Mustafa Kemal was appointed commander of all Ottoman armies in Syria in place of his former superior, Liman von Sanders.[37]

Mustafa Kemal, who had been a lieutenant colonel in virtual exile at the outset of the Great War, concluded it as a brigadier general and honorary aide-de-camp to the sultan. He regarded himself as the *beau sabreur* who had saved the empire in 1915,

[33] For an interesting analysis of this operation, see Gregory A. Daddis, "Armageddon's Lost Lessons: Combined Arms Operations in Allenby's Palestine Campaign," *Air Command and Staff College Wright Flyer Paper* 20 (February 2005), 1–2, 21–25.

[34] *A Brief Record of the Advance of the Egyptian Expeditionary Force under the Command of General Sir Edmund H. H. Allenby, G.C.B., G.C.M.G., July 1917 to October 1918* (London: His Majesty's Stationary Office, 1919), 25–36.

[35] *Atatürk ile İlgili Arşiv Belgeleri* (Ankara: Başbakanlık Osmanlı Arşivi Daire Başkanlığı, 1982), 20, 119.

[36] Süleyman Hatipoğlu, *Filistin Cephesi'nden Adana'ya Mustafa Kemal Paşa* (Istanbul: Yeditepe, 2009), 36–47.

[37] *Atatürk'ün Anıları: "Büyük Gazimizin Büyük Hayatından Hatıralar,"* 122–23.

halted the Russian advances in 1916, and organized an orderly retreat from Syria under desperately unfavorable circumstances created by the military's German generals. Though there were many
who took serious issue with this grandiloquent self-presentation,
nobody could ignore him. He had received a host of decorations,
gained even more fame, and become a prominent figure in the eyes
of the sultan, the military high command, and the high-level bureaucracy. In an interview he gave to the popular nationalist journal *Yeni Mecmua* (New Journal) in March 1918, he described his
actions on the first day of the initial Allied amphibious operation
at the Dardanelles as the turning point of this campaign, asserting,
"At that moment, we won."[38] During the interview the journalist,
whom Mustafa Kemal later made a parliamentary deputy, likened
him to previous Ottoman military heroes such as Gazi Osman
Pasha of Plevna.[39] In retrospect, this public recognition was a crucial step in Mustafa Kemal's ascent to political power.

Mustafa Kemal fully grasped the importance of becoming a
hero in the Ottoman context. He also knew that the military idols
of the CUP, whom large segments of the population held responsible for the Ottoman collapse, could not remain significant actors
after the war. This applied particularly to Enver Pasha, whom the
Allies treated as a war criminal. Furthermore, Mustafa Kemal well
understood that once the CUP leaders disappeared from the scene
he would become one of the men of destiny for the empire's Turkish population.[40] He felt that in the aftermath of defeat, it was the
military that had to lead the nation forward. Although a member
of the CUP, he had stayed out of politics and played no role in the
military blunders and civilian massacres committed by the CUP

[38] Ruşen Eşref [Ünaydın], *Anafartalar Kumandanı Mustafa Kemal ile
Mülâkat* (Istanbul: Hamit Matbaası, 1930), 26.

[39] Ibid., 48.

[40] Erik Jan Zürcher, "Atatürk as a Young Turk," *New Perspectives on Turkey*
22/41 (2009), 223–25.

leadership after 1914. Both his military skills and his loyalty to the nation had been proved on the battlefield. Just as the Germans would turn to Paul von Hindenburg in a time of political and social turmoil, he hoped that the Turks would turn to him.

In fact, he made his first bid for power two weeks prior to the Ottoman withdrawal from the war. He appealed to the sultan through the senior imperial aide-de-camp, and proposed the formation of a new government in which he would serve as minister of war. He argued that only such an emergency government could secure the future of the empire and enter into successful peace negotiations with the Allies.[41] Though he failed to secure approval for this scheme, he felt certain that his opportunity would come. In the meantime, he bided his time as honorary aide-de-camp to the sultan.

[41] Hikmet Bayur, "1918 Bırakışmasından Az Önce Muş[s]tafa Kemal Paşa'nın Başyaver Naci Bey Yulo [Yolu] ile Padişaha Bir Başvurması," *Belleten* 21/84 (October 1957): 563–65.

Muslim Communism? The Turkish War of Independence

The failure of the German spring offensive (Kaiserschlacht) between March and July 1918 put an end to the hopes sparked by Russia's withdrawal from the war in the wake of the Treaty of Brest-Litovsk (March 3, 1918), and thereby sealed the fate of the Ottoman Empire. Faced with disintegrating armies, more than a million deserters, major revolts in several Arab provinces, and the Allies advancing on all fronts except the Caucasus, the Ottoman leaders knew the war was lost. They also understood that what lay in store for them in defeat was different from anything they had faced in the past.

In November 1917, the Bolsheviks made public the secret Sykes-Picot-Sazanov agreement of 1916, which proposed the establishment of zones of influence in the postwar Ottoman Empire, thereby dashing the hopes of those Ottomans who had dreamed of a balanced settlement that showed some respect for the legacy of imperial power. A second blow came when Woodrow Wilson outlined his famous Fourteen Points in a speech delivered to the American Congress in January 1918: the American president called for the empire to be dismembered along ethnic lines. Finally there was the Armistice of Mudros, concluded on October 30, 1918, which marked the end not only of Ottoman participation in the Great War but effectively also of one of the longest-lasting empires in history. The Allies demanded that the Ottomans renounce their Arab provinces, grant the victors the right to seize "any strategic points" whenever they felt threatened, and provide them with carte blanche for the dismemberment of the empire.[1] From the Ottoman perspective, these were harsh terms indeed.

Still, in the autumn of 1918 very few people in the Ottoman government and public could realistically oppose such a settlement, since all of the Arab provinces outside Arabia were under an Allied occupation that was supported by Arab militia forces; only the leaders of Ḥā'il and the Yemen remained loyal Ottoman subjects to the bitter end. To be sure, this was not the first time that the Ottomans had lost control of Iraq, Syria, and the Ḥijāz. The Persians had occupied Baghdad for a while in the seventeenth century; the Wahhābis had conquered large parts of the Arabian peninsula, including the Ḥijāz, in the late eighteenth and early nineteenth centuries; and Mehmed Ali, the rebellious governor of Egypt, had occupied Syria and Palestine in the nineteenth century. But the circumstances in 1918 were vastly different. Anti-Ottoman sentiment, already exacerbated by Committee of Union and Progress (CUP) policies, had spread throughout the Arab provinces, leaving pro-Ottoman Arabs a dwindling minority. The Arab notables, intellectuals, and 'ulamā' fully supported their own nationalists. The prevailing notion of the time was that the age of polyethnic empires had come to an end, and that the future belonged to homogeneous nation-states. This idea gained momentum when Prime Minister David Lloyd George announced the British war aims in January 1918, Woodrow Wilson outlined his Fourteen Points in the same month, and the Bolsheviks, in their

---

[1] "Turquie: Convention d'armistice 30 Octobre 1918," *Guerre Européenne: Documents 1918: Conventions d'armistice passées avec la Turquie, la Bulgarie, l'Autriche-Hongrie et l'Allemagne par les puissances Alliées et associées* (Paris: Ministère des Affaires Étrangères, 1919), 7–9.

own way, promoted the cause of self-determination in postimperial Russia.

Under these circumstances, there were Ottoman statesmen who optimistically looked forward to a strict application of Wilson's principles in a manner that guaranteed the sovereignty and territorial integrity of the Turkish component of the empire. The crux of the matter obviously lay in delimiting the boundaries of this new Turkish nation-state. While such a settlement looked uncomplicated on paper, its implementation was exceedingly problematic. First, many provinces that the Ottoman administration considered Turkish, such as Mosul, had also been claimed by other ethnic groups. Similarly, thanks to the prodigal but vague promises made in early 1915 by Sir Edward Grey, the British foreign secretary, the Greek kingdom, which had fought the last eighteen months of the war on the Allied side, felt entitled to make claims on Western Anatolia, which was home to substantial Greek communities. Likewise, former Russian Armenia, which had become the Democratic Republic of Armenia in 1918, pressed for the annexation of a number of Ottoman provinces in the east. Meanwhile many Kurds who the Young Turks thought should be included in the Turkish state were dreading the prospect of minority status under Armenian, Arab or Turkish rule, and pressing for independence or foreign protection.

Disputes among the states of the region were not the only obstacles to overcome: delineation of the borders of the future Turkish state was rendered more difficult by disagreements between the British and French regarding the implementation of the Sykes-Picot Agreement, by conflicting promises given to Italy and Greece, and by significant differences of opinion among three major British institutions—the Foreign Office, the India Office, and the War Office—concerning the disposition of the empire and the fate of its capital. Not surprisingly, the negotiation of a peace treaty took almost two years. Only in August 1920, more than a year after the conclusion of the Treaty of Versailles, did the victorious Allies finally sign a peace treaty with the Ottoman Empire. It was the only postwar peace treaty never to be implemented.

In retrospect, it is probable that if the treaty had rested on a balanced application of Wilsonian principles, the Allies could have conceded less to Turkey than they were eventually compelled to surrender at Lausanne four and a half years after the armistice, and the first major conflict of the postwar era, or what the Turks term their war of independence, might have been avoided. Fighting between 1919 and 1922 on two principal fronts—against the British-backed Greeks in the West and the unsupported Armenians in the East—the nationalists, led by Mustafa Kemal, exploited the protracted conflict to solidify their hold on power. As İsmet İnönü, the chief Turkish delegate to the Lausanne peace conference, was to put it later, "The Mudros armistice had been signed because of our belief in Wilson's principles," but thereafter, tremendous injustices were inflicted on the Turkish nation.[2] Although İnönü vividly expressed the prevailing Ottoman sentiment at the time, the text of the armistice in fact made no reference to the Fourteen Points; and when in June 1919 the Ottoman grand vizier requested a peace based on Wilson's principles and the status quo antebellum, the Supreme Council of the Treaty of Versailles paid no heed.[3] Absent a strong U.S. interest in the postwar settlement in the Near East, the fate of the empire was left to the leaders of Great Britain and France, who had both told Wilson in 1917 that one of their principal objectives was the expulsion of the Ottoman Empire from Europe and the liberation of its subject peoples.[4]

---

[2] [İsmet İnönü], *İsmet İnönü : Lozan Barış Konferansı Konuşma, Demeç, Makale, Mesaj, Anı ve Söyleşileri*, ed. İlhan Turan (Ankara: Atatürk Araştırma Merkezi, 2003), 19–20.

[3] Harry N. Howard, *The Partition of Turkey: A Diplomatic History, 1913–1923* (Norman: Oklahoma University Press, 1931), 236–37.

[4] *The Ottoman Dominion* (London: T. Fisher Unwin, 1917), 3.

Illusions concerning the imminence of a just settlement based on the Wilsonian gospel were the main reason for the brief interlude between the Armistice of Mudros and the emergence of the movement for the Defense of National Rights, which became the engine of the Turkish War of Independence. Some Turkist members of the CUP were naive enough to form a "Wilson's Principles Society" in order to further the cause of a fair resolution.[5] They even considered the possibility of an American mandate for a fixed period, thinking that "America, which had turned a savage land like the Philippines into a machine capable of administering itself," would do a much better job in Turkey in a span of fifteen or twenty years.[6] However, the defeat of the Democratic Party in the congressional elections of November 1918 weakened Wilson, who now had to deal with his archenemy, Republican Senator Henry Cabot Lodge, as the new chairman of the Senate Foreign Relations Committee.[7] Furthermore, the U.S. public had little interest in the fate of the Ottoman Empire, against which their government had not declared war. By and large, Americans were strongly anti-Turkish, out of sympathy for the sufferings of the Ottoman Armenians. All this made an American commitment to the integrity of the Turkish portion of the empire very unlikely.

Thus, even before the convening in January 1919 of the Paris Peace Conference—at which the Ottoman Turks were the only representatives of the empire's peoples excluded from the deliberations—it had become abundantly clear that the fate of the empire lay in the hands of Great Britain and France. The Ottomans could expect little sympathy in either country. Lloyd George, who sought

[5] Tarık Zafer Tunaya, *Türkiye'de Siyasal Partiler*, vol. 2, *Mütareke Dönemi, 1918–1922* (Istanbul: Hürriyet Vakfı Yayınları, 1986), 245–48.

[6] *Nutuk: Gazi Mustafa Kemal Tarafından* (Ankara: n.p., 1927), 57.

[7] William C. Widenor, *Henry Cabot Lodge and the Search for an American Foreign Policy* (Berkeley and Los Angeles: University of California Press, 1980), 300ff.

to punish the Central Powers to the fullest extent, proposed that the Ottomans be expelled "bag and baggage" from the coastal areas of Anatolia, just as British statesman William Ewart Gladstone had proposed to expel them from Europe in 1876 during the "Bulgarian horrors."[8] Lloyd George, who was now dubbed "The Man Who Won the War," had been "one of the many who were lulled into a mood of false optimism by the apparent emergence of a partnership for peace,"[9] but subsequently became an ardent supporter of extreme punitive measures against the Central Powers. In 1917 he told the British War Cabinet that the Turks "are ruling lands which were the cradle of civilisation, the seminary of civilisation, the temple of civilisation, and, from the material point of view, lands which at one time were the granary of civilisation; and now those fair lands are a blighted desert, although once upon a time they were the richest in the world" and that they "must never be allowed to misgovern these great lands in the future."[10] They were, he had remarked elsewhere, "a human cancer, a creeping agony in the flesh of the lands which they misgoverned, rotting every fibre of life."[11] Such sentiments did not bode well for the Ottomans.

Lloyd George's French counterpart, Georges Clemenceau, had strongly defended CUP leaders in exile against the Hamidian regime not only in his dailies, *L'Aurore* and *Le Radical* but also in the French courts;[12] yet he became profoundly disillusioned with the

[8] W[illiam] E[wart] Gladstone, *Bulgarian Horrors and the Question of the East* (London: John Murray, 1876), 61–62.

[9] John Grigg, *Lloyd George: From Peace to War, 1912–1916* (Berkeley and Los Angeles: University of California Press, 1985), 132.

[10] David Lloyd George, *War Memoirs of David Lloyd George*, vol. 4, *1917* (Boston: Little, Brown, 1934), 42–43.

[11] David Lloyd George, *Through Terror to Triumph: Speeches and Pronouncements of the Right Hon. David Lloyd George, M.P., since the Beginning of the War*, ed. F. L. Stevenson (London: Hodder and Stoughton, 1915), 55.

[12] See *Procès contre le Mechveret et la Jeune Turquie* (Paris: Librairie Marescq Aîné, 1897), 25ff.

policies of the CUP leaders once they were in power. By the end of the Great War he had given up on the Turks.[13] In 1919, he was speaking of the Turks in language not significantly different from Lloyd George's: "There is no case to be found either in Europe or Asia or Africa, in which the establishment of Turkish rule in any country has not been followed by a diminution of material prosperity, and a fall in the level of culture; nor is there any case to be found in which the withdrawal of Turkish rule has not been followed by a growth in material prosperity and a rise in the level of culture."[14]

In short, the hope for a balanced settlement based on Wilson's principles was an Ottoman fantasy. Of all the claims made on Ottoman territory—by Arabs, Armenians, Greeks, Kurds, and Zionists—the most unacceptable, from the Ottoman perspective, were those made on Anatolia, the Turkish heartland of the empire. As soon as the far-reaching nature of the Allied proposals became apparent, Turkish public opinion stiffened against an imposed settlement. When in May 1919 Lloyd George—basing himself on a pledge that he had made on January 5, 1918—suggested leaving the sultan in Istanbul, he thought he was being magnanimous.[15] The Turks did not see it this way. Quite the opposite: in response to the Allied proposals for the dismemberment of the empire, they were preparing for war.

At this critical point, Mustafa Kemal emerged as one of the principal leaders of the popular struggle against partition. In November 1918, he had negotiated the surrender of Alexandretta to the British, and this episode deepened his suspicions concerning the real aims of the Allies.[16] Nevertheless, when he returned to

---

[13] İsmail Ramiz, "Ahmed Rıza Beyle Mülâkat," *Vakit*, September 16, 1922.

[14] Howard, *The Partition of Turkey*, 237.

[15] Ibid., 235–36.

[16] *Atatürk'ün Anıları: "Büyük Gazimizin Büyük Hayatından Hatıralar,"* ed. İsmet Görgülü (Ankara: Bilgi Yayınevi 1997), 137–55.

Istanbul later that month, he joined public opinion in expressing the hope that "the British would respect the freedom of our nation and the independence of our state" and that "there would not be a more benevolent friend of the Ottomans than the British."[17] Such hopes notwithstanding, Mustafa Kemal grasped more quickly than most of his colleagues that Allied diplomacy was pursuing objectives wholly at odds with those of the burgeoning Turkish nationalist movement.

In Istanbul, Mustafa Kemal found the political scene utterly transformed. The ruling CUP had disbanded and its leaders had fled the country. Their opponents, who wished to capitalize on the political vacuum, found it nearly impossible do so in a society that had been so thoroughly dominated by the CUP for a decade. From the boatmen's guilds to the boy scouts, and from the Academy of Historians to the Ottoman Red Crescent, the CUP had exercised control over every organization in Ottoman society and scrupulously inculcated its doctrine of Turkism. Although the sultan tried to deprive the CUP of its major power base by dismissing the Ottoman legislature on December 21, 1918,[18] the organization had woven itself so thoroughly into the fabric of society that this move had little practical effect. CUP members were still an overwhelming majority in the bureaucracy and the military, and kept the strategic services of intelligence, law enforcement, and communications entirely under their control. With all Arab provinces gone, and Armenian and Greek nationalists striving for territorial expansion, nobody was interested in the neo-Ottomanism of the CUP's opponents. The proponents of Ottomanism had fought a bitter war against their Turkist counterparts between 1908 and

---

[17] "Mustafa Kemal Paşa ile Mülâkat," in *Mustafa Kemal Atatürk'ün İlk Gazetesi Minber: Açıklamalı Çevirisi*, ed. Erol Kaya (Istanbul: Ebabil Yayınları, 2007), 334.

[18] "Meclis-i Meb'usanın Feshi Hakkında İrade-i Seniyye, December 21, 1918/no. 3425," in *Düstûr*, II/11 (Istanbul: Evkaf Matbaası, 1928), 72.

1918, but Ottoman territorial losses and the final dismemberment of the empire rendered their ideology a blatant anachronism in the postwar world.

Thus, contrary to what many foreign observers believed, the central political struggle in the Turkish portion of the empire soon became one for leadership of the Turkist movement, which had been decapitated by the exile of the CUP's inner circle. Whoever seized the mantle of Turkism would become the natural leader of the struggle against partition. There was some similarity between the Ottoman case and the patterns that prevailed in the other defeated Central Powers, where the wartime rulers initially lost power to liberals or socialists. Although Turkey experienced neither a revolution of the sort that took place in Germany in 1918 nor a reformist coup such as the one that occurred in Bulgaria, the critics of the CUP did briefly gain control of the central government. As in Hungary, the opponents of the regime at first benefited from public support based on the hope that they could deliver a merciful peace treaty; but once this hope faded, the public turned back to the nationalists. The difference was that in Turkey this transition took place more swiftly than anywhere else.

During his postarmistice stay in the capital, Mustafa Kemal's efforts at self-promotion met with little success. His attempts to become minister of war proved futile, and his numerous meetings with the sultan yielded no concrete results. Similarly, his brief career in journalism (November–December 1918), during which he purchased shares in a new daily, gave interviews, and wrote anonymous editorials, did not attract much public interest.[19] While he openly declared that he would remain a soldier and would not join the Teceddüd (Renovation) Party, an organization established by the CUP from behind the scenes in order to fill the political vacuum, he objected to the defamation of the CUP by the revan-

---

[19] See *Mustafa Kemal Atatürk'ün İlk Gazetesi Minber: Açıklamalı Çevirisi.*

chists. The CUP, he indignantly retorted, had made several mistakes, but it had nevertheless been "a patriotic organization."[20]

Meanwhile, the British—who thought differently of the CUP—pressed the Ottoman government to round up the remaining leaders of this organization and try them for war crimes. The arrest of the residual leadership of the CUP in early 1919 was thus followed by the replacement of a moderate government with a revanchist one, led by one of the archenemies of the organization. At the same time, the Armenians and Georgians seized the former Russian provinces of Kars and Ardahan, while the Greeks and Italians occupied Anatolian towns on the Aegean and Mediterranean coasts. All this did much to inflame nationalist emotion among the Turks. It was obvious that no settlement that would satisfy Turkish public opinion could be reached through negotiations between the sultan's government and the Allies. Public sentiment accordingly began to favor resistance.

Allied dominance in Istanbul meant that it was almost impossible to organize effective resistance to Entente schemes in the imperial capital itself. Anatolia, however, provided an extremely fertile ground for nationalist struggle. Indeed, starting in November 1918, local congresses and councils similar to those of the Bolshevik Soviets mushroomed throughout the Turkish portion of the empire, as well as in the former Russian provinces in eastern Anatolia that were coveted by the Armenians and Georgians.[21] These councils, convened by organizations called Societies for the Defense of National Rights, employed strong Islamic rhetoric to reject the dismemberment of the non-Arab Muslim portion of the empire and any attempt to hand out parts of Anatolia to furnish Greece and the Democratic Republic of Armenia

---

[20] *Atatürk'ün Anıları: "Büyük Gazimizin Büyük Hayatından Hatıralar,"* 187.
[21] For more information, see Bülent Tanör, *Türkiye'de Kongre İktidarları, 1918–1920* (Istanbul: Yapı ve Kredi Bankası Yayınları, 1998), 105ff.

with land.[22] Behind the scenes, it was the CUP network that was organizing these activities, and in many regions CUP branches turned themselves into Societies for the Defense of National Rights to oppose Allied schemes of partition.

Between June and October 1918 the CUP leadership had launched hasty but significant efforts to sow the seeds of a nationalist-Islamic resistance to partition. Until February 1919, action focused on Kars and Ardahan, which faced an imminent threat of annexation by the Democratic Republic of Armenia and the Democratic Republic of Georgia. Soon afterward, resistance spread to those parts of Western Anatolia that the Allies wished to hand over to the Greeks. But it was the Greek occupation of İzmir on May 15, 1919 that convinced the nationalists that the only option was yet another war. This event provided significant impetus to resistance activity and the spread of local resistance councils. Although in some ways these councils resembled the soviets of Bolshevik Russia or the Spartakist *Räterepubliks* of postwar Germany, they were not organizations bent on overthrowing the existing order. Rather, their common mission was to resist partition by the Allies and fight off Greek and Armenian encroachments. They did, however, challenge the imperial center's willingness to cooperate with the Entente, threatening to take matters into their own hands in the event of an ignominious capitulation.

This network of localized resistance needed to acquire two major assets if it were to become a full-fledged national movement: a central administration and a leadership. Though the organization benefited from the support of the CUP network, the covert guidance of expatriate CUP leaders, and the secret endorsement of the military command, none of this was enough to sustain a movement that could challenge the Allies and stave off total collapse.

[22] Erik Jan Zürcher, "The Vocabulary of Muslim Nationalism," *International Journal of the Sociology of Science* 137 (1999): 81–92.

Mustafa Kemal was looking for an appointment in Anatolia in order to join the resistance. The imperial government, however, asked him to go to Samsun for the totally different purpose of forestalling an Allied occupation of the Black Sea coast on account of clashes that had broken out between local Greeks and Muslims. The administration, seeing in Mustafa Kemal a capable commander who was close to the imperial palace and had been a vocal critic of both the CUP leaders and the German command in the past, thus made the glaring mistake of offering him an inspectorship to put a stop to Muslim-Christian strife, dissolve the nationalist councils, and collect all arms and ammunition. Mustafa Kemal conditioned his acceptance on the receipt of extraordinary powers that effectively subordinated the military and civilian administration in parts of Anatolia to his authority.[23] On May 16, 1919, one day after the Greek occupation of İzmir, Mustafa Kemal set sail for Samsun.

He arrived on May 19, 1919—a day later generations of Turks would celebrate as Youth and Sports Day and eventually Atatürk Commemoration Day. He immediately began acting as a resistance leader, attending meetings organized by the nationalists, backing Muslim bandit activity, and issuing subtle but strong statements criticizing the very government that had dispatched him to suppress nationalist activities.[24] Not surprisingly, he was soon summoned to return to Istanbul. Upon his refusal, the sultan discharged him from his position. In response to this, on July 8, 1919, Mustafa Kemal tendered his resignation and henceforth participated in the resistance movement, in open defiance of the imperial government. [25]

At this juncture, the nationalist-Islamic leadership in the east-

[23] *Atatürk ile İlgili Arşiv Belgeleri* (Ankara: Başbakanlık Osmanlı Arşivi Daire Başkanlığı, 1982), 22–25.

[24] Ibid., 26–32, 34–40; and *Nutuk*, 28.

[25] *Atatürk ile İlgili Arşiv Belgeleri*, 51–52.

ern provinces led an attempt to establish a central organization that would coordinate the various local resistance councils and create a national movement. These very provinces had led a constitutional revolt between 1905 and 1907, during the last years of the Hamidian regime, and in one of them, Erzurum, a local administration—similar to the *Anjuman*s (councils of peasants and craftsmen) that emerged during the Iranian Constitutional Revolution—had administered the province for more than a year. They, too, were now once more in open defiance of the central government.[26]

Mustafa Kemal seized the opportunity offered by the eastern leaders' initiative to hold the first regional congress of the resistance in Erzurum. Although he envisaged a national congress not restricted to the eastern provinces, he recognized the significance of this first attempt to coordinate the resistance and determined to use this meeting as a first step toward a national convention. Significantly, the organizers chose to convene the congress on the eleventh anniversary of the Young Turk Revolution, July 23, 1919. In the absence of competition from the expatriate leaders of the CUP, the attendees selected Mustafa Kemal as the chairman of the congress. Two weeks of heated deliberations produced an announcement that the Eastern Anatolian and Eastern Black Sea provinces were united against any foreign intervention; that henceforth national forces would serve as the shield of the caliphate, the sultanate, and the territorial integrity of the empire; that national sovereignty should reign supreme; that the central government should comply with the national will; that Muslims in the region would fight against any cession of land to the Armenians and Greeks; and that Muslims would not accept any schemes conferring privileges on non-Muslims. The congress further de-

[26] M. Şükrü Hanioğlu, *Preparation for a Revolution: The Young Turks, 1902–1908* (New York: Oxford University Press, 2001), 109–114.

clared the establishment of an organization named the Eastern Provinces Defense of Rights Society, which considered all Muslims its natural members.[27] At the same time Mustafa Kemal was selected for a seat on a nine-man executive committee, called the Board of Representatives—a name designed to emphasize the representative character of the new organization. Mustafa Kemal's prominence at the congress signaled to the entire movement his intention of assuming a leading role in the nationalist struggle.

In the immediate wake of this momentous event, Mustafa Kemal led the initiative to convene an all-Turkey congress in Sivas. Despite the central government's relentless efforts to apprehend him and his comrades, he succeeded in holding it between September 4 and 11, 1919.[28] The most important achievement of this second congress was to announce the formation of a parallel government in Anatolia. Mustafa Kemal headed the Board of Representatives, now a sixteen-man executive committee established to oversee a new national resistance movement called the Anatolia and Rumelia Defense of Rights Society; under its aegis all local Defense of National Rights organizations were to unite.[29] The congress also defined the geographical boundaries of the country, declaring that those areas that had not fallen under occupation on the day of the Armistice of Mudros belonged to the Muslims and would be defended; no concessions would be made to non-Muslims.[30] The Board of Representatives contained former deputies of the Ottoman chambers, bureaucrats, and army commanders, as

[27] "Erzurum Kongresinin Tutanak ve Kararları," ed. Hayri Mutluçağ, *Belgelerle Türk Tarihi Dergisi* 11/61 (October 1972): 6–8.

[28] *Nutuk*, 75ff.

[29] *Sivas Kongresi Tutanakları*, ed. Uluğ İğdemir (Ankara: Türk Tarih Kurumu Yayınları, 1969), 101–102.

[30] Faik Reşit Unat, "Anadolu ve Rumeli Müdafaai Hukuk Cemiyetinin Kuruluşuna Ait Vesikalar: Umumî Kongre Beyannâmesidir," *Tarih Vesikaları* 1/1 (June 1941): 7–8.

well as local leaders; most of them had close ties with the CUP. In the small hours of the last day of the congress, the members sent an ultimatum to the central government and warned that unless it facilitated direct correspondence with the sultan, the nation would cut all its ties with Istanbul. The grand vizier ignored this demand, and the Board of Representatives instructed all officials and commanders to stop communicating with the central government and instead report to the Board pending the establishment of a legitimate administration.[31] Despite a few protests, most governors and commanders followed these instructions. The Board of Representatives, acting as a provisional government, also appealed to the Allies and requested a fair implementation of the Wilson principles.

The sultan, hopelessly outmaneuvered by these bold strokes, replaced the antinationalist government with a moderate one under a former general who immediately contacted the new organization in Anatolia. The two parties, each asserting its legitimacy as the lawful government of the country, finally reached an agreement in October 1919. As a result of their accord, the imperial government recognized the Anatolia and Rumelia Defense of Rights Society as a provisional authority in Anatolia, accepted the resolutions of the Erzurum and Sivas Congresses, promised fresh, fair elections to form a new Chamber of Deputies, and undertook working toward a peace settlement in accordance with the Wilson principles. In return, Mustafa Kemal and his colleagues declared that they would allow local administrators to communicate with the capital and would assist the central administration. On the insistence of the central government, they publicly declared that they had no relations with the CUP and that they would not oppose the trial of the war criminals.[32] The road to elections now lay open.

[31] *Nutuk*, 82–85.
[32] Ibid., 145–49.

The nationalists knew that without a network, the revanchists were no match for them. As it happened, the major antinationalist organization, the Liberal Entente Party, decided to boycott the elections so as to save face. In December 1919, taking advantage of the effectiveness of their network, the supporters of the Defense of National Rights movement won a landslide victory, much to the dismay of the effete revanchists and the flabbergasted Allies. Winston Churchill carped contemptuously that "the Turks had voted. Unhappily . . . almost all of them voted the wrong way."[33] Mustafa Kemal was elected deputy for Erzurum, but opted not to risk traveling to Istanbul.[34] The new chamber convened in January 1920. The following month it accepted the resolutions of the Erzurum and Sivas Congresses and unanimously adopted a new resolution, known as the National Pact, that contained two main provisions. The first declared that the territories that had not been under occupation at the signing of the Armistice of Mudros formed the indivisible homeland of the non-Arab Ottoman Muslims (this area was to be called Turkey for the first time in 1921 in the text of the Treaty of Moscow signed between the nationalist government and the Soviet Union).[35] The second stated that the future of the occupied Arab provinces, of the former Russian provinces of Kars, Ardahan, and Batumi, and of Western Thrace (which the empire had left to Bulgaria after the Balkan Wars, and which was awarded to Greece in 1919) would be determined through plebiscites.[36]

[33] Winston S. Churchill, *The World Crisis, 1918–1928: The Aftermath* (New York: Charles Scribner's Sons, 1929), 397.

[34] "Kendisinin ve Rauf Beyin İstanbul'a Gitmiyeceklerine Dair, 7.I. 1920," in *Atatürk'ün Tamim Telgraf ve Beyannameleri,* vol. 4, *1917–1938,* ed. Nimet Arsan (Ankara: Türk İnkılâp Tarihi Enstitüsü Yayınları, 1964), 149–50.

[35] "Rusya ile Mün'akid 16 Mart 1337 Tarihli Muhadenet Mu'ahedenâmesi ve Bunu Musaddık Kanun" (Law #141, 21 July 1921), in *Türkiye Cumhuriyeti Sicill-i Kavânini,* ed. Karakoç Sarkiz, vol. 1 (Istanbul: Cihan Matbaası, 1926), 73–78.

[36] Kâzım Karabekir, *İstiklâl Harbimiz,* (Istanbul: Merk Yayıncılık, 1988), 426–27.

This was astonishing bravado from a defeated nation. In March 1920, the British responded heavy-handedly, occupying the Ottoman capital, arresting leading nationalist deputies, and banishing them to Malta. The other deputies adjourned and dispersed, although technically the chamber was not dissolved.

The overbearing British action played into the hands of the nationalists. In fact, on the day following the adjournment of the Ottoman chamber, Mustafa Kemal sent a circular to all provinces and army corps commanders inviting them to organize elections to choose deputies to join those who would be able to reach Ankara from Istanbul.[37] The new assembly in Ankara was to have extraordinary powers. The local authorities followed these instructions, and elections were held to elect additional deputies for the assembly, which met in Ankara on April 23, 1920. The sultan had tried to avert this fait accompli by dismissing the Ottoman chamber twelve days prior to this date, but it was too late.[38]

The new chamber was named the Grand National Assembly to emphasize its extraordinary powers. Following the lead of Mustafa Kemal, the new deputy from Ankara, it adopted a strong Islamic tone from the outset. The opening was deliberately scheduled for a Friday, following prayers at the central mosque. Accompanied by a crowd, the deputies marched to the old CUP club, in which the new assembly was to be located. Before they entered the building, which contained a replica of the Prophet's banner and a piece of hair from his beard, clerics completed a recitation of the full text of the Qur'ān. The Islamic character of these opening ceremonies outdid any comparable solemnity in Ottoman history and gave no inkling of the secular revolution that would follow in the years to come.[39] The assembly proceed-

[37] *Nutuk*, 365.
[38] "Meclis-i Meb'usanın Feshi Hakkında İrade-i Seniyye, April 13, 1920/no. 3826," in *Düstûr*, II/12 (Istanbul: Evkaf Matbaası, 1927), 38–39.
[39] Karabekir, *İstiklâl Harbimiz*, 426–27.

ings—with an imām leading prayers, deputies summoned to pray five times a day, constant reference to religious sources, and placards displaying Qur'ānic quotations (such as *wa-amruhum shūrā baynahum* [Qur'ān, 42:38] commending those "whose affairs are decided by mutual consultation.")—resembled old *meşveret* (consultation) meetings at the house of the Şeyhülislâm (the chief mufti) more than meetings of the Ottoman chambers after 1877. The Grand National Assembly also issued a law banning the production, sale, and use of alcohol throughout the country and mandating beatings for offenders.[40] In so doing it surpassed any Ottoman administration since the inception of the Tanzimat in 1839 in the enforcement of Islamic morals.

Ironically, it was the staunch Westernist Mustafa Kemal who took the lead in this regard. He addressed the entire Muslim world in these words: "Following the fall of the caliphates in Damascus, Cordoba, Cairo, and Baghdad, the last center of the Muslim caliphate has fallen under the shadow of enemy weapons . . . Anatolia, the union and independence of which we are trying to defend, is a land of refuge for many Muslim communities driven out of their homelands. . . . Hundreds of muftis and scholars have issued fatwās to show the right direction to our nation and the Islamic world. . . . Please hear this voice of sharī'a."[41]

This pretense of pious pan-Islamism, coming from an avowedly secular leadership dedicated to the cause of Turkish nationalism, is perhaps not so surprising when the historical circumstances are taken into account. First was the need to challenge the imperial government, which had obtained a fatwā from the Şeyhülislâm declaring Mustafa Kemal and his comrades brigands and proclaiming their killing a duty incumbent upon all Muslims. In the embit-

[40] "Men'-i Müskirât Kanunu" (Law #22, September 14, 1920), in Karakoç, ed., *Sicill-i Kavânin*, vol. 1, 12–13.
[41] "Büyük Millet Meclisinin Bütün İslâm Âlemine Beyannamesi, 9.V.1920," in *Atatürk'ün Tamim Telgraf ve Beyannameleri*, vol. 4, 323–26.

tered struggle for legitimacy, both sides vied for fatwās issued by religious scholars and competed to be more Islamic than the other.[42] Mustafa Kemal shrewdly exploited this dynamic with the help of nationalist-leaning 'ulamā' in the assembly. For instance, instead of defending his claims on the basis of national unity or Ottoman brotherhood, he delegitimized the government's attacks, citing the Qur'ānic injunction *Wa-in jā'akum fāsiqun bi- naba'in fa-tabayyanū* ("If a corrupt person comes to you with news, investigate it"; Qur'ān, 49:6).[43]

Another concern of the nationalists was to maintain the support of the Muslims in Central Asia and India who had raised considerable funds to support the nationalist struggle in order to protect the Ottoman Caliphate from Western occupation. The Khilāfat movement in India gained momentum in 1920, especially after the issuance of the All India Khilāfat Committee's Khilāfat manifesto inviting Indian Muslims to unite in supporting the Ottoman Caliphate;[44] and it acquired further strength following the alliance of the movement with the Indian National Congress and its leader Mohandas Gandhi. The Khilāfat movement's handsome donation of £125,000, kept as emergency reserve by the nationalist government in Ankara, and its consistent pressure on the British government throughout the years 1920–22, depended on an understanding of the Anatolian struggle as a jihād to free the caliph-sultan from the hands of Christian crusaders.[45] Mustafa Kemal's pan-Islamic rhetoric was calculated to reinforce this

[42] Karabekir, *İstiklâl Harbimiz*, 607–609; Klaus Kreiser, *Atatürk: eine Biographie* (Munich: Verlag C. H. Beck, 2008), 153–55.

[43] "B.M.M. Şeriye Encümeni Tarafından Hazırlanan ve Mecliste Kabul Edilen İslâm Alemine Beyanname, 9. V. 1920," in *Atatürk'ün Tamim Telgraf ve Beyannameleri*, vol. 4, 322.

[44] See M. Naem Qureshi, *Pan-Islam in British Indian Politics: A Study of the Khilafat Movement, 1918–1924* (Leiden, Netherlands: Brill, 1999), 439–42.

[45] Ibid., 246–48; Alptekin Müderrisoğlu, *Kurtuluş Savaşının Malî Kaynakları* (Ankara: Atatürk Kültür, Dil ve Tarih Yüksek Kurumu, 1990), 558ff.

understanding and preserve the valuable support of the Khilāfat movement.

Finally, the appeal to religious sentiment sought to mobilize the force of Islam in a struggle against the Allies and the non-Muslim Ottoman groups they supported. A narrower Turkish nationalist or pan-Turkist message would have endangered the vital support of the Kurds, especially in the southeastern parts of Anatolia, and would have annoyed Soviet leaders, who viewed pan-Turkism as a major threat to the Bolshevization of Central Asia and the Caucasus. Mustafa Kemal felt it necessary to emphasize that the group of people whom the nationalists were attempting to save comprised not only Turks but also many other Muslim ethnic groups such as Kurds and Circassians, who together formed an "Islamic community" and whose struggle had nothing to do with pan-Turkism.[46]

At the same time just as he used an extreme Islamist and pan-Islamic rhetoric despite his scientistic and Turkist proclivities, so also Mustafa Kemal augmented his nationalist opposition to imperialism with a purely rhetorical socialism. All in all, during this period he gave the impression of being a Muslim communist. In this he closely resembled Mirsäyet Soltangäliev, who attempted to reconcile Islam and socialism, and argued that the Muslim proletariat of the East had been enslaved by Western bourgeois colonizers.[47] In a letter to Georgy Chicherin, the Soviet People's Commissar of Foreign Affairs, Mustafa Kemal wrote, "Our nation has

[46] "Türk Milletini Teşkil Eden Müslüman Öğeler Hakkında, May 1, 1920," in *Atatürk'ün Söylev ve Demeçleri*, vol. 1, *T.B. M. Meclisinde ve C.H.P. Kurultaylarında, 1919–1938* (Istanbul: Türk İnkılâp Tarihi Enstitüsü Yayımları, 1945), 70–71.

[47] For more information, see Alexandre Bennigsen and Chantal Lemercier-Quelquejay, *Sultan Galiev, le père de la révolution tiers-mondiste: les inconnus d'histoire* (Paris: Fayard, 1986), 129 ff; and A[rtur] V[ladimirovitch] Sagadaev, *Mirsait Sultan-Galiev i ideologinatsional'no-osvoboditel'nogo dvizheniiaa: Nauchno-analiticheskii obzor* (Moscow: Akademiia nauk, 1990), 33ff.

become a vicious target of European imperialists due to its defense of Muslim countries . . . I strongly believe that . . . when the enslaved peoples of Asia and Africa comprehend that international capital exploits them for their masters' maximum profit and their own enslavement . . . the power of the bourgeoisie will come to an end."[48] He expressed similar views in the Grand National Assembly: "Bolshevism includes the most exalted principles and rules of Islam."[49] The assembly itself declared in November 1920 that the aim of its work was to "liberate the people of Turkey from the oppression and cruelty of capitalism and imperialism."[50] Mustafa Kemal further assured the Soviet envoys who met with him that he and his "comrades favor communism, but circumstances compel [them] to be silent about this fact."[51] Like Soltangäliev, who advocated a special form of communism for Muslims in Russia, Mustafa Kemal frequently emphasized that there was a need for a distinctive form of communism in Turkey.[52] As his official newspaper elucidated, he and his friends had adopted the "most advanced form of communism," but instead of "imitating" the Russian archetype they preferred a "communism without a bloody workers' dictatorship," which would better fit the social structure of Anatolia and Turkey.[53]

[48] "RSFSC Dışişleri Halk Komiseri Çiçerin'e, October 22, 1920," in *Atatürk'ün Bütün Eserleri*, vol. 10, *1920–1921* (Istanbul: Kaynak Yayınları, 2003), 64.

[49] "Erzurum Milletvekili Durak ve Arkadaşlarının, Şark Cephesi Kuvvetlerinin Mütecavizlere Karşı Mukabele Etmemeleri Sebeplerinin Bildirilmesi Hakkındaki Sual Takriri Üzerine, August 14, 1920," in *Atatürk'ün Söylev ve Demeçleri*, vol. 1, 92.

[50] Tarık Zafer Tunaya, *Devrim Hareketleri İçinde Atatürk ve Atatürkçülük* (Istanbul: Turhan Kitabevi, 1981), 95–97.

[51] Mehmet Perinçek, *Atatürk'ün Sovyetler'le Görüşmeleri: Sovyet Arşiv Belgeleriyle* (Istanbul: Kaynak Yayınları, 2005), 272.

[52] Ibid., 274, 277, 299–301.

[53] "İki Komünizm," in *Kurtuluş Savaşı'nın İdeolojisi: Hakimiyeti Milliye Yazıları*, ed. Hadiye Bolluk (Istanbul: Kaynak Yayınları, 2003), 90–91.

Figure 8. True Bolsheviks and pretenders: A Bolshevik delegation in Ankara (1921). Source: Clarence K. Streit Papers, Library of Congress, DLC/PP 1994: 064.150.

Mustafa Kemal's appeal to socialist principles stemmed in part from a desire to forestall the emergence of socialist rivals. In fact, a small but genuine communist organization did emerge to threaten his supremacy. At the Congress of Eastern Peoples, held in Baku in September 1920, the exiled CUP leadership also sought to use communism as a tool to regain control of the national movement in Anatolia, which was slipping from their grasp. But the Bolsheviks were not impressed by the statement read on behalf of Mustafa Kemal's delegate at the congress: "Long live revolutionary Russia ... and revolutionary Russia's backer–the Revolutionary East!"[54] They feared the well known pan-Turkist proclivities of the CUP's Enver Pasha (who had attended the Baku Congress as a

[54] *Congress of the Peoples of the East, Baku, September 1920: Stenographic Report*, trans. Brian Pearce (London: New Park, 1977), 82.

representative from Libya), and backed a group of Turkish émigrés in Russia who went on to form the Communist Party of Turkey there.[55] This initiated an uneasy relationship between Mustafa Kemal and the real communists. Under pressure from Moscow, he opened a dialogue with the leaders of the Communist Party of Turkey and grudgingly allowed them to return to Anatolia. The communist leaders, however, faced an extremely hostile reception from the nationalists and were subsequently murdered.[56] It is still uncertain whether it was the former CUP leadership or the Ankara government that gave the orders, but this was an extremely welcome development for Mustafa Kemal; he had already ordered some of his close associates to form an official Communist Party of Turkey,[57] and had conveyed a straightforward message to the Soviet leaders that "everyone should understand that in Turkey even communism is our business."[58] While promoting an official nationalist form of Bolshevism, Mustafa Kemal banned any other form of socialist discourse, and at his behest many socialists were arrested.[59] Not surprisingly, the Comintern refused to accept Mustafa Kemal's ersatz communist party into its ranks.[60] Despite these ideological differences, the Soviet leaders maintained cordial relations with Mustafa Kemal on pragmatic grounds. The Soviets not only supported his struggle against Western encroachment on their southwestern flank but much preferred his government to the likely alternative: a servile puppet regime under British control.

Although the circumstances of the time compelled Mustafa Kemal to act like an Islamist and a Bolshevik, he actually despised

[55] Mete Tunçay, *Türkiye'de Sol Akımlar I, 1908–1925*, vol. 1 (Istanbul: BDS Yayınları, 1991), 100.
[56] Ibid., 102.
[57] Ibid., 92–94.
[58] Mehmet Perinçek, *Atatürk'ün Sovyetler'le Görüşmeleri*, 273.
[59] Tunçay, *Türkiye'de Sol Akımlar I*, vol. 1, 104–105.
[60] Ibid., 94.

both ideologies and possessed little knowledge of either. For the most part, he repeated the clichés of Ottoman Islamists and the slogans of Soviet ideologues. At the same time, he avoided expounding his Turkist ideals. This pattern of dissimulation was undoubtedly part of a deliberate strategy to align the nationalists with the most powerful and broad-based ideologies of resistance while obfuscating the exclusionary objectives of the movement. This ideological mishmash was crucial to Mustafa Kemal as he performed his difficult role as political leader, diplomat, and supreme military commander. The following charts provide a fascinating illustration of his short-lived resort to Bolshevik and Islamist rhetoric. The precipitous decline in such references after the establishment of the republic in 1923 (and even more so following his consolidation of power in 1925) speaks volumes about the opportunistic character of this policy.[61]

As a political leader, Mustafa Kemal began with apparently little theoretical knowledge of politics, state, and administration. He idealized the principles of the French Revolution of 1789 and at the bottom of his heart harbored a strong sympathy for republicanism and populism; he further attempted to reconcile these ideas with a structure that was under his absolute control. He knew so little about theoretical discussions on these subjects, however, that in his speeches he confused the Baron de Montesquieu with Jean-Jacques Rousseau.[62] He admired the Genevan philosopher's notion that sovereignty is indivisible and inalienable, that every legitimate government is republican, and that every government in the world, once clothed in public power, sooner or later usurps sovereign authority.[63] He was struck by this sentence in par-

---

[61] For more detailed information, see Taha Akyol, *Ama Hangi Atatürk* (Istanbul: Doğan Yayıncılık, 2008), 214–98.

[62] Mete Tunçay, "Atatürk'e Nasıl Bakmak," *Toplum ve Bilim* 1/4 (1977): 90–91.

[63] *Atatürk'ün Okuduğu Kitaplar*, ed. Recep Cengiz, vol. 7 (Ankara: Anıtka-

TABLE 1

Mustafa Kemal's Use of Socialist Terminology, April 1920–January 1923

Time Frame	Prole-tariat	Workers	Bour-geoisie	Imperi-alism	Capital-ism
April 23, 1920– September 30, 1920	—	—	—	31	5
October 1, 1920– January 31, 1921	3	5	2	44	6
February 1, 1921– September 30, 1921	—	1	—	6	2
October 5, 1921– March 3, 1922	—	8	1	21	15
March 4, 1922– October 15, 1922	—	—	—	—	—
October 16, 1922– January 23, 1923	—	—	—	—	1
Total	3	14	3	102	29
Grand Total					151

Source: Taha Akyol, *Ama Hangi Atatürk* (Istanbul: Doğan Kitap, 2008), 543.

ticular from *Du contrat sociale*: "I therefore give the name 'Republic' to every State that is governed by laws, no matter what the form of its administration may be: for only in such a case does the public interest govern, and the *res publica* rank as a *reality*. Every legiti-

bir Derneği Yayınları, 2001), 313, 320; J[ean]-J[acques] Rousseau, *Du Contrat sociale ou principes du droit politique* (Amsterdam: Mark Michel Rey, 1762), 31ff, 137. See also *Atatürk'ün Okuduğu Kitaplar*, vol. 8, ed. Recep Cengiz, 262ff; Babanzâde İsmail Hakkı, *Hukuk-i Esasiyye* (Istanbul: Müşterekü'l-Menfa'a Osmanlı Matbaası, 1329 [1911]), 274ff.

TABLE 2
Mustafa Kemal's Use of Socialist Terminology, January 1923–
November 1927

Time Frame	Prole-tariat	Workers	Bour-geoisie	Imperi-alism	Capital-ism
January 24–June 30, 1923	—	2	—	—	—
July 1, 1923–September 17, 1924	—	—	—	3	—
September 18, 1924–September 27, 1925	—	—	—	—	—
September 28, 1925–October 12, 1927	—	—	—	2	
October 19, 1927–November 1, 1929	—	—	—	—	1
Total	—	2	—	5	1
Grand Total					8

Source: Taha Akyol, *Ama Hangi Atatürk* (Istanbul: Doğan Kitap, 2008), 546.

mate government is republican."[64] This was, of course, a rather out-
dated version of republicanism in the 1920s, but it fit the model
Mustafa Kemal had in mind: a peculiar sort of republicanism in
which he, as supreme leader, would strive to implement a grand
program of social engineering. He repeatedly stated that in this
model the motor of change would be state-sponsored populism.

[64] *Atatürk'ün Okuduğu Kitaplar*, vol. 7, ed. Recep Cengiz, 288; Rousseau, *Du Contrat sociale ou principes du droit politique*, 49. The English translation provided here is taken from *The Social Contract*, trans. G.D.H. Cole (Stilwell, KS: Digireads, 2005), 25.

TABLE 3
Mustafa Kemal's Use of Islamic Terminology, April 1920–January 1923

Time Frame	God	Prophet Muḥammad	Muslim(s)	Islam	Reli-gious
April 23–July 7, 1920	—	4	35	149	—
July 8–September 30, 1920	9	4	13	34	13
October 1, 1920–January 31, 1921	7	—	19	16	13
February 1, 1921– October 4, 1921	24	1	16	32	13
October 5, 1921– May 5, 1922	11	3	3	29	19
May 6, 1922– October 15, 1922	22	—	5	15	7
October 16, 1922– January 27, 1923	41	—	17	147	71
Total	114	12	108	422	136
Grand Total					792

Source: Taha Akyol, *Ama Hangi Atatürk* (Istanbul: Doğan Kitap, 2008), 548.

Thus, the names chosen by Mustafa Kemal for the official newspapers of the national movement—*Hakimiyet-i Milliye* (National Sovereignty) and *İrade-i Milliye* (National Will)—expressed this embrace of populism, which purported to speak for the people. Likewise, he submitted a petition to the national assembly following its formation that requested the construction of a "popular government," and later prepared a "populism program" with strong

TABLE 4

Mustafa Kemal's Use of Islamic Terminology, April 1923–November 1929

Time Frame	God	Prophet Muḥammad	Muslim(s)	Islam	Religious
April 23–June 30, 1923	47	—	25	78	121
July 1, 1923– September 17, 1924	8	—	10	17	25
September 18, 1924– September 27, 1925	3	1	—	3	10
September 28, 1925– October 12, 1927	3	—	—	—	10
October 19, 1927– November 1, 1929	1	—	—	—	—
Total	62	1	35	98	166
Grand Total					362

Source: Taha Akyol, *Ama Hangi Atatürk* (Istanbul: Doğan Kitap, 2008), 549.

étatist underpinnings.[65] Nevertheless, as an elitist sympathizer of Gustave Le Bon, he never desired a government of the people or sought to promote genuine grassroots populism. Like many intellectual members of his generation, he ignored Le Bon's mortal antipathy for revolutions in general and the French Revolution of 1789 in particular,[66] and thought that this pseudosociologist's elitism and the ideas of the Revolution could be reconciled.

[65] *Atatürk'ün Bütün Eserleri*, vol. 9, *1920* (Istanbul: Kaynak Yayınları, 2002), 323–27.
[66] See Gustave Le Bon, *La révolution française et la psychologie des révolutions*

Mustafa Kemal's fascination with the "Grande Révolution" and his commitment to the indivisibility of power, concentrated in a single authority, prompted him to attempt to construe the Grand National Assembly as an Assemblée nationale constituante similar to that of revolutionary France. Likewise, he closely watched the convention of the short-lived Vserossiiskoe Uchreditel'noe Sobranie (All-Russian Constituent Assembly) in 1918.[67] Although he did not say so explicitly, he undoubtedly viewed the events that unfolded after the Erzurum and Sivas congresses as a revolution in which the people had claimed sovereignty.[68] When drafting the circular inviting the provinces to institute elections for a new assembly in March 1920, he attempted to use the phrase "constituent assembly" to define the nature of the new chamber.[69] However, in response to intense opposition from many leaders of the nationalist movement, who feared the radical implications of the term, he was compelled to change the expression to "an assembly with extraordinary powers."[70]

This opposition to Mustafa Kemal's proposal had a precedent. When, at a congress in 1907, the CUP and the Armenian Revolutionary Federation negotiated the form of the assembly to be convened in the imperial capital after their revolution, the CUP strongly objected to the Armenian proposal to call the prospective chamber an *Assemblée constituante*, fearing that such an assembly

---

(Paris: E. Flammarion, 1912), passim. Le Bon commented, "Quoique l'expérience de la Révolution ait été catégorique, beaucoup d'esprits, hallucinés par leurs rêves, souhaitent de la recommencer" (321).

[67] See M[ark] V[en'iaminovich] Vishniak, *Vserossiiskoe uchreditel'noe sobranie* (Paris: Sovremennyia zapiski, 1932).

[68] *Gazi Mustafa Kemal Paşa Hazretleri'nin Bir Hitabesi: Halkçılık, Halk Hükûmeti, Hakimiyet Bilâ Kayd ü Şart Milletindir* (Ankara: Hakimiyet-i Milliye Matbaası, 1338 [1922]), 40.

[69] "Faik Reşit Unat, "Atatürk'ün Toplamak İstediği 'Meclisi Müessisan,'" *Belleten* 21/83 (July 1957): 483–87.

[70] *Nutuk*, 366.

would threaten sultanic rule and attempt to alter the political and social structures of the country.[71] In 1920, similar fears were harbored by many deputies; after all, they were going to Ankara to save the caliph-sultan, which Mustafa Kemal had proclaimed to be the paramount aim.

The Grand National Assembly emerged as the body in control of legislative, executive, and judicial powers. As its elected speaker, Mustafa Kemal gained extraordinary authority. Such an all-powerful government could not be reconciled with the Ottoman Constitution of 1876, which was accordingly replaced by a new document in January 1921, euphemistically referred to as the Law of Fundamental Organization.[72] While Mustafa Kemal and his friends refrained from using the word *constitution*, the twenty-three articles of this document in practice served as a constitution until April 1924. The first article totally ignored the sultan and his role as caliph, stating unequivocally, "Sovereignty belongs without restriction to the nation, and the method of administration depends on the people's direct administration of its own destiny." This already implied the possibility of adopting a nonmonarchical regime. In 1922, Mustafa Kemal used this article to force the Grand National Assembly to abolish the 623-year-old sultanate— although the caliphate, for the moment, remained. The second article empowered the assembly to take charge of executive and legislative powers as the sole and genuine representative of the nation. The Law of Fundamental Organization considered the speaker of the parliament to be the natural director of the cabinet, which was composed of selected deputies. Deputies also manned the whimsical Independence Courts, whose purpose was to try traitors, deserters, and opponents of the national movement.[73]

---

[71] Hanioğlu, *Preparation for a Revolution*, 195.

[72] "Teşkilât-ı Esasiye Kanunu" (Law #85, January 20, 1921), in Karakoç, ed., *Sicill-i Kavânin*, vol. 1, 39–41.

[73] "İstiklâl Mahkemeleri Hakkında Kanun" (Law #21, September 11, 1920),

Thus Mustafa Kemal assumed practically all legislative, executive, and judicial powers on behalf of an assembly resembling, in many aspects, France's Convention nationale of 1792–95. Then, in August 1921, the assembly appointed Mustafa Kemal as the supreme commander of the armed forces for a renewable three-month period.[74] After a few renewals, in July 1922 it reappointed him to the same position with no specific deadline for renewal. By 1921, Mustafa Kemal wielded more power than any Ottoman sultan or statesman since 1839.

This peculiar all-powerful assembly governed without the presence of political parties. The public had a rather low opinion of parties, which it blamed for the collapse of the Ottoman order between 1908 and 1918. In the eyes of the average person, the parties that emerged after the Young Turk Revolution had brought about polarization and superfluous conflict. In this climate, various political groupings emerged, but none went so far as to present itself as a party.[75] The so-called People's Group advanced socialist ideas, the Solidarity Group promoted nationalist objectives, and the Reform Group espoused a modernization program. There was also a conservative faction closely aligned with the CUP; this faction was extremely critical of Bolshevism.[76] Mustafa Kemal, maintaining his aloofness as national leader, refrained from any formal affiliation and acted instead as a broker among these groups. But in 1921, seeking to solidify his power base, he decided to form a group of his own. This was the Anatolia and Rumelia Defense of Rights Group, the primary objective of which was independence

---

ibid., 11–12; and "İstiklâl Mehâkimi Kanunu" (Law #249, July 31, 1921), ibid., 139–42.

[74] See *T.B.M.M. Gizli Celse Zabıtları*, vol. 2 (17 Mart 1337 [1921]–25 Şubat 1337 [1922]; Ankara: T. İş Bankası Kültür Yayınları, 1985), 164–85.

[75] *Nutuk*, 369–70.

[76] İhsan Güneş, *Türkiye Büyük Millet Meclisi'nin Düşünsel Yapısı, 1920–1923* (Eskişehir: Anadolu Üniversitesi Yayınları, 1985), 116–35.

for Turkey.[77] Many deputies flocked to what became known as the First Group; like the others, it denied that it was a party, but in practice it served as the ruling party.

Within the First Group Mustafa Kemal formed an unofficial executive committee made up of his close followers, and this functioned as a party central committee. His opponents referred to it as the Comité de salut public after the de facto government of France during the Terror.[78] These dissidents disliked his concentration of all power in his own hands and formed a rival group called the Second Group, accusing him of becoming a dictator.[79] The social and political backgrounds of the deputies in both groups were nearly identical; the main bone of contention was not ideological but personal. Mustafa Kemal resented the dissent, but he was not yet powerful enough to quash it. Later, when he read in Erich Ludendorff's *Kriegführung und politik* that during Germany's postwar parliamentary experiment "the government drowned in the small swamp of domestic politics and surrendered to the annoying influence of German parliamentarians," he jotted down a marginal note that this reminded him of the first Turkish Grand National Assembly.[80] For him, parliamentarism was not an aim in itself but a means for the transformation of society. Thus, a chamber with an effective opposition was not an asset but an obstacle to be overcome.

While he was busy consolidating power as a politician, Mustafa Kemal quickly learned the ropes as a diplomat. Although he had no previous experience in this field, he easily outshone the

---

[77] *Nutuk*, 370.

[78] Ahmet Demirel, *Birinci Meclis'te Muhalefet: İkinci Grup* (Istanbul: İletişim Yayınları, 1995), 381–91.

[79] Ibid., 379ff.

[80] *Atatürk'ün Okuduğu Kitaplar*, ed. Recep Cengiz, vol. 6, 43; Erich Ludendorff, *Kriegführung und Politik* (Berlin: Verlag von E. S. Mittler und sohn, 1922), 58.

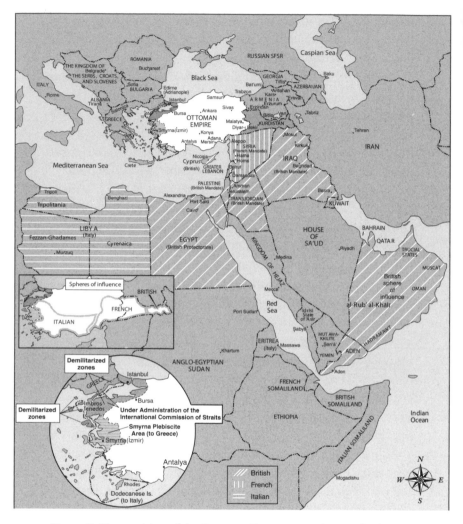

Figure 9. The partition of the Ottoman Empire according to the Sèvres Treaty of 1920.

sultan's defeatist diplomats, who had seen only one option: surrender. In August 1920 they signed the draconian Treaty of Sèvres, which handed over substantial portion of the land claimed by the National Pact to Greeks, Armenians, and Kurds while establishing foreign spheres of influence and domination in much of the rest. An unfaltering Westernist at heart, Mustafa Kemal would eventually do his utmost to make Turkey a member of the Western club of nations. But at this point, conditions forced him to establish different alliances, which he negotiated with remarkable skill. His main achievement was the formation of an unlikely alliance with the Soviet Union. Addressing Lenin, Stalin, and other Soviet leaders as his comrades, he overcame his own private loathing for communism in order to capitalize on the strategic convergence of interests between Turkey and the Soviet Union brought about by the Allied occupation.[81] In order to win over the suspicious Soviets and gain their support for his war in the west, he wisely made territorial concessions to them in the east. Prudently setting aside his Turkist proclivities, he also abandoned the Azerbaijani nationalists to their fate at the hands of the Soviets.

Mustafa Kemal's cunning negotiations with the Soviet leadership issued in the Treaty of Moscow. Signed between the nationalists and the Soviet government in March 1921, the treaty marked a turning point in the international recognition of the nationalist regime in Turkey. In return for Turkish agreement to the establishment of Soviet control over most of the former Russian Caucasus, the Soviets recognized the borders of Turkey as described in the Turkish National Pact, approved the abrogation of the Ottoman capitulations (grants by the sultans to Christian nations, confer-

---

[81] See, for example, Mustafa Kemal's letter to Stalin, dated December 14, 1920, and his letter to "Comrade Lenin," dated December 18, 1920, in *Atatürk'ün Bütün Eserleri*, vol. 10, 160, 171.

ring rights on those of their subjects who lived or traded in Ottoman territory), and pledged that they would not honor any international treaty concerning Turkey unless the Turkish Grand
National Assembly had ratified it.[82] In addition to settling the
northeastern boundaries of Turkey, the Russians secretly pledged
to provide ten million gold rubles, as well as sufficient weaponry
and ammunition to arm two divisions, in order to help the nationalist government fight Western imperialism.[83] It was the reliable
flow of Russian gold and armaments that made possible the pros-
ecution of the war against the Greeks and thus secured the independence of Turkey.

The connection to the Soviets also helped Mustafa Kemal establish cordial relations with other Muslim nations. The Turco-
Afghan Treaty, signed in March 1921 under Soviet auspices in
Moscow,[84] was deliberately aimed at annoying the British, who
had reluctantly granted full sovereignty to Afghanistan through
the Treaty of Rawalpindi in 1919. It gained the Turkish nationalists crucial recognition by a Muslim power at the expense of the
Ottoman imperial government.

Mustafa Kemal had to surmount more serious diplomatic problems with the Allies, who occupied parts of the Turkish heartland
after the Armistice of Mudros. He turned for insight to the centuries-old Ottoman tradition of playing off one power against another in order to create a space for diplomatic maneuvering. He
had also learned from his Ottoman predecessors that dealing with
the liberal democracies of Europe was easier than grappling with
Russian despotism or Austrian autocracy. Although elections

[82] "Rusya ile Mün'akid 16 Mart 1337 Tarihli Muhadenet Mu'ahedenâmesi
ve Bunu Musaddık Kanun," in Karakoç, ed., *Sicill-i Kavânin*, vol. 1, 73–78
   [83] "M. V. Frunze's Mission to Turkey," *International Affairs* 6/7 (July 1960):
119–22.
   [84] "Afganistanla Mün'akid 1 Mart 1337 Tarihli İttifak-ı Tedafüî
Mu'ahedenâmesi ve Bunu Musaddık Kanun" (Law #140, July 21, 1921), in Karakoç, ed., *Sicill-i Kavânin*, vol. 1, 72–73.

made democracies unpredictable, their frequent changes of government could be used to good advantage. One example of this was the French election of 1920, which replaced Clemenceau with leaders more favorably disposed toward Turkey—statesmen such as Alexandre Millerand, Aristide Briand, and Raymond Poincaré.

But the shift in French attitudes did not result merely from a change in leadership. Turkish victories over the token colonial forces of the French (and the Armenian militiamen they had dressed in French uniform) convinced them that they had little to gain from continued hostilities. Moreover, Mustafa Kemal shrewdly exploited his contacts with Syrian nationalists to convince the French that it was not in their interest to oppose Turkish nationalism. On the contrary, under the circumstances, an accommodation might gain Turkish recognition of the French mandate in Syria and protection for French religious and educational institutions in Turkey. Mustafa Kemal did not make it easy for the French: he failed to ratify an early agreement signed by his representative and Briand in March 1921.[85] But when the tide of the Greco-Turkish War turned toward the Turks, the French lost their appetite for protecting the Armenians and instead proposed peace conditions acceptable to the nationalists. In the Ankara Accord of October 1921, they abandoned all their claims to Cilicia and those southeastern Turkish provinces that had been occupied by their forces, and provided guarantees for a special administration of the *sanjak* (subprovince) of Alexandretta. In return, the Turkish nationalists recognized the French mandate in Syria and undertook to respect French interests in Turkey.[86] In addition the French left behind their military equipment, including ten airplanes, as a gift for the nationalists, and promised to

[85] *Nutuk*, 384.

[86] "Türk-Fransız Anlaşması," in *Tarihçeleri ve Açıklamaları ile Birlikte Türkiye'nin Siyasal Andlaşmaları*, vol. 1, *1920–1945*, ed. İsmail Soysal (Ankara: Türk Tarih Kurumu Yayınları, 1983), 50–60.

sell them arms. In the words of a leading British diplomat, "the French had . . . ratted."[87] This accord marked another milestone on the road to international recognition for the new nationalist regime. The only negative consequence of this rapprochement between the Turkish nationalists and a Western colonial power was that it raised the suspicions of Mustafa Kemal's new Soviet allies at a time when the nationalists were still masquerading as communists.

In another diplomatic coup, Mustafa Kemal deftly exploited the resentment of the Italians against "Perfidious Albion" in order to keep them out of the war. The Italians felt betrayed by Lloyd George's open-ended endorsement of Greece, and had never really supported Great Britain's desire to implement the Treaty of Sèvres to the letter. Like the French, the Turcophile Italian foreign minister, the Count Carlo Sforza, signed an agreement with the nationalists in March 1921. According to the terms of the accord, the Italians were to withdraw their troops from Anatolia, recognize Turkish sovereignty, and support a peace acceptable to the nationalists in Ankara. In return, Turkey was to grant Italy economic concessions within the region designated by the Treaty of Sèvres as the Italian sphere of influence, and even outside it (specifically in the Heraclea coal mines). In the event, Mustafa Kemal refused to ratify this agreement because he found the economic concessions too reminiscent of the reviled capitulations.[88] The replacement of the government of Giovanni Giolitti with that of Ivanoe Bonomi, whose foreign minister, Marquis Pietro Tomasi della Torretta, promoted a more pro-British policy, rendered a Turkish-Italian accord more difficult thereafter. Indeed, the Italians, frustrated by the maximalist demands of the Turkish nationalists, went so far as

[87] Nevile Henderson, *Water under the Bridges* (London: Hodder & Stoughton, 1945), 109.

[88] Mevlüt Çelebi, *Milli Mücadele Döneminde Türk-İtalyan İlişkileri* (Ankara: Dışişleri Bakanlığı, SAM, 1999), 227–38.

to conclude a secret commercial treaty with the imperial Ottoman government in April 1922, though they avoided any armed clash with the nationalists.[89] Although he had overplayed his hand with the Italians in 1921, Mustafa Kemal successfully kept them at bay during the entire war with Greece.

Another of Mustafa Kemal's diplomatic goals was to secure the friendship of the United States. Despite his vehement critique—behind closed doors—of those who wished to secure an American mandate, he never overtly rejected the idea. As a tactical maneuver, he even sent a telegram to the U.S. Senate after the Sivas Congress in 1919, inviting a Senate committee to come to Turkey to investigate the situation.[90] Later he welcomed an American military mission through which he conveyed the message to Washington that peace in Turkey was unattainable without an understanding with the nationalists. Subsequently, American lack of interest in the Near Eastern settlement, and disinclination to intervene, came at the expense of the Armenians. This new policy was a significant relief to Mustafa Kemal, who reacted by proposing closer economic and commercial relations with the United States.

Thus, through hard diplomatic work, Mustafa Kemal managed to reduce an ominous struggle against the victors of the Great War to a more manageable war with the Greeks, who were fighting a proxy war on behalf of Great Britain. Unlike the pusillanimous Ottoman defeatists, he rightly deduced that the war-weary Entente Powers could not afford a major military confrontation in the Near East, and that the Greeks, despite all the material support that they might receive, could not on their own win a prolonged struggle against Turkey in the Turkish heartland. Turkish efforts also benefited from the alienation of Allied public opinion from

[89] Ibid., 311–18.
[90] "Sivas Kongresi Kararları ve Bir Amerikan Tetkik Heyetinin Gönderilmesi Hakkında, 9.IX. 1919," in *Atatürk'ün Tamim, Telgraf ve Beyannameleri*, vol. 4, 57.

the Greek adventure in Anatolia following the return to power of the pro-German King Constantine (who in 1917 had been forced to turn over power to his second son); this took place after the death of King Alexander in October 1920. The subsequent resignation of the Greek premier Eleuthérios Venizélos, whom Lloyd George had considered "the greatest Greek statesman since Pericles,"[91] further estranged Entente public opinion. By late 1921, the "Welsh Wizard" seemed to be the only leader who continued to believe that a Greek victory would shortly impose the terms of the Treaty of Sèvres on the impenitent Turkish nationalists. Lloyd George declared that "the Greeks are the people of the future in the Eastern Mediterranean.... They represent Christian civilisation against Turkish barbarism."[92] These blandishments were deemed irrelevant by many conservatives within his national liberal coalition, and in any case they meant little in the struggle for life and death between the Greek irredentists and the Turkish nationalists.

If Mustafa Kemal emerged as a political leader and statesman during the Turkish struggle for independence, he also came into his own as commander in chief. The invasion of the Turkish heartland by a formidable Greek expeditionary force in the spring of 1919, armed by Great Britain and aided by Ottoman Greek volunteers, necessitated a coordinated response on a national scale. The Greek troops, who were welcomed as liberators by the Greek communities of the Aegean coast, had high hopes of accomplishing the century-old *Megali Idea* (the Great Ideal) of Greek irredentism, which envisaged a vast state encompassing all ethnic Greeks. The enthusiasm of their Greek partners was a boon to the British. But at the same time, the far-reaching expansionist ambitions of the Greeks and their "cross against crescent" rhetoric ensured a de-

[91] Desmond Stewart, *The Middle East: Temple of Janus* (Garden City, NY: Doubleday, 1971), 230.
[92] Churchill, *The World Crisis, 1918–1928: The Aftermath*, 415.

termined reaction to their enterprise. The disembarkation of the Greek troops at İzmir in May 1919 thus had the effect of galvanizing Turkish public opinion in favor of resistance, thereby triggering the Turkish War of Independence.

When Mustafa Kemal assumed leadership of the nationalist movement, local bands supported by regular units had already started resistance against the Greek occupation. The Aegean districts of Anatolia were famous for their bandits. One such brigand, the infamous Çakırcalı Mehmed Efe, had terrorized the region during the Hamidian era and carved out an autonomous sphere of influence as a warlord. During the Young Turk Revolution, the CUP, which had transformed Muslim bandits into revolutionary strike forces in Macedonia, sought to recruit Mehmed Efe as well, but without success.[93] The Greek invasion, however, encouraged such local brigands to support the nationalist cause. Their ranks were already swollen with army deserters and draft dodgers from the Great War, and they now began to transform themselves into nationalist resistance bands. Simultaneously, regular army officers distributed arms to nationalist volunteers organized by local CUP networks into "national forces." These local bands and volunteer units, who knew the terrain well and benefited from the support of the Muslim population, harassed the advancing Greeks and slowed them down. They also helped the nationalists to suppress revolts backed by the government in Istanbul.

Although Mustafa Kemal appreciated the contribution of these irregular forces to the war effort, he firmly opposed assigning them a key role in the war on the western front. Local militias were invaluable in meeting the first wave of the Greek onslaught, but they were incompatible with centralized government. Obstreperous and rapacious, they meted out capricious punishments, extorted money from the rich, levied taxes at will, and resisted the chain of

---

[93] Hanioğlu, *Preparation for a Revolution*, 226–27.

command. As a cadet Mustafa Kemal had studied guerrilla units and their tactics,[94] and as an Ottoman officer from Macedonia he had observed what in his time was still the greatest guerrilla war in modern history. He knew that the Christian bands in Macedonia had waged a tenacious, decades-long struggle against the Ottoman state, but that in the end the Ottomans had surrendered Macedonia not to these irregular units but to the superior, better-equipped armies of the Balkan powers. At first, he decided to train the Anatolian guerrilla bands and place them under strict army command. Later, he opted for their dissolution. This prompted a small-scale civil war in which Mustafa Kemal and the Ankara government prevailed.[95] In the meantime a Greek offensive started in June 1920, and quickly brought a large portion of Western Anatolia and Eastern Thrace under Greek control. Now the two early capitals of the empire, Bursa and Edirne were under Greek occupation along with a host of other major cities. The military outlook was bleak in the extreme.

The Greeks started a second offensive aimed at shattering the remains of the Turkish western front in January 1921. This time, however, the Turkish troops stood firm, halting the advancing Greeks at İnönü. A renewed Greek offensive in the same area in March failed to make headway; but a general offensive launched in July overwhelmed the Turkish positions. In response, Mustafa Kemal immediately took command in person and decreed an orderly retreat across the entire front. The army as a whole withdrew northeast of the Sakarya (Sangarius) River in order to mount a strategic defense of Ankara. On August 4, 1921, Mustafa Kemal introduced a bill stipulating his right to employ all the powers and prerogatives of the Grand National Assembly, and in addition granting him the command of the army. Despite acerbic opposi-

---

[94] Afet [Âfet İnan], "Gerilla Hakkında İki Hatıra," *Belleten* 1/1 (January 1, 1937): 11.
[95] *Nutuk*, 318–41.

tion on the part of many deputies who feared that these measures would make him a dictator, the bill passed.[96]

Mustafa Kemal then moved from the chamber to the front. The area that the Turkish troops wished to defend was not fortified, so he ordered all his armies to stand their ground without holding to any particular defense line. All available reserves were dispatched to the front. In August, the superior Greek forces attempted to shatter Turkish resistance and take Ankara. But despite staggering casualties, including 80 percent of the officer corps, Turkish troops continued to fight with élan, forcing the Greeks, after three bloody weeks of slaughter in September 1921, to retreat and form a defensive line of their own to the west of the Sakarya River. In honor of this victory, the Turkish Grand National Assembly promoted Mustafa Kemal to the rank of field marshal. It also and bestowed upon him the title of Gazi; notwithstanding his dislike of religious symbols, he cherished this title, and was later to make it part of his official name.[97]

At this point in the war, despite the strong urge to continue the momentum and counterattack, Mustafa Kemal made a risky decision to pause in order to better prepare his troops for an all-out offensive against the Greeks. He declared a general mobilization and started a draft on a large scale. One of his contemporaries, Winston Churchill, later wrote that this bold decision demonstrated that "he also was able and indeed content to wait, and capable of compelling others to wait with him."[98] Since his years as a cadet at the Royal Military Academy, Mustafa Kemal had wished to lead a nation in a Japanese-style offensive. His time had finally

[96] *T.B.M.M. Gizli Celse Zabıtları*, vol. 2, 164–85.

[97] "Büyük Millet Meclisi Re'isi Başkumandan Mustafa Kemal Paşa Hazretleri'ne Gazilik Ünvânı İta´ ve Rütbe-i Müşirî Tevcihine Dair Kanun" (Law #153, September 19, 1921), in *Türkiye Büyük Millet Meclisi Kavânin Mecmuası*, vol. 1 (Ankara: Büyük Millet Meclisi Matbaası, 1925), 179.

[98] Churchill, *The World Crisis, 1918–1928: The Aftermath*, 435.

come: the long-awaited offensive began on August 26, 1922. This was the first time Ottoman or Turkish forces had gone on an all-out attack since 1897. The Turkish troops reached İzmir on September 9. The Greeks had suffered a devastating defeat, and Mustafa Kemal, who had assumed all the powers and responsibilities of the Grand National Assembly, was victory incarnate.

The Greek defeat in turn precipitated the so-called Chanak (Çanak) Affair, in which Great Britain stood poised to intervene in order to forestall a nationalist victory that would end Allied control of the strategically vital Straits. The crisis reached its climax when Mustafa Kemal refused to recognize the Allied neutral zone and ordered his troops to prepare to cross into European Turkey. In the end, a number of circumstances combined to avert a clash of arms: Mustafa Kemal's skill at aggressive brinkmanship, French mediation, strong antiwar sentiment in Britain and its dominions, and the reluctance of the British commander in Istanbul to use force.[99] On October 11, the nationalist government prudently agreed to sign an armistice in return for a complete Greek withdrawal from Eastern Thrace and a return to the pre–Great War borders there. At long last the guns were silent.

As politician, diplomat, and commander, Mustafa Kemal had fought and won a protracted and arduous struggle on three fronts. In less than four years, he had risen from being the rebel general of a dying empire to become supreme leader of a resurgent nation. He now had the unprecedented opportunity to craft a new nation-state out of the ruins of an old sultanate.

[99] See David Walder, *The Chanak Affair* (London: Hutchinson, 1969), 187 ff; and Charles Harington, *Tim Harington Looks Back* (London: John Murray, 1940), 112–17; 150ff.

6

The Secular Republic

By the autumn of 1922, Mustafa Kemal had become a household name throughout the Islamic world, where he was recognized as a hero who had led his nation to a victory on the scale of the Japanese triumph of 1905. He had stood up to the seemingly unassailable victors of the Great War and forced them to abandon their schemes for an imposed settlement; he had created a new, fully independent Muslim nation in a world dominated by Christian powers; and he had triumphed in a war presented as an Islamic struggle against Western imperialism. Mustafa Kemal remained a role model for the third-world intelligentsia and leaders as different as the atheist Hindu statesman Jawaharlal Nehru and the pious, anti-Western Muslim Punjabi poet Muhammad Iqbal. Similarly, the much-touted anti-imperialist character of the war of independence earned Mustafa Kemal the lasting respect of socialists—his high-handed suppression of the Turkish Left notwithstanding. The figure of Mustafa Kemal continued to loom large in the Muslim world long after his radical secular reforms had made a mockery of his early Islamic posturing. When he died, the All India Muslim League, which had reacted to his abolition of the caliphate with sonorous anguish, expressed its deep sorrow at the death of "a truly great personality in the Islamic world, a great general and a great statesman." His memory, the League declared,

Figure 10. A postcard depicting Mustafa Kemal as a Muslim hero (1922); left to right: Sheikh Aḥmad al-Sanūsī (d. 1933), Field Marshal Mustafa Kemal, Sultan Ṣalāḥ al-Dīn Yūsuf ibn Ayyūb (d. 1193). Source: Clarence K. Streit Papers, Library of Congress, DLC/PP 1994: 064.173.

would "inspire Muslims all over the world with courage, perseverance and manliness."[1]

If popular expectations were any guide, two paths to global leadership lay wide open to Mustafa Kemal in 1922: he could either capitalize on Ottoman possession of the caliphate in order to seize the mantle of pan-Islamic leadership, or he could set himself up as an anti-imperialist model for Asian and African socialists. But it was at this juncture that Mustafa Kemal's Turkist, scientistic, and pro-Western leanings became manifest, leading

[1] *Resolutions of the All India Muslim League from October 1937 to December 1938*, ed. Liaquat Ali Khan (Delhi: Muslim League Printing Press, n.d. [1944]), 65.

him and the Turkish nation down an uncharted path that combined intense nationalism with an extreme commitment to Western secularism.

The popular philosophy of scientism, serving as a deus ex machina, provided the overall framework of this new secularism and shaped Mustafa Kemal's views of Islam. In addition, he combined insights from German vulgar materialism with those of positivism, reading carefully such works as Leone Caetani's *Annali dell'Islām* in Turkish renditions.[2] He seems to have fully agreed with the Italian orientalist that revelation was a myth fabricated by Muslim tradition;[3] that the Qur'ān represented Muḥammad's own composition;[4] that the Prophet adopted many practices from Judaism;[5] and that the driving force behind Islamic expansion was not religious zeal but the rapacity of the Arab tribesmen.[6] As president of the Republic, he went so far as to make cautious use of

---

[2] *Atatürk'ün Okuduğu Kitaplar*, ed. Recep Cengiz, vol. 3 (Ankara: Anıtkabir Derneği Yayınları, 2001), 132–490; vol. 4, 1–422. The translation of Caetani's multivolume study on Islam prompted strong criticisms from conservative circles. For a detailed refutation of Caetani's theses, see M. Âsım Köksal, *Müsteşrik Caetani'nin Yazdığı İslâm Tarihi'ndeki İsnad ve İftiralara Reddiye* (Ankara: Balkanoğlu Matbaacılık, 1961). The Turkish Directorate of Religious Affairs republished this refutation in 1986.

[3] *Atatürk'ün Okuduğu Kitaplar*, ed. Recep Cengiz, vol. 3, 210 ff; Leone Caetani, *Annali dell'Islām*, vol. 1, *Introduzione dell'anno 1. al 6. H.* (Milan: Ulrico Hoepli, 1905), 202–208. See also Mustafa Kemal's personal notes in *Atatürk'ün Bütün Eserleri*, vol. 24, *1930–1931* (Istanbul: Kaynak Yayınları, 2008), 198, and a typed note in his personal library. *Atatürk'ün Okuduğu Kitaplar*, ed. Recep Cengiz, vol. 9, 58–62; Caetani, *Annali dell'Islām*, vol. 1, 198ff.

[4] *Atatürk'ün Okuduğu Kitaplar*, ed. Recep Cengiz, vol. 3, 204ff.; Caetani, *Annali dell'Islām*, vol. 1, 200–203. See also *Atatürk'ün Okuduğu Kitaplar: Özel İşaretleri, Uyarıları ve Düştüğü Notlar İle*, ed. D. Gürbüz Tüfekçi (Ankara: Türkiye İş Bankası Kültür Yayınları, 1983), 341; Caetani, *Annali dell'Islām*, vol. 1, 218.

[5] *Atatürk'ün Okuduğu Kitaplar*, ed. Recep Cengiz, vol. 3, 264–65; Caetani, *Annali dell'Islām*, 1, 375–76.

[6] *Atatürk'ün Okuduğu Kitaplar*, ed. Recep Cengiz, vol. 3, 291–93; Caetani, *Annali dell'Islām*, vol. 1, 390–91.

Caetani's words when drafting a chapter on the origins of Islam for the official high school history textbook.[7]

In Mustafa Kemal's vision, nationalism was to replace religion through a radical reinterpretation of Islam from a Turkish nationalist perspective. Following Caetani, he believed that Islam had become a "real religion and belief system" only when the Muslim Arabs turned to subjugating non-Arab peoples.[8] A chapter for the high school textbook prepared under his supervision described this process as the start of the "Arab-Turkish struggle," in which "torrents of Bedouins overflowing from the Arabian deserts moved toward cultivated and prosperous [Turkish cities] through Iranian valleys."[9] As he later explained in more straightforward terms, Islam was an Arab faith and a vehicle for Arab domination: "The Turks, too, had been a great nation before accepting the religion of the Arabs." However, the "Arab religion . . . loosened the national ties of the Turkish nation" and "benumbed national feelings and enthusiasm for the nation, because the aim of the religion established by Muḥammad prompted an Arab nationalist policy. . . . Those who accepted Muḥammad's religion had to suppress their identities and devote their lives to the exaltation of the name of Allāh everywhere. . . . Under these circumstances, the Turkish nation resembled those who commit the Qur'ān to memory without understanding the meaning of a single word of it and thus become senile."[10]

Needless to say, the realization of Mustafa Kemal's project to

---

[7] See his notes taken in 1930 in *Atatürk'ün Bütün Eserleri*, vol. 24, 60–65; *Tarih II: Ortazamanlar* (Istanbul: Devlet Matbaası, 1931), 79ff. Mustafa Kemal's notes summarized various parts of the first volume of Caetani's magnum opus, and provided the skeleton of the narrative on Islam in the textbook.

[8] *Atatürk'ün Okuduğu Kitaplar*, ed. Recep Cengiz, vol. 3, 291ff. Caetani, *Annali dell'Islām*, vol. 1, 391.

[9] *Tarih II: Ortazamanlar*, 143.

[10] Âfetinan [Ayşe Âfet İnan], *Medenî Bilgiler ve M. Kemal Atatürk'ün El Yazıları* (Ankara: Türk Tarih Kurumu Yayınları, 1969), 364–66.

"reawaken" that benumbed nation by the construction of a secular nation-state, republican in structure and scientistic in principle, would have been a daunting enterprise anywhere in the non-Western world—let alone in a conservative Muslim society of the 1920s. In a way, the challenge was even greater than that faced by the Bolsheviks, since Marxism-Leninism lent itself to the development of an effective set of tools for state building more easily than crass scientism. Mustafa Kemal did, however, benefit from one significant advantage: the elaborate blueprints for a future society prepared by the Ottoman proponents of scientism during the Second Constitutional Period. Although much of Ottoman society dismissed these visions as the ruminations of marginal intellectuals, while the religious establishment denounced them as outright heresy, the momentous victory of 1922 brought into being the revolutionary situation necessary for their implementation by a true believer.

The nationalist victory of 1922 rendered Ottoman ideology meaningless. The supranational identity promoted by Ottomanism did not fit the circumstances of the postwar era, since only one noteworthy ethnic group other than Turks remained in Turkey—namely, the Kurds. Similarly, the ancient institution of the caliphate, though still respected in many regions outside the former Ottoman realm, could be of little practical use for domestic Turkish purposes now that major Muslim groups vital for the maintenance of Ottoman rule in the Balkans and the Fertile Crescent—namely, the Albanians and the Arabs—had separated themselves from the empire. These practical realities, reinforced by Mustafa Kemal's Turkish nationalist sentiments and his profound belief that reform in one country was the only feasible project, prompted the hero of the War of Independence to move toward abandoning Ottoman ideology altogether.

The first stroke came immediately after victory. Since its inception the Ankara government had functioned as a republican institution—without, however, formally declaring that the new state was a republic. At the time, Mustafa Kemal had justifiably feared that any reference to republicanism—with its implication that the time-honored sultanate was to be abandoned—would gravely jeopardize the success of the war effort. Once victory was accomplished, however, he felt confident enough to prepare public opinion for the eventual abolition of the sultanate and the establishment of a republic in its stead. Like Jean-Jacques Rousseau, he considered the principal aim of a republic not to assure individual liberty but to give expression to the "general will."[11] Like Niccolò Machiavelli, he thought that a true republic should pursue national strength even at the expense of individual freedom. He further believed that dynastic rule was an anachronism due to be replaced by republicanism, "the final remedy that humanity has produced after a four-hundred-year struggle."[12] His archetype was France's Troisième République (1870–1940), which he viewed as a genuine republic and the most successful regime in the history of humankind. He approved of official France's militant anticlericalism, its pugnacious *laïcité*, and its idealistic *solidarité* as described by Alfred Fouillée.[13] Mustafa Kemal also looked with favor upon France's étatism, descriptions of which he read in the works of

[11] *Atatürk'ün Okuduğu Kitaplar*, ed. Gürbüz Tüfekçi, 246; Babanzâde İsmail Hakkı, *Hukuk-i Esasiyye*, 133.

[12] Afet [Âfet İnan], *Vatandaş İçin Medenî Bilgiler*, vol. 1 (Istanbul: Devlet Matbaası, 1931), 41–42. When Mustafa Kemal read Voltaire's verses "La mort du fils des rois suffit à ma vengeance / Étouffons dans son sang la fatale semence," he commented, "The people will live to annihilate the kings." See *Atatürk'ün Okuduğu Kitaplar*, ed. Recep Cengiz, vol. 24, 3; *Théatre de Voltaire*, vol. 2 (Paris: Librairie Garnier Frères, 1927), 124.

[13] Mustafa Kemal read a Turkish rendition of Fouillée's well-known study of national character *Esquisse psychologique de peuples Européens*, which deftly attacked anthroposociology and its assertion that the struggle for life was the major law of society, with great interest and "in a single night." See *Atatürk'ün Okuduğu Kitaplar*, ed. Recep Cengiz, vol. 5, 303–54.

Charles Gide.[14] The extent to which he found in contemporary France a political model worthy of emulation may be gauged from the fact that he had special translations of studies on political parties in the Third Republic prepared especially for his perusal.[15]

The primary institutional obstacle to transplanting the Third Republic to Turkey was the six-centuries-old sultanate. In an appeal to the Turkish nation issued immediately after the victory, Mustafa Kemal hinted at his plans in this regard: "The reason you do not find the Greek king among our prisoners of war is that royal sovereigns are inclined to partake only of their nation's pleasures. In times of catastrophe, they think of nothing but their palaces."[16] In a more direct reference to the Ottoman sovereign, he reminded his audience that the authorities who had surrendered to the Greeks such major cities as İzmir and Bursa had no ties to the nation, and that the salvation of the homeland had not started until "the nation's own will and vote started to determine its destiny without restriction."[17] Like a sniper lying in ambush, Mustafa Kemal took aim at his target, but held his fire for the moment.

Had the sultan of the Ottomans not been at the same time the caliph of Sunnī Islam, removing him would have been less complicated. But in the fall of 1922, on the heels of a war ostensibly fought on behalf of Islam, a radical shift to a republic without a caliph would have prompted a major hue and cry. Mustafa Kemal therefore proceeded circumspectly, directing the Turkish Grand National Assembly first to separate the caliphate from the sultanate and then to abolish the latter on November 1–2, 1922. In doing so he seized upon the opportunity presented by the request

[14] Mustafa Kemal skimmed the Turkish rendition of Charles Gide's *Cours d'économie politique*. See *Atatürk'ün Okuduğu Kitaplar*, ed. Recep Cengiz, vol. 7, 335–42.

[15] *Atatürk'ün Okuduğu Kitaplar*, ed. Gürbüz Tüfekçi, 470.

[16] "Millete Beyanname, September 12, 1922," in *Atatürk'ün Bütün Eserleri*, vol. 13, *1922* (Istanbul: Kaynak Yayınları, 2004), 274.

[17] Ibid., 275.

of the grand vizier in Istanbul (first addressed to Mustafa Kemal, and then to the Turkish Grand National Assembly) that the Ankara government should cooperate with the Istanbul government in dispatching a joint delegation to the peace negotiations in Lausanne.[18] The assembly, which had no intention of sharing its victory and enhanced power with the paper government of the sultan, reacted furiously.

From a doctrinal standpoint, separating the caliphate from the sultanate, and thereby creating a religious figurehead who reigned but did not rule, had become extremely difficult by the twentieth century. Despite the original fusion of religion and politics in the early Islamic state, such a separation would not have been problematic a few centuries later, when the caliphate and sultanate were typically quite distinct institutions. Indeed al-Māwardī (d. 1058) in the eleventh century had in effect legitimized such a separation,[19] and the 'ulamā' in Mamluk Egypt had accepted a similar arrangement.[20] Yet the premise of the inseparability of the caliphate and sultanate gradually became the mainstream assumption about the relationship between the two institutions. The Ottoman tradition expanded on this point in later years to justify the Ottoman sultan's possession of both titles. Hence, members of the 'ulamā' in the Turkish Grand National Assembly, who had vehemently defended this point of view, spoke out against the proposed separation. During a particularly turbulent session of the Sharī'a and Justice Commission, Mustafa Kemal cut the discussion short by

[18] *Nutuk: Gazi Mustafa Kemal Tarafindan* (Ankara: n.p., 1927), 420.

[19] Qamaruddin Khan, *Al-Mawardi's Theory of the State* (Lahore, Pakistan: Islamic Book Foundation, 1983), 42–43.

[20] In 1250 the Mamluk 'ulamā' played a prominent role in legitimizing the rule of Sayf al-Dīn Quṭuz, the third Mamluk ruler, as the amīr of the Muslim army. See Yūsuf ibn Tagrī-Birdī, *al-Nujūm al-zāhirah fī mulūk Miṣr wa-al-Qāhirah*, vol. 7 (Cairo: Maṭba'at Dār al-Kutub al-Miṣriyya, 1938), 72–73. After the installation of a pseudocaliphate in Cairo, the caliphs nominally appointed the Mamluk rulers; ibid., 111–13.

jumping on a table and issuing a peremptory warning: "sovereignty and sultanate are not granted to anyone through discussion and debate. . . . Now the Turkish nation . . . seizes its own sovereignty. This is . . . a fait accompli. . . . If the assembly . . . accepts this naturally, it would be better in my opinion. If not, this truth will . . . be expressed in due course, although probably some heads will be cut off."[21] In response, the commission members, aghast at this outburst of candor, hurried to explain that they had merely been discussing the issue from a theoretical viewpoint, and were "enlightened" by Mustafa Kemal's explanation. They accepted the proposal immediately and forwarded it for deliberation in the assembly.[22]

In order to rally support for his radical proposal during the deliberations that followed in the assembly, Mustafa Kemal spoke both like a Muslim scholar and like a nationalist ideologue. The religious content for his well-rehearsed peroration was based on his extensive reading as of 1920 on the first twenty-four years of the Islamic state.[23] The Turkist substance was taken from his own interpretation of the Turkist theses advanced during the Second Constitutional Period, and from Joseph de Guignes's eighteenth-century study *Histoire générale des Huns, des Turcs, des Mogols et des autres Tartares occidentaux*.[24] In a lengthy, detailed, and innovative speech, Mustafa Kemal extolled the magnificent past of the Turkish people. According to this account, Noah had a grandson named Turk, who was the ancestor of the Turkish nation. Although the prehistoric achievements of this great nation were somewhat obscure, the Turks had established

[21] *Nutuk*, 422.

[22] Ibid.

[23] [Halide Edib], *The Turkish Ordeal: Being the Further Memoirs of Halidé Edib* (New York: Century, 1928), 168.

[24] Mustafa Kemal seems to have taken much of the information from the first tome of Joseph de Guignes's multivolume study, which he read with interest. See *Atatürk'ün Okuduğu Kitaplar*, ed. Recep Cengiz, vol. 16, 323ff. He later read the Turkish rendition of the same volume; see vol. 6, 103ff.

major states in Central Asia over 1,500 years ago. Then came the encounter with the Arabs, another great people, and one inspired to adopt a new religion by their leader Muḥammad who was sent as the last prophet to mankind. Following his death the caliphate emerged as an institution of government, but Islam's swift expansion made its continuation in this form impossible after the four Rightly Guided Caliphs.[25] Consequently, rival sultanates laying claim to this sacred office emerged throughout the Muslim world. It was during this period that the Turks penetrated the Caucasus, Anatolia, Iran, and Iraq, and reduced the ʿAbbāsid caliphs to vassalage. Thereafter, Turkish rulers tolerated the existence of the caliphate as a separate institution within their magnificent state. Had the great Turkish ruler Melikşah (d. 1092) wished to seize this title for himself, he could easily have done so. Yet he preferred to let the caliph remain in Baghdad, intervening only to advocate the appointment of one of his own grandsons as caliph. The situation in 1922, Mustafa Kemal dexterously argued, was remarkably similar. Accordingly, it was entirely appropriate that the Turkish Grand National Assembly, which represented national sovereignty and worldly government, should coexist with a caliph bereft of temporal power. In fact, he argued, the religious status of such an authority would exceed that of Melikşah's caliph, while the separation would forestall any recurrence of the treasonous behavior exhibited by the current sultan Mehmed VI.[26]

In the course of this theologically inclined disquisition, Mus-

---

[25] Mustafa Kemal later opposed the use of the phrase "rightly guided" for the first caliphs and proposed that they should simply be called the "four caliphs." See *Atatürk'ten Düşünceler*, ed. Enver Ziya Karal (Ankara: Türkiye İş Bankası Kültür Yayınları, 1956), 92.

[26] *Hilâfet ve Saltanat Mes'elesi Hakkında Türkiya Büyük Millet Meclisi Re'isi Gazi Mustafa Kemal Paşa Hazretleri'nin Nutukları* (Ankara: Türkiya Büyük Millet Meclisi Matbaası, 1341/1338 [1922]); *Nutuk Muhteviyâtına Aid Vesâik: Gazi Mustafa Kemal Tarafından* (Ankara: n.p., 1927), 269–76.

tafa Kemal had made three significant points. First, he had presented the development of the caliphate strictly within the context of *history*, and not as a *religious* issue. Second, he had
presupposed a fundamental dichotomy between sovereignty and
the caliphate. Third, he had implicitly rejected the accepted view,
propounded by the 'ulamā', that the caliphate and sultanate
were inseparable. How much this position was out of line with
mainstream Muslim views in a country such as Egypt was to be
seen three years later, when 'Alī 'Abd al-Rāziq, an al-Azhar-edu-
cated Egyptian jurist and the qāḍī of Manṣūra, made similar
claims in his book *al-Islām wa-uṣūl al-ḥukm* (Islam and the Fun-
damentals of Government).[27] The al-Azhar 'ulamā' responded
by revoking his title of scholar and pressuring the government to
dismiss him from his post. The high praise for 'Abd al-Rāziq's
work in the republican Turkish press and the popularity of his
book in Turkish modernist circles did not help him much in defending his minority opinion.[28] The fusion of political and religious authority in the early Islamic state overrode the later medieval precedents; as Fazlur Rahman put it, 'Abd al-Rāziq's view
was tantamount to an attempt to "prove the impossible, viz. that
Muḥammad, when he acted as a law-giver or a political leader,
acted extra-religiously and secularly."[29]

[27] 'Alī 'Abd al-Rāziq, *al-Islām wa-uṣūl al-ḥukm: baḥth fī al-Khilāfah wa-al-
ḥukūmah fī al-Islām* (Cairo: Maṭba'at Miṣr, 1925). For a detailed discussion on
'Abd al-Rāziq's central argument, see Souad T. Ali, *A Religion Not a State: Ali
'Abd al-Rāziq's Islamic Justification of Political Secularism* (Salt Lake City: University of Utah Press, 2009), 70–89.

[28] Mahmut Esat Bozkurt, *Atatürk İhtilâli: Türk İnkılâbı Tarihi Enstitüsü
Derslerinden* (Istanbul: İstanbul Üniversitesi Yayınları, 1940), 442–43. The
translator of 'Abd al-Rāziq's book made the following comment: "This work is a
torch illuminating the new horizons opened by the grand Turkish revolution in
the world of science and philosophy." Ömer Rıza [Doğrul], "Mütercimin İfadesi,"
in 'Alī 'Abd al-Rāziq, *İslâmiyet ve Hükûmet: Din ve Devlet, Hilâfet ve Saltanat,
Siyaset ve İslâmiyet* (Istanbul: Kütübhane-i Sûdî, 1927), 5.

[29] Fazlur Rahman, *Islam* (London: Weidenfeld and Nicolson, 1966), 229.

Although he sounded like a Muslim scholar when addressing the assembly, Mustafa Kemal cared little about the strength of his argument from an Islamic viewpoint; his objectives were over-whelmingly political. Following Mustafa Kemal's speech, the assembly issued a decree separating the caliphate from the sultanate, and declaring the latter retroactively annulled from the time of the Allied occupation of Istanbul in March 1920.[30] A fortnight later, the last Ottoman sultan, Mehmed VI, who had become the bête noire of the nationalists, left Istanbul aboard a British man-of-war. Subsequently the Turkish Grand National Assembly approved a fatwā, issued by the Ministry of Sharī'a Affairs and Pious Foundations, legitimizing the deposition of Mehmed VI as caliph, and then chose his cousin Abdülmecid as the new spiritual leader of the Sunnī Muslims.[31] Symbolically, Abdülmecid was told not to roam the palace girded with a sword, thereby underscoring his lack of temporal powers. Mustafa Kemal gave him a further idea of the limitations of his powers by instructing him what to say and not to say in his first public appeal to the Muslim world.[32] Initial reactions from his coreligionists were relatively positive. The 'ulamā' of al-Azhar recognized the new caliph, and Indian Muslims, who at first refused to believe the somber news since it came through Reuters, comforted themselves by looking forward to a new era symbolized by a Muslim League of Nations under Mustafa Kemal's leadership.[33] They even went so far as to confer the titles Sayf

[30] "Saltanatın İlgası ve Hilâfetin Hanedân-ı Âl-i Osman'a Aidiyeti Hakkında Büyük Millet Meclisi Kararı" (November 1–2, 1922), in *Türkiye Cumhuriyeti Sicill-i Kavânini,* ed. Karakoç Sarkiz, vol. 1 (Istanbul: Cihan Matbaası, 1926), 149–50.

[31] *T.B.M.M. Gizli Celse Zabıtları,* vol. 3 (6 Mart 1338 [1922]–27 Şubat 1338 [1923]) (Ankara: T. İş Bankası Kültür Yayınları, 1985), 1042–65.

[32] *Nutuk,* 424–25.

[33] The renowned jurist 'Abd al-Razzāq Aḥmad al-Sanhūrī theoreticized this concept following the abolition of the caliphate in 1924. See A[hmad] Sanhoury,

al-Islām (Sword of Islam) and Mujaddid-i Khilāfat (Renovator of the Caliphate) on him at the Khilāfat Conference in December.[34] Likewise Rashīd Riḍā, who had championed Islamic republicanism, subtly agreed with Mustafa Kemal by making a strict distinction between the Rightly Guided Caliphs and their successors, but proposed a revival under new caliphs exercising both spiritual and temporal authority on behalf of an Islamic State in Ankara.[35] However, Mustafa Kemal soon gave Muslims outside Turkey reason to think again, asking them not to expect anything from the caliphate but rather "to strive toward saving themselves," and going on to condemn the caliphate as "a calamity [which had] befallen the [Turkish] nation."[36] Nevertheless, Mustafa Kemal refrained from proclaiming Turkey a republic for almost a year, and waited sixteen months before abolishing the caliphate. Before taking such drastic steps, he felt the need to secure full international recognition of Turkey in the context of a comprehensive peace settlement, and to establish complete control over Turkish politics.

In spite of arduous negotiations, a two-and-a-half month interruption, and the unresolved issue of the former Ottoman province of Mosul, the Lausanne Peace Treaty was signed on July 24, 1923. His significant concessions notwithstanding, Mustafa Kemal thereby capped his military victory with a diplomatic one. Finally accomplished long after the conclusion of the Great War, the treaty recognized the emergence of an independent country that had freed itself from the vestiges of Western judicial and commercial control,

---

Le Califat: son évolution vers une société des nations orientale (Paris: P. Geuthner, 1926), 586–607.

[34] M. Naem Qureshi, Pan-Islam in British Indian Politics: A Study of the Khilafat Movement, 1918–1924 (Leiden, Netherlands: Brill, 1999), 336–41.

[35] Rashīd Riḍā, al-Khilāfa aw al-imāma al-ʿuẓmā (Cairo: Maṭbaʿat al-Manār, 1341 [1923]), 76, 90–106.

[36] Gazi Mustafa Kemal Atatürk'ün 1923 Eskişehir-İzmit Konuşmaları, ed. Arı İnan (Ankara: Türk Tarih Kurumu Yayınları, 1982), 65, 71.

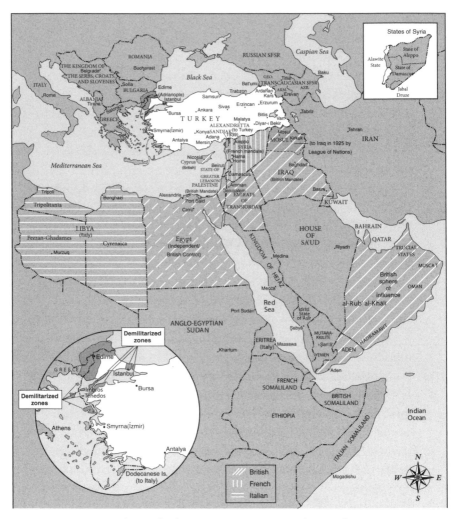

Figure 11. Turkey and other successor states according to the Lausanne
Treaty of 1923.

and purged the last remnants of the Allied occupation. On October 2, 1923, the band of the Coldstream Guards played the tune "Mustafa Kemal Pasha," originally composed in the name of Enver Pasha, to appease the jubilant Turkish spectators watching the departure of the last Allied troops from the Ottoman capital.[37] Four days later Mustafa Kemal's soldiers triumphantly paraded in Istanbul. By this time such Western statesmen as Georges Clemenceau, Lloyd George, and Woodrow Wilson had lost not only their public offices but also the leadership of their parties or movements. In contrast, Mustafa Kemal not only became the supreme guide of a nation but also the leader of its single ruling party, and for the rest of his life no tune other than his would be played in his country.

In December 1922, he announced that following the peace he would establish a new political party. This new organization, he promised, would encompass all social classes, including farmers, workers, capitalists, industrialists, and intellectuals, and would serve as a vehicle for the implementation of a major program of transformation.[38] Clearly, such an all-encompassing party would render the existence of any other political organization pointless. In the meantime the assembly, acting at his behest, called for new elections in April 1923. Mustafa Kemal declared that after the elections the Anatolia and Rumelia Defense of Rights organization would be reconstituted as the People's (later Republican People's) Party.[39] Following his landslide victory in the elections, which had a turnout of 60 percent and excluded many dissident figures, a new, obsequious assembly was convened in August 1923, and the People's Party officially came into being in September. With a party and assembly under his complete control, Mustafa

---

[37] David Walder, *The Chanak Affair* (London: Hutchinson, 1969), 351.

[38] "Halk Partisi'ni Kurmak Hakkındaki Kararını Açıklaması, 6.XII. 1922," in *Atatürk'ün Söylev ve Demeçleri*, vol. 2, *1906–1938*, ed. Nimet Unan (Ankara: Türk İnkılâp Tarihi Enstitüsü Yayımları, 1952), 46–48.

[39] *Nutuk*, 436–37.

Kemal now achieved total domination of politics, an ascendancy that lasted until his death. Although the system was theoretically open to the participation of other political organizations, in reality it was a single-party regime. The dissidents, who came together in a new party called the Progressive Republican Party in November 1924, faced tremendous difficulties in opposing the policies of the Republican People's Party and its leader.[40]

In June 1925, seizing on the pretext of a Kurdish uprising with strong Islamist undertones, the government banned the opposition party after it had been in existence for only six and one-half months. In 1926, following a foiled attempt on his life, Mustafa Kemal throttled his remaining opponents, including many prominent figures of the War of Independence and former CUP leaders. Kangaroo courts tried all significant dissidents, linking them to the assassination plot; some were executed while others received various terms of imprisonment. Leading generals of the War of Independence, although acquitted by the magistrates, were compelled to quit politics. The opposition was either literally or figuratively dead. In October 1927 Mustafa Kemal delivered his famous thirty-six-and-a-half-hour *Speech* (later deemed his magnum opus), in which he claimed sole authorship of the War of Independence and of the major reforms implemented in its wake, and condemned everyone who opposed him in the harshest terms. Even those who had played significant roles in the War of Independence did not escape his censure. Mustafa Kemal seems to have genuinely desired a multiparty democracy, but could not tolerate any criticism of his policies. Thus his organization remained the single party. Later, in August 1930, he attempted to form a spurious opposition party composed of his close associates; but the extraordi-

[40] Erik Jan Zürcher, *Political Opposition in the Early Turkish Republic: The Progressive Republican Party, 1924–1925* (Leiden, Netherlands: Brill, 1991), 80–94.

nary support given to this new organization by all classes of people prompted its worried founders to dissolve it a mere three months after its inception.[41] Less significant initiatives toward establishing small parties were similarly abandoned.[42]

With his absolute political supremacy assured, Mustafa Kemal now acted to implement his comprehensive program of political and social transformation. Although the need to proceed vigilantly had prevented him from publicizing his intentions earlier, he had in fact provided clues about his revolutionary program immediately following the military victory. One such clue was his abrupt dismissal of the imām assigned to the Turkish Grand National Assembly. "We do not need such things [prayers] here," explained Mustafa Kemal. "You may perform them in a mosque. We did not win the war with prayers, but with the blood of our soldiers."[43] Another example of his volte-face was the only Friday sermon (khuṭba) ever delivered by a Turkish head of state; this took place at a mosque in Balıkesir during the election campaign. While praising Islam as a progressive religion to appease the conservative electorate, Mustafa Kemal used this singular opportunity to promote scientistic and nationalist theses, such as the need for scientific khuṭbas in Turkish. To repeat the sermons of a thousand years ago, he explained, was to preserve backwardness and promote nescience.[44] And when Mustafa Kemal expressed himself in less sanctified surroundings he spoke like a staunch Darwinist and Turkist. For example, he instructed an audience in İzmir that "Life

[41] Ali Fethi Okyar, *Serbest Cumhuriyet Fırkası Nasıl Doğdu, Nasıl Fesh Edildi?* (Istanbul: n.p., 1987), 79–83.

[42] Mete Tunçay, *T.C.'nde Tek Parti Yönetimi'nin Kurulması* (Istanbul: Cem Yayınevi, 1989), 273–82.

[43] Bozkurt, *Atatürk İhtilâli*, 139.

[44] "Balıkesir'de Halkla Konuşma, 7.II. 1923," in *Atatürk'ün Söylev ve Demeçleri*, vol. 2, 93–95.

means struggle," and spoke of advancing a "Turanian" national policy incompatible with the disastrous policy of Islamism.[45]

After the elections, Mustafa Kemal came out openly and vigorously in favor of his republican agenda. First, he instructed the Turkish Grand National Assembly to declare Ankara the capital of the new country.[46] Even though Ankara had served as the de facto capital of the nationalist state since 1920, this was a significant symbolic change, since Istanbul had served as the capital of two majestic empires and administered Anatolia for centuries. Replacing Istanbul with a provincial town in Anatolia had seemed unthinkable. Then, in late October 1923, Mustafa Kemal seized the opportunity presented by a government crisis to propose a law officially establishing Turkey as a republic. The assembly unanimously accepted this proposal and elected Mustafa Kemal as the first president of the new republic on October 29.[47] If we disregard the short-lived experiments of Azerbaijan, Tripoli of Barbary, and Rif in republicanism (Azərbaycan Xalq Cümhuriyyəti of 1918, al-Jumhūriyya al-Ṭarāblusiyya of 1918, and al-Dawla al-Jumhūriyya al-Rīfiyya of 1923), this marked the first time that a modern Muslim society adopted a republican form of government. This was enormously significant. In Ottoman parlance, the term *republicanism* had generally been used in a derogatory sense and was held to be antithetical to Islam. Acting to shield himself from public criticism in the immediate wake of this revolutionary change, Mustafa Kemal added a new clause to the constitution on the day of the promulgation of the republic, declaring Islam "the religion of the state."[48]

---

[45] "İzmir'de Halka Nutuk, February 2, 1923," in *Atatürk'ün Bütün Eserleri*, vol. 15, *1923* (Istanbul: Kaynak Yayınları, 2005), 58–61, 68.

[46] "Ankara Şehrinin Makarr-ı İdare İttihazı Hakkında Karar" (October 13, 1923), in Karakoç, ed., *Sicill-i Kavânin*, vol. 1, 336.

[47] "20 Kânûn-i Sânî 1337 Tarihli Teşkilât-ı Esasiye Kanunu'nun Bâzı Mevaddının Tavzihen Ta'diline Dâir Kanun" (Law #364, October 29, 1923), in Karakoç, ed., *Sicill-i Kavânin*, vol. 1, 348.

[48] Ibid.; see also *Nutuk*, 435–36.

The president nevertheless went on to make the new republic secular. Although he had strongly defended the caliphate when proposing its separation from the sultanate, the new Vatican-style institution remained a major obstacle to the secular transformation he wished to bring about. Emblematic of the president's view of the caliphate was his truculent response to the new caliph's request to don a turban at Friday prayers like that worn by Sultan Mehmed II (d. 1481); Mustafa Kemal blithely recommended that Abdülmecid Efendi wear a frock coat instead.[49] On another occasion, he termed the caliphate "nonsense."[50] Nonsense or not, the caliphate was a tremendously important symbol, and its abolition was incomparably more difficult than the termination of the sultanate. Sultan Abdülhamid II had successfully revitalized the institution, and large numbers of Sunnī Muslims all over the Islamic world viewed it as the paramount Muslim establishment charged with the defense of their rights against Western encroachment. Even the CUP leaders who dethroned Abdülhamid II strove to benefit from the caliphate despite their secular proclivities. During the Great War in particular, Ottoman propaganda had exploited the caliphate to the fullest extent, while the nationalists portrayed the Turkish War of Independence as a struggle to revive the institution. Moreover to many educated Muslims, the abolition of the caliphate meant a return to the leadership vacuum that had followed the destruction of the ʿAbbāsid caliphate by the Mongols in 1258 (an event that Mustafa Kemal unkindly described in 1923 as the "punishment of a deceitful ruler ... by a Turk").[51] Thus the abolition of the caliphate was not a decision to be undertaken lightly, and it had the potential to trigger a dangerous backlash at home and abroad.

[49] *Nutuk*, 425.
[50] Ibid., 512–13.
[51] "Konya Gençleriyle Konuşma, 20.III.1923," in *Atatürk'ün Söylev ve Demeçleri*, 2, 146.

Mustafa Kemal was nevertheless determined to deal with the issue when the opportunity arose. As conservative criticism of Abdülmecid's reduced stature mounted, and the caliph himself escalated his demands for a more active role in administration, the president felt compelled to act. Hence, only a year and a half after mounting a vigorous defense of the nontemporal caliphate coexisting with secular governance, Mustafa Kemal began to stress its irreconcilability with republican principles and popular sovereignty.[52]

The separation of the caliphate from the sultanate had caused criticism and dismay in conservative circles. A leading Islamist, Eşref Edib (Fergan), penned a pamphlet titled *Hilâfet-i İslâmiye ve Büyük Millet Meclisi* (The Islamic Caliphate and the Grand National Assembly) and published it under the name of a deputy, İsmail Şükrü (Çelikalay), since the latter had parliamentarian immunity. Eşref Edib maintained that the caliphate and legislative authority were inseparable.[53] He further argued that it was up to the caliph to approve the laws issued by the assembly and to appoint preachers and imāms.[54] Mustafa Kemal immediately denounced these arguments, emphasizing that the assembly was responsible only to the nation,[55] and that "the law of the revolution [was] above all other laws."[56] He further instructed Justice Minister Çelebizâde Mehmed Seyyid, a former CUP member and leading *fiqh* scholar, to refute Eşref Edib's assertions. Using *hadīth*s and classical fiqh works such as the *Hidāyah* of the authoritative jurist al-Marghīnānī (d. 1197), Mehmed Seyyid strenuously contested the claim that there was any temporal authority vested in the ca-

---

[52] *Nutuk*, 429ff.

[53] [Eşref Edib], *Hilâfet-i İslâmiye ve Büyük Millet Meclisi* (Ankara: Ali Şükrü Matbaası, 1339 [1923]), 8–11, 22–23.

[54] Ibid., 27–28.

[55] *Nutuk*, 429, 431–32, 436; and *1923 Eskişehir-İzmit Konuşmaları*, 61–62.

[56] *1923 Eskişehir-İzmit Konuşmaları*, 83.

liph.[57] He cited the process resulting in Abū al-Qāsim Aḥmad's (d. 1262) assumption of the caliphal title *al-mustanṣir* while the Mamluk Sultan Baybars (d. 1277) reigned in Cairo.[58] According to him the pledge of allegiance given by a scholar like 'Izz al-Dīn ibn 'Abd al-Salām (d. 1279) to the new 'Abbāsid caliph, who was in no way a temporal ruler, unequivocally proved the separate nature of the caliphate.[59] His conclusion, that "today there is no need to discuss the question of the caliphate . . . [which] is nothing but a matter of politics and tradition," hinted at the possible abolition of the institution.[60]

Soon afterward, in November 1923, Agha Khan III, the Indian leader of the Nizārī Ismā'īlī sect, and his compatriot Sayyid Amīr 'Alī, the renowned Shī'ite scholar who had founded the National Mohammedan Association in 1877 and had served on the judicial committee of the Privy Council since 1909, sent a joint letter to the Turkish prime minister, İsmet İnönü. The two noted with regret that Islam was losing its influence as a "moral and cohesive force" among large sections of the Sunnī population, "owing to the diminution in the Caliph's dignity and prestige," and warned that "if Islam is to maintain its place in the world as a great moral force, the Caliph's position and dignity should not, in any event, be less than that of the Pontiff of the Church of Rome."[61] The prime minister and the leaders of the ruling party reacted with predictable fury, accusing the two Muslim leaders of intervening in the domes-

[57] [Çelebizâde Mehmed Seyyid], *Hilâfet ve Hakimiyet-i Milliye* (Ankara: n.p., 1923), 75.

[58] Ibid., 58–59.

[59] Ibid., 59–60. Reliable sources do indeed support this claim; see Ismā'īl ibn Kathīr, *al-Bidāyah wa-al-nihāyah fī al-Tarīkh,* vol. 13 (Cairo: Maṭba'at al-Sa'adah, n.d. [1939]), 231–32; and Tāj al-Dīn Subkī, *Ṭabaqāt al-Shāfi'īyah al-kubrā,* vol. 3 (Cairo: Maṭba'at 'Īsā al-Bābī al-Ḥalabī wa shurakā', n.d. [1964]), 215, 245.

[60] [Çelebizâde Mehmed Seyyid], *Hilâfet ve Hakimiyet-i Milliye,* 72.

[61] Arnold J. Toynbee, *Survey of International Affairs, 1925,* vol. 1 (Oxford: Oxford University Press, 1927), 571–72.

tic affairs of Turkey, questioning their competence as Shī'ites to discuss the Sunnī caliphate, and denouncing them as lackeys of British imperialism.[62] In December, the prosecutor of the Independence Court ordered the arrest of the editors of the Istanbul dailies that had published the translation of the missive. While these events were moving quickly toward their dénouement, the *Jam'īyyat al-'Ulamā'* in India proposed an international congress of Muslim scholars to discuss the future of the caliphate.[63] Under attack at home and abroad, Mustafa Kemal, after receiving assurances of the military's support, launched the abolition process.

In late February 1924, the official newspaper of the government featured an article declaring that the caliphate was irreconcilable with national sovereignty and the republican regime.[64] This was a clear signal of imminent action. On March 2, the parliamentary group of the ruling People's Party approved three draft bills and passed them on to the assembly. Among other things, they proposed the abolition of the caliphate and the Ministry of Sharī'a Affairs and Pious Foundations, the unification of the religious and secular educational systems, and the expulsion of all members of the Ottoman royal house from Turkey. Instead of personally engaging in the process, as he had done during the debate over sultanate, Mustafa Kemal asked Mehmed Seyyid to defend the abolition of the caliphate from an Islamic viewpoint at the parliamentary group meeting.[65]

After reiterating Mustafa Kemal's thesis that the Turkish Revolution was the greatest revolution in the history of humankind, let alone in that of the Muslim peoples, Mehmed Seyyid once again

---

[62] *T.B.M.M. Gizli Celse Zabıtları*, vol. 4 (2 Mart 1339 [1923]–25 Teşrin-i evvel 1939), (Ankara: T. İş Bankası Kültür Yayınları , 1985), 314ff.

[63] Toynbee, *Survey of International Affairs, 1925*, 59.

[64] "İnkılâbın Mübrem Mantıkı," *Hakimiyet-i Milliye*, February 27, 1924.

[65] Mete Tunçay, "İkinci Meclis Tutanaklarında İlginç Bir Montaj Olayı," *Toplumsal Tarih* 10/105 (2002): 24–25.

stressed that the question of the caliphate was political and temporal in nature, and had nothing to do with the sharī'a or the Muslim system of belief.[66] According to his explanation, which echoed Mustafa Kemal's speech during the sultanate debate, after the Rightly Guided Caliphs there had been no caliphs in a real sense. The caliphate was an instrument in the hands of the nation, which could alter the arrangement in accordance with the necessities of the age.[67] It was telling, he argued, that the later sultan-caliphs had all used the title "sultan X, son of sultan Y" and not "caliph X, son of caliph Y."[68] He also underscored the importance of issuing laws that were "in conformity with the traditions and customs of Turkishness." Here he made one fatal mistake in an otherwise brilliant defense of Mustafa Kemal's position. Underestimating the president's commitment to Westernization, he mentioned the Swiss Civil Code as a clear example of something that could not possibly be adopted by a truly Turkish legislature.[69] As a result, he lost his cabinet portfolio three days later. In an ironic twist of fate, he died shortly before the Turkish assembly adopted a slightly modified version of the Swiss Civil Code in 1926. Keeping abreast of Mustafa Kemal's avant-garde program was not easy.

On March 3, bowing to the force of Mustafa Kemal's will and Mehmed Seyyid's reasoning voiced at the parliamentary group of the People's Party, the Turkish Grand National Assembly voted for the abolition of the caliphate and proclaimed that "the caliph

---

[66] [Mehmed Seyyid], *Türkiye Büyük Millet Meclisi'nin 3 Mart 1340 Tarihinde Mün'akid İkinci İctima'ında Hilâfetin Mahiyet-i Şer'iyyesi Hakkında Adliye Vekili Seyyid Bey Tarafından İrâd Olunan Nutuk* (Ankara: Türkiye Büyük Millet Meclisi Matbaası, n.d. [1924]), 4, 10–11. For a detailed analysis of Mehmed Seyyid's line of thought, see Sami Erdem, "Cumhuriyet'e Geçiş Sürecinde Hilafet Teorisine Alternatif Yaklaşımlar: Seyyid Bey Örneği, 1922–1924," *Dîvân* 1/2 (1996): 119–46.

[67] *Seyyid Bey Tarafından İrâd Olunan Nutuk*, 13–14.

[68] Ibid., 52.

[69] Ibid., 62–63.

has been deposed from his post. Since the [essence of the] caliphate is subsumed under the concepts of government and republic,
the institution of the caliphate has been abolished."[70] The name of
the caliph was now replaced in the Friday prayers by the phrase
"Government of the Turkish Republic." When Indian Muslim organizations petitioned Mustafa Kemal to become the new caliph,
he refused point-blank.[71] The abolition marked the virtual end of
the Indian Khilāfat movement; it also prompted a ferocious struggle among various Arab leaders led by Sharīf Ḥusayn of Mecca and
King Fu'ād of Egypt for recognition as the greatest spiritual leader
in the Sunnī Muslim world.[72] Within Turkey, it transformed the
whole question of religious reform into a domestic one over which
Mustafa Kemal now exercised complete control.

Signaling his desire to move forward immediately with religious reform, Mustafa Kemal authorized the establishment of the
Directorate of Religious Affairs on the very same day that the caliphate was abolished.[73] This institution, placed from the beginning under the firm guidance of the administration, replaced the
old religious establishment, which had given relatively free rein to
differing interpretations of Islam. In taking this step, Mustafa
Kemal embraced one of the mottoes of the Westernizers of the
Second Constitutional Period: "Religion is the science of the
masses, whereas science is the religion of the elite." He did not

---

[70] "Hilâfetin İlgasına ve Hanedân-ı Osmanî'nin Türkiye Cumhuriyeti
Memâliki Haricine Çıkarılmasına Dair Kanun" (Law #431, March 3, 1924), in
Karakoç, ed., *Sicill-i Kavânin*, vol. 1, 448.

[71] "Telgraf, March 1924," in *Atatürk'ün Bütün Eserleri*, vol. 16, *1924* (Istanbul: Kaynak Yayınları, 2005), 236–37; *Nutuk*, 515.

[72] See Sylvia G. Haim, "The Abolition of the Caliphate and Its Aftermath," in
Thomas W. Arnold, *The Caliphate* (New York: Barnes and Noble, 1967),
224–44.

[73] "Şer'iye ve Evkaf ve Erkân-ı Harbiye-i Umumiye Vekâletlerinin İlgasına
Dâir Kanun" (Law #429, March 3, 1924), in Karakoç, ed., *Sicill-i Kavânin*, vol. 1,
446.

wish to ridicule religion in the eyes of the masses as the Soviet leaders were doing; instead he wished to tame its power, harness it to his own program of reform, and exploit it to raise the moral standard of the masses. This is why, in writing an official textbook of civics to be taught in schools, he muted his adverse views on Islam.[74] He understood that criticism of religion was best left to the elite, for whom there should be no guide other than science. He was also interested in the Turkification of Islam along the lines described by Ziya Gökalp in his *Yeni Hayat* (New Life, 1918) and *Türkçülüğün Esasları* (The Principles of Turkism, 1923). These were confusing times, in which the state was sponsoring antireligious publications such as the Baron d'Holbach's *Le Bon sens* and extreme antireligious journals such as *İctihad* and *Hür Fikir* (Libre Pensée), while simultaneously promoting major religious reform.

The main idea behind this initiative was that a religious reform program similar to that of the Protestant reformation of the sixteenth century would prompt a Turkish renaissance in the twentieth century. Thus, unlike puritanical Muslim movements such as Wahhābism and Salafism, which proposed a return to the original sources of Islam in order to create a new orthodoxy, Mustafa Kemal wished to reinterpret the Muslim tradition so as to facilitate a Turkish renaissance. His goal was to achieve much more than a mere theoretical reconciliation of modernity and Islam. Oblivious of the strongly Christian underpinnings of the Reformation, the president, like the Late Ottoman Westernists before him, sought to bring about the sort of secularizing change set in motion by the Lutheran and Calvinist movements in Christendom. The U.S. ambassador to Turkey, Charles Sherrill, who compared Mustafa Kemal to Martin Luther and John Wycliffe, was not far off the mark.[75] Mustafa

[74] Afet [Âfet İnan], *Vatandaş İçin Medenî Bilgiler*, vol. 1 (Istanbul: Devlet Matbaası, 1931), 12.
[75] Charles H. Sherrill, *A Year's Embassy to Mustafa Kemal* (New York: Charles Scribner's Sons, 1934), 193–96. See also Rıfat N. Bali, *New Documents on*

Kemal is said to have remarked, "I do not want to become a Luther,"[76] but in fact he did.

In 1923, Mustafa Kemal declared that "contemporary mujtahids"—those qualified to make new interpretations of Islamic law—would now turn to a fresh library of books drawn from three continents as a source for reforming Islam.[77] In 1925 the Turkish Grand National Assembly commissioned a Turkish translation of the Qur'ān, a multivolume Turkish commentary of the text, and a compilation of sound ḥadīths in Turkish translation.[78] The assumption was that the availability of such sources in the vernacular would have an impact similar to that of Luther's Bible of 1534. It was not that the Qur'ān had never before been translated into Turkish; early renderings into Turkic languages went back many centuries, just as did translations of the Bible into Germanic languages. In addition, a number of contemporary versions in a more contemporary Turkish had appeared after 1841. But the hope was that a new translation would pave the way for a purification of the religion, a Turkish *Ralliement*, and a renaissance among the masses. In a similar vein, starting in 1927 the Directorate of Religious Affairs not only decided the topics of khuṭbas to be delivered at Friday prayers, but also required that prayers and direct quotations

---

Atatürk: Atatürk as Viewed through the Eyes of American Diplomats (Istanbul: Isis Press, 2007), 156.

[76] Şevket Süreyya Aydemir, *Tek Adam: Mustafa Kemal*, vol. 3, *1922–1938* (Istanbul: Remzi Kitabevi, 1981), 496.

[77] "Dördüncü Toplantı Yılını Açarken, March 1, 1923," in *Atatürk'ün Söylev ve Demeçleri*, vol. 1, *T.B.M. Meclisinde ve C.H.P. Kurultaylarında, 1919–1938* (Istanbul: Türk İnkılâp Tarihi Enstitüsü Yayımları, 1945), 289.

[78] A nine-volume *tafsīr* (Qur'ān commentary), entitled *Hak Dini Kur'an Dili* (The Religion of God and the Language of Islam), by Elmalılı Muhammed Hamdi Yazır, appeared between 1935 and 1938, and a twelve-volume translation of Aḥmad ibn Aḥmad Zabīdī's (d. 1488) *al-Tajrīd al-ṣarīḥ li-aḥādīth al-Jāmi' al-ṣaḥīḥ* (an abridged version of the famous compilation of sound ḥadīths, the Ṣaḥīḥ of Bukhārī) by Babanzâde Ahmed Naʿim (vols. 1–3) and Kâmil Miras (vols. 4–12) was published between 1928 and 1948.

from the Qur'ān and *ḥadīth*s with Turkish translations. Any admonitions or interpretations were henceforth to be given only in Turkish. However, attempts at a full switch to Turkish met with little enthusiasm, and were abandoned after 1928. A similar fate befell Mustafa Kemal's stipulation in 1932 that khuṭbas be given in frock coats and without any headgear.[79] Legal changes made in the same year nevertheless required the use of Turkish at three stages of the ritual prayer: the call to prayer (*adhān*), the invitation to prayer at the mosque (*qad qāmat al-ṣalāt*), and the recitation of the phrase "God is Great (*Allāhu Akbar*)."[80]

Mustafa Kemal and the republican leaders assumed that the original sources, now available in Turkish, would render the orthodox religious establishment (the 'ulamā') and the *Ṣūfī ṭurūqs* obsolete, and thus help to privatize religion as well as produce a Turkified Islam.[81] In addition, the republican authorities closed down the madrasahs in 1924 and outlawed all ṭarīqas and dervish lodges (*tekye*s and *zāwiya*s) in 1925.[82] In Mustafa Kemal's words, "The most truthful ṭarīqa is the ṭarīqa of civilization," and "Primitive individuals seeking moral and material prosperity through the guidance of such and such a sheikh despite the enlightenment of science, technology, and civilization as a whole should not exist in

[79] Dücane Cündioğlu, *Türkçe Kur'an ve Cumhuriyet İdeolojisi* (Istanbul: Kitabevi, 1998), 239–40.

[80] Dücane Cündioğlu, *Bir Siyasî Proje Olarak Türkçe İbadet*, vol. 1, *Türkçe Namaz, 1923–1950* (Istanbul: Kitabevi, 1999), 92–93.

[81] Mustafa Kemal seems to have been impressed by Goethe's epigram "Tel est l'homme, tel est son Dieu"; when he read it in a Turkish rendition of one of Fouillée's works, he jotted down a marginal note reading, "National soul—religion, philosophy, literature." See *Atatürk'ün Okuduğu Kitaplar*, ed. Recep Cengiz, vol. 5, 324; Alfred Fouillée, *Psychologie du peuple Français* (Paris: Félix Alcan, 1898), 200.

[82] "Tekye ve Zâviyelerle Türbelerin Seddine ve Türbedârlıklar ile Bir Takım Ünvanların Men' ve İlgasına Dair Kanun" (Law #677, November 30, 1925), in *Türkiye Cumhuriyeti Sicill-i Kavânini*, ed. Karakoç Sarkiz, vol. 2 (Istanbul: Cihan Matbaası, 1926), 18.

Turkish society."[83] It was thought that the elimination of the orthodox and *Ṣūfī* religious establishments, along with traditional
religious education, and their replacement with a system in which
the original sources were available to all in the vernacular language,
would pave the way for a new vision of Islam open to progress and
modernity and usher in a society guided by scientism and Turkism.
The Directorate of Religious Affairs was to spearhead this process
and ensure its success. Those 'ulamā' who agreed to help the new
regime accomplish this goal would receive individual recognition,
but not respect as a class.

In retrospect, the republican leaders grossly overestimated the
potential of the genre of modern Qur'ānic interpretation. In the
Arab world, for instance, Rashīd Riḍā's unfinished commentary
written in light of Muḥammad 'Abduh's views had little effect on
the masses,[84] despite its noteworthy impact on Muslim thinking.
And even there, the idea of a return to the original sources, which
was championed by the Salafīs, had negligible influence. The new
Turkish political elite also pinned too much hope on Turkish versions of Islamic scripture. Efforts toward the Turkification of Islam
made limited headway among the masses. In general, pious Muslims adopted a negative stance vis-à-vis these attempts at indoctrination by the elite. As a result, the republican leaders never implemented the final phase of the reform program, in which Turkish
was to become the sole language of liturgy.

The early republican leaders also seriously underestimated the
strength of Islamic social networks, assuming fallaciously—like

[83] "Kastamonu'da İkinci Bir Konuşma, 30. VIII. 1925," in *Atatürk'ün Söylev
ve Demeçleri*, vol. 2, 218.

[84] Rashīd Riḍā, *Tafsīr al-Qur'ān al-ḥakīm al-mushtahar bi-sm Tafsīr al-
Manār*, (Cairo: Dār al-Manār [1947], 1954), 12 vols. Parts of this commentary
were translated and published during the Second Constitutional Period. See Muḥammad 'Abduh, "'Asr Sure-i Celîlesinin Tefsîri," *Sırat-ı Mustakim* 3/73 (January 27, 1910): 323–24ff.

many fin-de-siècle Western intellectuals—that religion would soon fade into a distant memory. There was something naive about this assumption that the role of religion in society could be gradually diminished until such time as the world attained a higher stage of human evolution and was ready to accept the "world religion" of science. In Mustafa Kemal's words, "The advancement of all mankind in experience, knowledge, and thinking, and the establishment of a world religion through the abandonment of Christianity, Islam, and Buddhism" constituted the ultimate ideal.[85] In the meantime, however, the existing religions must be reformed. In the event, Mustafa Kemal and his colleagues achieved their goal of making "science" the religion of the elite; however, their attempts at reforming religion, the so-called science of the masses, produced mixed results at best. The downfall of the single ruling party in the first free Turkish elections held in 1950 was to mark the end of the religious reforms, and the return of the Arabic call to prayer in Turkey.

Alongside the indoctrination of the masses Mustafa Kemal sought to establish the secular character of the republican regime, thereby creating the first such state in the Muslim world. The 1924 Constitution, which emulated the Polish Constitution of 1921, preserved the articles declaring Islam to be the religion of the state and entrusting the implementation of the sharīʿa to the Turkish Grand National Assembly.[86] This, however, was little more than lip service intended to assuage conservative circles that were by

[85] *Nutuk*, 434. Here Mustafa Kemal quoted H. G. Wells, *The Outline of History: Being a Plain History of Life and Mankind*, vol. 4 (New York: Review of Reviews, 1924), 1297. Mustafa Kemal seems to have been deeply impressed by the subsection titled "The Next Stage of History" (1289ff). At his behest a Turkish translation of this subsection was prepared for his personal perusal. See *Atatürk'ün Okuduğu Kitaplar*, ed. Recep Cengiz, vol. 8, 327–37.

[86] "Teşkilât-ı Esasiye Kanunu" (Law #491, April 20, 1924), in Karakoç, ed., *Sicill-i Kavânin*, vol. 1, 538, 540–41.

now thoroughly alarmed; both articles were removed in a constitutional amendment of 1928.[87] In parallel, a series of measures laid the foundations for a secular legal system. In 1924, the Sharīʿa Courts were abolished,[88] and the legal dualism that had prevailed especially since 1864 came to an end. The adoption of a modified version of the 1912 Swiss Civil Code, and the acceptance of the 1881 Swiss Code of Obligations in 1926, thoroughly secularized private law and ended many Islamic practices such as polygamy. The constitutional amendment of 1928 replaced the phrase "by God (waʾllāhi)" in the oath of office with "on my honor."[89] By 1930, the entire legal system had been stripped of any religious references and resembled that of secular Western European countries. A year later the Republican People's Party formally adopted the French republican principle of laïcité as one of the pillars of the organization.[90] In 1937, this principle was enshrined in the constitution as a central tenet of the Turkish Republic.[91]

[87] "20 Nisan 1340 Tarihli Teşkilât-ı Esasiye Kanun[un]un 2, 16, 26 ve 38nci Madde-i Kâimeleri Hakkında Kanun" (Law #1222, April 11, 1928), in *Türkiye Cumhuriyeti Sicill-i Kavânini,* ed. Karakoç Sarkiz, vol. 4 (Istanbul: Cihan Matbaası, 1928), 229–30. While primarily basing his decision to remove the article declaring Islam to be the state religion on the anticlerical French concept of laïcité, Mustafa Kemal was also influenced by John Stuart Mill—or, more precisely, a Turkish rendition of his *On Liberty* in which the translator has him condemn the idea of state religion. See *Atatürk ʾün Okuduğu Kitaplar,* ed. Recep Cengiz, vol. 8, 430; John Stuart Mill, *On Liberty* (London: Longmans, 1921), 32.

[88] "Mehâkim-i Şerʿiyenin İlgasıyla Mehâkimin Teşkilâtına Aid Ahkâmı Muʿaddel Kanun" (Law # 469, April 8, 1924), in Karakoç, ed., *Sicill-i Kavânin,* vol. 1, 509–11.

[89] Law #1222, April 11, 1928, in Karakoç, ed., *Sicill-i Kavânin,* vol. 4, 230.

[90] *Cümhuriyet Halk Fırkası Nizamnamesi ve Programı* (Ankara: T.B.M.M. Matbaası, 1931), 31.

[91] "20 Nisan 1340 Tarihli Teşkilatı Esasiye Kanununun Bazı Maddelerinin Değiştirilmesine Dair Kanun" (Law #3115, February 13, 1937), in *Türkiye Cumhuriyeti Sicilli Kavanini,* ed. Sarkiz Karakoç, vol. 18 (Istanbul: Cihan Kitaphanesi, 1938), 76.

In addition to such secularizing legislation, Mustafa Kemal promoted reforms aimed at introducing new secular mores. Many of these changes entailed abolishing symbols associated with Islam and replacing them with equivalents associated with Christianity. The adoption of the Gregorian calendar in 1925 including the concepts "BC" and "AD," the replacement of the fez with the European hat in 1926, the switch from the Arabo-Persian Ottoman script to a modified Latin alphabet in 1928, and the acceptance of Sunday as the weekly holiday instead of Friday in 1935—all these further sidelined Islam in Turkish society and strengthened a secular way of life.

Like many Young Turks, Mustafa Kemal was profoundly influenced by the triumph of laïcité in France in 1905 and, viewing the French model as the authentic form of secularism, wished to apply it to the letter in Turkey. On the model of its French counterpart, Turkish laïcité strove to control religion and reduce it to a private affair, instead of merely creating a separation between mosque and state. Mustafa Kemal's achievements in this regard should not be underrated. He worked as if he were Leo the Isaurian, Martin Luther, the Baron d'Holbach, Ludwig Büchner, Émile Combes, and Jules Ferry rolled into one. He took a society in which religion had played a dominant role and led its transformation into a society administered by a strict scientistic and secular ideology. The major shortcoming of this exceptional accomplishment—unparalleled anywhere else in the Islamic world outside the Muslim territories of the Soviet Union—was its limited penetration of the masses.

Nationalism and Kemalism

The elimination of Islam as an ideological pillar of the main Ottoman successor state created a legitimacy vacuum at the center of
the regime. Although the policy of Ottomanization had already
diminished the role of religion within official state ideology in the
nineteenth century—citizenship, for example, was not defined in
denominational terms—Islam nonetheless maintained its pride of
place in official ideology until the very end of the empire. The new
republic, however, strove to remove religion from the public
sphere and confine it entirely to the private realm. An effective
modern state, so the argument went, no longer required the fiction
of religion in order to gain the support of its populace. To illustrate the point, Mustafa Kemal cited the example of Jesus, describ-
ing him as "a weak ruler . . . who need[ed] religion to uphold his
government."[1] Likewise, the founder of the republic is said to have
developed an admiration for the first Umayyad Caliph, the sharp-
witted Mu'āwiya I (d. 680), who rose to prominence through cunning political maneuvers at the expense of his more pious rivals.[2]
Mustafa Kemal himself wished to see religion "at the bottom of
the sea."[3] However, he knew well that he needed a replacement for
it. Crass scientism, so obviously deficient when it came to the for-

[1] Grace Ellison, *Turkey To-Day* (London: Hutchinson, n.d. [1928]), 24.
[2] [Halide Edib], *The Turkish Ordeal: Being the Further Memoirs of Halidé
Edib* (New York: Century, 1928), 168.
[3] Ellison, *Turkey To-Day*, 24.

mation of identity, would not suffice as the sole precept of the new state ideology. Furthermore, the abolition of the sultanate and the dissolution of the Committee of Union and Progress (CUP) had given rise to a second void necessitating the creation of substitute foci for popular allegiance—both personal and institutional. Mustafa Kemal sought to fill this lacuna with a new civic religion buttressed by a number of cults.

The new ideology, unsurprisingly, was a modified, scientifically sanctioned version of Turkish nationalism. There were several associated cults: a Turkish cult of reason, reminiscent of those of the French and American revolutions, based on Enlightenment ideas as well as on late nineteenth and early twentieth century scientism; an institutional cult of the republic, which aspired to create a sentiment reminiscent of the French *esprit républicain*; a personality cult surrounding Mustafa Kemal, "the savior Gazi"; and a further institutional cult around his own Republican People's Party. In the 1930s, his followers and party pulled together various strands of these cults to create Kemalism, an all-encompassing state ideology based on the sayings and writings of Mustafa Kemal.[4]

The new Turkish nationalism had its roots in the Turkism that had gained substantial ground in Ottoman intellectual circles from the last quarter of the nineteenth century onward, but it carried this nascent current to new heights. Mustafa Kemal wished to infuse Turkish nationalism with scientism, fashionable racial concepts, and popular Darwinian theories of evolution. This reinvigorated form of nationalism, it was assumed, would supersede religion in the formation of identity. An official history book of the time emphasized that Turks should "rectify their thoughts by abandoning superstitions" that were based mainly on "Jewish myths" and understand that their evolution stemmed from "deep

---

[4] [Munis] Tekin Alp [Moiz Kohen], *Kemalizm* (Istanbul: Cumhuriyet Matbaası, 1936), 18–21.

racial roots."[5] Borrowing a page from H. G. Wells's popular scientistic book, *The Outline of History*, the high school textbooks prepared under Mustafa Kemal's guidance to educate the new generation dismissed religion as an obsolete institution devised in a bygone era in order to protect human beings from their fear of the unknown, a fear that was no longer justified in an age in which "scientific inventions enlighten their minds."[6]

Like Wells's study, which profoundly impressed Mustafa Kemal,[7] early Republican textbooks attempted to situate the human in "space and time" by using theories advanced by Thomas Henry Huxley and Ernst Haeckel; but they provided a different explanation of the latest phases of human evolution and history. Skipping from the appearance of mammals and the start of toolmaking to the emergence of civilized life in the Turkish homeland in 9000 BC, they asserted that "the real evolution of humankind will be properly illuminated when the pickaxe of science breaks ground in Central Asia . . . the Turkish homeland."[8] Far from being an unpretentious ideology, the Turkish nationalism produced under Mustafa Kemal's guidance amounted to a comprehensive explanation, backed by Darwinian evolutionary theories, of the whole of human history. According to this interpretation, the Turks, with their "brachycephalic skulls," should be proud of

[5] *Türk Tarihinin Ana Hatları*, ed. Afet et al. (Istanbul: Devlet Matbaası, 1930), 1–3.

[6] *Tarih*, I: *Tarihtenevvelki Zamanlar ve Eski Zamanlar* (Istanbul: Devlet Matbaası, 1931), 23–24; H. G. Wells, *The Outline of History: Being a Plain History of Life and Mankind*, vol. 1 (New York: Review of Reviews, 1924), 121–36.

[7] *Atatürk'ün Okuduğu Kitaplar*, ed. Recep Cengiz, vol. 2 (Ankara: Anıtkabir Derneği Yayınları, 2001), 134–490. Mustafa Kemal initially skimmed through the French translation of the book, *Esquisse de l'histoire universelle* (Paris: Payot, 1925). See *Atatürk'ün Okuduğu Kitaplar*, ed. Recep Cengiz, vol. 12, 433–53. Mustafa Kemal's personal library also included two copies of the 1925 English edition. *Atatürk'ün Özel Kütüphanesinin Kataloğu: Anıtkabir ve Çankaya Bölümleri* (Ankara: Başbakanlık Kültür Müsteşarlığı, 1973), 464.

[8] *Tarih*, I, 35–36.

membership in "such a great historical race that evolved into a nation," a "great strength and honor not enjoyed by many human groups."[9] Henceforth, accordingly, Turkish identity was to be founded not on the alien import of Islam but on this "scientific" theory of Turkish peoplehood.

State-sponsored historical studies played an important role in advancing the new Turkish nationalism. Mustafa Kemal charged the Turkish History section of the Turkish Hearths (a Turkist society that had helped the CUP advance the cause of Turkism during the last years of the empire) with producing a new nationalist and scientistic interpretation of Turkish history. He placed a premium on findings that highlighted Turkish involvement in the origins and evolution of human civilization. Like the great archeologist Jacques Jean-Marie de Morgan, the founder of the republic wished to find the beginnings of human life and the cradle of civilization, but with the hope of discovering major Turkish involvement in both of them. The result appeared in 1930's *Türk Tarihinin Ana Hatları* (The Outlines of Turkish History). This was a Wellsian oeuvre of 606 pages that sought to reconcile scientism, Darwinism, racial theories, and the Turkic past and to explain world history from the emergence of the cosmos to the establishment of the Turkish Republic under "Mustafa Kemal's flag."[10] It was also a Turkish summary of the volumes of Henri Berr's ambitious L'Évolution de l'Humanité series, but with a strong focus on the Turks.[11] Only one hundred copies of this mas-

[9] Ibid., 20.
[10] *Türk Tarihinin Ana Hatları*, 606.
[11] Mustafa Kemal read a number of books published in this series, including *L'évolution de l'humanité: Synthèse collective: Introduction générale* (1920); J[oseph] Vendryes, *Le langage: Introduction linguistique à l'histoire* (1921); Lucien Febvre, *La terre et l'évolution humaine* (1922); L[ouis] Delaporte, *La Mésopotamie: les civilisations babylonienne et assyrienne* (1923); Gustave Glotz, *La civilisation Égéenne* (1923); A[uguste] Jardé, *La formation du peuple Grec* (1923); A[lexandre] Moret and G[eorges] Davy, *Des clans aux empires* (1923); Jacques de

sive study were published for official historians and statesmen, but it served as the basis of further works, including a four-volume history textbook for high schools published in 1931.[12] Under Mustafa Kemal's personal guidance, a more elaborate version of these ideas known as the Turkish history thesis was advanced and vigorously promoted, especially after the establishment of the Society for the Examination of Turkish History in 1931 (this became the Turkish Historical Association in 1935) and the convening of the first Turkish History Congress in 1932. In 1938, the absolute victory of the thesis was declared, and criticisms—officially termed "incongruous nonsense"—were denounced as "dependent on foreign works" and judged "incontestably unscientific" (a stance reminiscent of anti-Mendelian, Michurinist Lysenkoism in the Soviet Union).[13]

According to the Turkish history thesis, the cradle of human civilization was Central Asia, the Turkish homeland. From here the Turks had migrated to all Old World continents, establishing major states, such as the Sumerian and Hittite empires, and helping "backward" human groups such as the Chinese and Indians to produce impressive civilizations. Similarly, the Turks could take substantial credit for the achievements of Greco-Roman civilization, which was the product of Turkic peoples who had migrated to Crete and Italy. Although not all of the peoples of China, India, or the Mediterranean basin were racially Turkic, they owed their

---

Morgan, *L'humanité préhistorique* (1924); Eugène Pittard, *Les races et l'histoire* (1924); Clément Huart, *La Perse antique et la civilisation Iranienne* (1925); A[lexandre] Moret, *Le Nil et la civilisation Égyptienne* (1926); Ferdinand Lot, *La fin du monde antique et le début du moyen âge* (1927); and Henri Hubert, *Les Celtes et l'expansion Celtique* (1932).

[12] *Tarih*, I: *Tarihtenevvelki Zamanlar ve Eski Zamanlar*; II: *Ortazamanlar*; III: *Yeni ve Yakın Zamanlarda Osmanlı-Türk Tarihi*; IV: *Türkiye Cümhuriyeti* (Istanbul: Devlet Matbaası, 1931).

[13] Şemsettin Günaltay, "Türk Tarih Tezi Hakkındaki İntikatların Mahiyeti ve Tezin Kat'î Zaferi," *Belleten* 2/7–8 (October 1938): 337–65.

civilization to Turkish immigration, which had been prompted by environmental changes. This thesis, resembling the *Kulturkreise* (culture circles) hypothesis of the German diffusionist school of anthropology,[14] further maintained that "Turks lived clothed during the stone [Neolithic] age in 12000 BC, while Europeans reached that stage 5,000 years later."[15] Thus, the Turks were not merely the founders of "world civilization" but also the people who spread it throughout the world. Had there been no Turkish migration, the other regions of the world might long have continued to live in primitive conditions. In other words, the twentieth-century Turk in Anatolia was the descendant of "the race that first gave humankind fire, bread, clothing, tools, and domesticated animals."[16]

One of the most useful attributes of this revisionist interpretation of human history was that it bypassed the Ottoman past. To validate the new regime, Mustafa Kemal wished to erase any traces of Ottoman history. The best way to accomplish this goal was to present the Ottoman experience as no more than a modest footnote to a long and glorious past, and in the process subvert the role of Islam entirely, transforming it from the cement of Ottoman power to the principal cause of Turkic decline. An added advantage of this invented past was that it served to preempt claims by rival nationalisms that the Turks were latecomers to Anatolia and the Balkans. The thesis of a Turkic *mission civilisatrice* originating in the Neolithic age also solidified Turkey's position as an integral

[14] For interesting similarities, see Fritz Graebner, *Das Weltbild der primitiven; eine Untersuchung der Urformen weltanschaulichen Denkens bei Naturvölkern* (Munich: Verlag Ernst Reinhardt, 1924), 105ff.

[15] "Maarif Vekili Esat Beyefendinin Açma Nutku," in *Birinci Türk Tarih Kongresi: Konferanslar Müzakere Zabıtları* ([Ankara]: Maarif Vekâleti, 1932), 6.

[16] M. Saffet Engin, *Kemalizm İnkilâbının Prensipleri: Büyük Türk Medeniyetinin Tarihî ve Sosyolojik Tetkikine Methal*, vol. 1 (Istanbul: Cumhuriyet Matbaası, 1938), 52. See also "Ulusal Ökonomya Kurumlu Ökonomyadır," *Kadro* 3/35–36 (December 1934–January 1935): 4.

part of the West, replacing Greece as the fountain of Western civilization. Tellingly, the new republic based its claim to the Alexandretta Sanjak, awarded to Syria under the French mandate, on the fact that the region had once been an integral part of the old Hittite empire, and that a Turkic people, the Hurrians, had settled there long before the Semite Arabs.[17] In Mustafa Kemal's own words, "the Turkish homeland of four thousand years [Alexandretta] cannot remain a prisoner in the hands of the enemy."[18] Similarly, when the regime sought an understanding between Turkey and Greece, it would claim that the Turks were the founders of the so-called Greek civilization, and that Greeks and Turks were racially similar. Alternatively, when the regime wished to underscore problems between the two countries, it would trace the conflict back to the Trojan War, maintaining that the horse-taming Trojans were of Turkish origin.[19]

Anthropology, especially racial and physical anthropology, also played a significant role in reconstructing the past and shaping the new Turkish identity. Mustafa Kemal himself had developed a strong interest in racial anthropology and read extensively on this subject. Upon carefully examining the Comte de Gobineau's *Essai sur l'inégalité des races humaines*, he agreed with the main thesis but had no use for the French aristocrat's treatment of the Turkic races.[20] Similarly, he glanced at Alfred Cort Haddon's works and was impressed by his approach—using Darwinian biogeography to deduce an evolution of racial types—as well as by his thesis that Anatolian

[17] Nureddin Ardıç, *Antakya-İskenderun Etrafındaki Türk Davasının Tarihî Esasları* (Istanbul: Tecelli Matbaası, 1937), 7ff.

[18] Tayfur Sökmen, *Hatay'ın Kurtuluşu İçin Harcanan Çabalar* (Ankara: Türk Tarih Kurumu Yayınları, Ankara 1978), 70.

[19] This claim was also based on the Renaissance belief that the Turks descended from Trojans. For detailed information, see Margaret Meserve, *Empires of Islam in Renaissance Historical Thought* (Cambridge, MA: Harvard University Press, 2008), 22ff.

[20] See *Atatürk'ün Okuduğu Kitaplar*, ed. Recep Cengiz, vol. 21, 123–215.

civilizations had been produced by a brachycephalic race.[21] Another anthropologist who influenced Mustafa Kemal was George Montandon, the Swiss-born, former Bolshevik physician-anthropologist who is considered one of the founders of French ethnoracism. Montandon's theses, including his conception of the Turanian race and his contention that the population of France was composed of different races,[22] would serve the Turkish case well.

In addition to these scholars, Eugène Pittard, a respected Swiss anthropologist and the founder of the Musée d'Ethnographie de Genève, deeply affected Mustafa Kemal.[23] Like Pierre-Marcellin Boule, from whom he took his definition of race,[24] Pittard thought that anthropological realities were obscured by ethnographic, linguistic, and historical facts. He attempted to prove that human evolution and the formation of national groups were different processes.[25] In tandem with Montandon, Pittard maintained that pure race was a myth. Yet despite his subtle criticism of racism and its use of the category of race in explaining human evolution, Pittard had contributed significantly to anthropometrical research.[26]

---

[21] Alfred C. Haddon, *The Races of Man and Their Distribution* (Cambridge: Cambridge University Press, 1924), 27, 96. Mustafa Kemal read the French version of this study and highlighted these parts as well as many other sections. See *Atatürk'ün Okuduğu Kitaplar*, ed. Recep Cengiz, vol. 23, 1–30.

[22] George Montadon, *La race les races: mise au point d'ethnologie somatique* (Paris: Payot, 1933), 233–36. When he perused this study, Mustafa Kemal found the section on the Mongoloid race important. See *Atatürk'ün Okuduğu Kitaplar*, ed. Recep Cengiz, vol. 23, 58ff.; and George Montadon, *L'ethnie française* (Paris: Payot, 1935), 9.

[23] Mustafa Kemal read Pittard's *Les races et l'histoire* (Paris: La Renaissance du Livre, 1924), published in Henri Berr's L'évolution de l'humanité series, with the utmost interest and underlined almost every sentence. See *Atatürk'ün Okuduğu Kitaplar*, ed. Recep Cengiz, vol. 22, 225–486.

[24] Eugène Pittard, *Race and History: An Ethnological Introduction to History* (New York: Alfred A. Knopf, 1926), 3–4, 116.

[25] Ibid., 17ff.

[26] See, for example, Eugène Pittard, "Quelques nouveaux crânes Grisons de la Valée du Rhin," *Bulletin de la Société d'anthropologie de Lyon* 21 (1902): 249–68.

His work in the Balkans on the eve of the Balkan Wars, when a significant portion of the peninsula was still under Ottoman rule, led him to conclude that "the Turks are certainly one of the handsome races of Eur-Asia"[27] and "a tall, brachycephalic or sub-brachycephalic people."[28] He further maintained that Turks and Greeks had many racial similarities and proposed that the existence of a large number of light-eyed Turks could be seen as stemming from their arrival in Europe earlier than many other races.[29] The founders of the republic seized upon these favorable remarks. Mustafa Kemal's adopted daughter Âfet İnan prepared her dissertation under Pittard's supervision. For her graduate work she conducted an extensive, state-sponsored research project to produce an anthropometrical map of Turkey for which Pittard wrote an introduction;[30] it was entitled *L'Anatolie, le pays de la "Race" turque: Recherches sur les caractères anthropologiques des populations de la Turquie: Enquête sur 64.000 individus* and published in Geneva in 1939.[31] In his personal exchanges with the Swiss anthropologist, Mustafa Kemal expressed lively interest in Pittard's hypothesis that

---

Pittard encouraged Turkish anthropologists to use anthropometry to determine the ancestors of the Turkish people. See Eugène Pittard, "Neolitik Devirde Küçük Asya ile Avrupa Arasında Antropolojik Münasebetler," *Belleten* 2/5–6 (April 1938): 38.

[27] Pittard, *Race and History*, 320.

[28] Ibid., 324 ; see also Eugène Pittard, *Les peuples des Balkans: esquisses anthropologiques* (Paris: Attinger Frères, n.d. [1916]), 95.

[29] Pittard, *Race and History*, 323ff., Pittard, *Les peuples des Balkans*, 95 ff; Pittard, "Comparaison de quelques caractères somatologiques chez les Turcs et les Grecs," *Revue Anthropologique* 25 (1915): 447–54.

[30] He made the following statement: "Mlle Afet en prit l'initiative. Atatürk en fut le réalisateur." See "Préface," Afet [İnan], *L'Anatolie, le pays de la "Race" turque: Recherches sur les caractères anthropologiques des populations de la Turquie: Enquête sur 64.000 individus* (Geneva: Imprimerie Albert Kundig, 1939), vii.

[31] An enlarged Turkish edition appeared in 1947.

Figure 12. Eugène Pittard at the Second Turkish History Congress (1937). Source: *La Turquie Kemaliste* 21–22 (December 1937): 4.

the brachycephalic peoples of Europe must have come from Asia.[32] Many Turkish scholars also viewed his use of anthropometry as a key to understanding the past and establishing scientific bases for Turkish identity.[33] As a token of the widespread appreciation of his work, Pittard was made honorary chairman of the Second Turkish History Congress held in 1937.[34]

Meanwhile, Turkish anthropologists, who started educating

[32] Eugène Pittard, "Atatürk'ün Hatırâsını Tazim," *Belleten* 3/10: 187–88. See also Hans-Lukas Kieser, "Türkische Nationalrevolution, anthropologisch gekrönt: Kemal Atatürk und Eugène Pittard," *Historische Anthropologie* 14/1 (2006): 105–18.

[33] Şevket Aziz, "Antropoloji Tedrisatı Hakkında," *Türk Antropoloji Mecmuası* 7/12 (September 1931): 114.

[34] *İkinci Türk Tarih Kongresi, İstanbul 20–25 Eylül 1937: Kongrenin Çalışmaları, Kongreye Sunulan Tebliğler* (Istanbul: Türk Tarih Kurumu Yayınları, 1943), v, xxxix.

history students in 1932 at Mustafa Kemal's behest,[35] busied themselves finding proofs for the official history. Chief among them
was one of the students of Georges Papillault, Şevket Aziz (Kansu),
whom Mustafa Kemal made a member of the Society for the Examination of Turkish History in 1932 following the first Turkish
Historical Congress, at which he passionately defended Turkish
racial superiority and claimed that "European man" was of Turkic
origin. (Şevket Aziz went so far as to bring a peasant family with a
blond child from a nearby village to prove to the attendees that
Turks were descended from a brachycephalic Alpine race).[36] The
anthropologists focused on craniological, morphological, and anthropometrical research, and even investigations into degrees of
prognathism.[37] They sought to prove that ancient civilizations
such as those of the Hittites and Sumerians had been established
by genuine Turkic races migrating from Central Asia; that Turks
were a Caucasian, Aryan (Alpine), brachycephalic race superior to
all others because of their highly developed cranial structures (thus
posing a major challenge to popular race theories claiming the superiority of the Nordic race over the other European—including
Alpine—races); and that civilized life had started much earlier in
Anatolia than was commonly thought. They buttressed their findings with the major vulgar materialist and Darwinist theses of scientistic thinkers such as Huxley and Karl Vogt.[38] To prove their
point, they carried out meticulous measurements of Hittite and
Seljuk skulls,[39] and compared the bone structures of cadavers in

[35] Şevket Aziz Kansu, *Türk Antropoloji Enstitüsü Tarihçesi* (Istanbul: Maarif
Matbaası, 1940), 4.

[36] Şevket Aziz, "Türklerin Antropolojisi," *Birinci Türk Tarih Kongresi*,
277–78.

[37] See, for example, Şevket Aziz, "Alelade Prognatisma ve Türk Kafalarının
Prognatisması," *Türk Antropoloji Mecmuası* 6/9 (March 1930): 5–14.

[38] See, for example, Şevket Aziz, "Antropoloji Tedrisatı Hakkında," 115.

[39] Şevket Aziz Kansu, "Anadolu'nun Irk Tarihi Üzerine Antropolojik Bir Tetkik," *Belleten* 3/9 (January 1939): 127–31; Şevket Aziz Kansu, "Hittite'lerin

Turkish, Jewish, and Greek cemeteries to establish the racial superiority of the Turks.[40] Republican scholars also attempted to document the racial origins of many leading Ottoman figures in order to reinforce their racial claims. For instance, in 1935, a group of anthropologists and historians exhumed the remains of the illustrious Ottoman architect Sinan (d. 1588) to conduct anthropometrical measurements on his cadaver. Although the architect himself had written that he was a *devşirme* (a Christian boy seized by the state) taken in Kayseri in the early sixteenth century,[41] the anthropologists found that "the investigation made on the genius's skull showed that the grand architect was not only culturally, but racially Turkish."[42] Like the Soviet anthropologist Mikhail Gerasimov's later examination of the cadaver of the great conqueror Timur (d. 1405),[43] the eccentric work of Turkish anthropologists (utterly despised by devout Muslims) demonstrated how scientism could be applied to theorizing about the past.

Another subject that the early republican Turkish anthropologists focused on was language—or, more precisely, the common origin of all languages.[44] Not surprisingly, language was a pillar of the new Turkish nationalism forged under Mustafa Kemal's guidance. The switch in 1928 from the Arabo-Persian Ottoman script

Kraniolojik Tetkikatına Methal," *Türk Antropoloji Mecmuası* 6/10 (September 1930): 3–16.

[40] Nureddin et. al., "Türk Irkı ile İstanbul'da Yaşayan Diğer Irkların Tedkikleri," *Türk Antropoloji Mecmuası* 1/2 (March 1926): 5–8.

[41] *Sâî Mustafa Çelebi, Yapılar Kitabı: Tezkiretü'l-Bünyan ve Tezkiretü'l-Ebniye (Mimar Sinan'ın Anıları)*, ed. Hayati Develi (Istanbul: K Kitaplığı, 2003), 122.

[42] "Mimar Sinan: Büyük Mimarın Kafa Tası Mezarından Çıkarıldı," *Akşam*, August 5, 1935.

[43] M[ikhail] M[ikhailovich] Gerasimov, "Portret Tamerlana: opyt skul'pturnogo vosproizvedeniya na kraniologicheskoi osnove," *Kratkie soobshcheniia istorii material'noi kul'tury* 17 (1947): 14–21.

[44] See Saim, "Dilbirliği," *Türk Antropoloji Mecmuası* 7/12 (September 1931): 1–62.

to a modified Latin alphabet (called the Modern Turkish Alphabet or the Gazi Alphabet) had other objectives besides facilitating linguistic reform. The comparative study of the Turkic and Indo-European languages, with a view to highlighting the centrality of language in Turkish nationalism, can be traced back to the initial Turkist essays of the nineteenth century. One of the first efforts in this field, *Les Turcs anciens et modernes* (1869), was written by Mustafa Celâleddin Pasha (Konstanty Polklozic-Borzęcki), a Pole who converted to Islam and became an Ottoman subject after fleeing to the empire in the wake of the unsuccessful 1848 revolution.[45] In it he claimed to find similarities between Turkish and Latin, and hinted at the Turkic origins of the Romance languages.[46] Mustafa Kemal read this essay with great interest. He was particularly entranced by the parts discussing the problems stemming from the Turks' adoption of the Arabo-Persian alphabet. His examination of Bernard Carra de Vaux's study, *La langue étrusque; sa place parmi les langues* (1911), left no doubt in his mind that Latin had originated from proto-Turkish.[47] In 1930 Mustafa Kemal, who attached the greatest importance to the Turkic origins of the tongues of major civilizations, especially the Indo-European languages, ordered one of his journalist confidants to translate a conference paper by David-Léon Cahun on the Turanian origins of the language that

[45] Jerzy S. Łątka, *Pasza z Lechistanu: Mustafa Dzêlaleddin (Konstanty Borzęcki)* (Kraków: Społeczny Instytut Historii i Kultury Turcji, 1993), 113ff.

[46] *Atatürk'ün Okuduğu Kitaplar*, ed. Recep Cengiz, vol. 17, 368 ff; Moustapha Djelaleddin, *Les Turcs anciens et modernes* (Paris: Libraire Internationale, 1870), 252ff.

[47] In addition to reading this study, Mustafa Kemal personally studied two Latin dictionaries, A. Ernout and A. Meillet, *Dictionnaire Étymologique de la langue Latin: Histoire des mots* (Paris: Librairie C. Klincksieck, 1932); and L[ouis] Quicherat and A[médée] Daveluy, *Dictionnaire Latin-Français* (Paris: Librairie Hachette, 1910) to find similarities between Turkish and Latin. See *Atatürk'ün Okuduğu Kitaplar*, ed. Recep Cengiz, vol. 22, 63–102.

had preceded the Aryan tongues in France.[48] Another study that he carefully perused, Hilaire de Barenton's (Étienne Boulés's) two-volume work, *L'Origine des langues, des religions et des peuples* (1932), focused on the Sumerian language and the linguistic derivatives of this ancient tongue.[49] These essays convinced Mustafa Kemal that modern Turkish was the culmination of an evolutionary process beginning with the initial tongue of civilized humanity, from which all other languages derived.

In 1932, at Mustafa Kemal's behest, the Society for Examining the Turkish Language (which became the Turkish Language Association in 1936) was established to conduct further research in this field and furnish additional support for the official Turkish history thesis. The first director of the society, Samih Rif'at, who was personally appointed by Mustafa Kemal, had long claimed that the Indo-European and Semitic languages derived from the proto-Turkish spoken in Central Asia thousands of years ago.[50] The first Turkish Language Congress, held in 1932 and broadcast live by radio to crowds summoned to city and town centers,[51] made numerous references to this theory, and adopted as its priority a large-scale mobilization to collect authentic Turkish vocabulary. The government duly requested the entire bureaucracy to participate in gathering and submitting "pure Turkish words" to the authorities. These words were to be collected from the various local dialects of the Turkic world, and also from folktales and ancient texts; they were to be used to provide substitutes for the

[48] Léon Cahun, *Fransa'da Arî Dillere Takaddüm Etmiş Olan Lehçenin Turanî Menşei*, trans. Ruşen Eşref [Ünaydın] (Istanbul: Cumhuriyet Matbaası, 1930).

[49] *Atatürk'ün Okuduğu Kitaplar*, ed. Recep Cengiz, vol. 22, 57–62.

[50] He reiterated his thesis at the first Turkish Language Congress; see "Türkçenin Ârî ve Samî Lisanlarla Mukayesesi," in *Birinci Türk Dili Kurultayı: Tezler Müzakere Zabıtları* (Istanbul: Devlet Matbaası, 1933), 21–64.

[51] Ruşen Eşref Ünaydın, *Türk Dili Tetkik Cemiyeti'nin Kuruluşundan İlk Kurultaya Kadar Hâtıralar* (Ankara: Recep Ulusoğlu Basımevi, 1943), 35.

many foreign words that were currently "polluting" the Turkish language—especially those derived from Arabic and Persian. When no authentic Turkish word could be found to replace a foreign one, the Society for Examining the Turkish Language would coin a new word based on an existing Turkish root.[52] A similar attempt to collect "pure" Turkish words to replace their Arabic and Persian equivalents had already been made during the Hamidian period in 1894, with limited results;[53] but this time a determined initiative with strong nationalist undertones aimed at nothing less than a full-scale purge.

The idea of simplifying the stilted Ottoman language and stressing its Turkish foundations may be traced back to the Tanzimat period. However, the subsequent popularization of new genres of literature such as the novel, the reception of Western scientific knowledge, and the efforts to codify Ottoman law based on Western models, resulted in an even more artificial language and further borrowings from Persian and Arabic. After the Young Turk Revolution, a literary movement called *Genc Kalemler* (Young Pens) emerged in Mustafa Kemal's hometown of Salonica. Its followers developed a program called New Language, which advocated the use of simple language based solely on Turkish grammatical rules.[54] Despite the existence of a minority advocating wholesale purification through the replacement of Arabic and Persian words with ancient Turkish vocabulary, the majority— including Ziya Gökalp, whose nationalist ideas deeply influenced Mustafa Kemal—opted for a gradual simplification without a

[52] See "Türk Dili Tetkik Cemiyeti Nizamnamesi," *Türk Dili* 1/1 (April 1933): 11–15; "Söz Derleme Talimatnamesi," *Türk Dili* 1/1 (April 1933): 49–51; and "Söz Derleme Talimatını Tamamlayıcı Tamim," *Türk Dili* 1/1 (April 1933): 52.

[53] Agâh Sırrı Levend, *Türk Dilinde Gelişme ve Sadeleşme Evreleri* (Ankara: Türk Dil Kurumu Yayınları, 1960), 143ff.

[54] Yusuf Ziya Öksüz, *Türkçenin Sadeleşme Tarihi: Genç Kalemler ve Yeni Lisan Hareketi* (Ankara: Türk Dil Kurumu Yayınları, 1995), 85ff.

major purge.[55] As in many other fields, though, Mustafa Kemal adopted the most radical approach on offer: in an endorsement to a 1930 study on language reform, he stressed the need for "liberating Turkish from the yoke of foreign tongues."[56] Undoubtedly, his actual aim was far more grandiose than mere linguistic reform. In his own words, he was "going to defeat the Ottoman [language]."[57]

Lists of Turkic words collected from various dialects or from ancient books and mythology appeared in the *Tarama Dergisi* (Combing Journal), which started publication in 1934. The authorities requested that this new vocabulary replace the Ottoman words of Arabic and Persian origin appearing in one of the prime modern Ottoman dictionaries, the *Kâmûs-i Türkî* of Şemseddin Sami Frashëri. In most cases, more than one alternative was offered for an Arabic or Persian word, and people were asked to indicate their preferences to the linguistic authorities. In addition, radio stations and dailies were asked to collect suggestions from their listeners and readers. Soon 125,000 ostensibly authentic Turkish words were collected to replace roughly 7,000 foreign terms existing in the language.[58] By the time of the second Language Congress in 1934, linguistic chaos reigned. Official declarations had become virtually incomprehensible, and even the educated public could not follow many newspaper articles. Pocket Ottoman-Turkish and Turkish-Ottoman dictionaries were published in 1935 in the hope of helping people find pure Turkish synonyms for the purged Arabic and Persian words; these dictionaries in effect treated Ottoman as a for-

[55] Ibid, 150–51.

[56] Sadri Maksudi, *Türk Dili İçin: Türk Dilindeki Sözleri Toplama, Dizme, Türk Dilini Ayırtlama, Türkçe Köklerden Bilgi Sözleri Yaratma İşi Üzerinde Düşünceler* (Istanbul: Türk Ocakları İlim ve Sanat Heyeti Neşriyatı,1930), i–ii; and " Gazi ve Türk Dili," *Öz Dilimize Doğru* 1/1 (May 15, 1932): 3.

[57] Geoffrey Lewis, *The Turkish Language Reform: A Catastrophic Success* (New York: Oxford University Press, 1999), 49.

[58] *Tarih* IV: *Türkiye Cümhuriyeti*, 264.

eign language.[59] In 1934, Mustafa Kemal decided not to use his birth name, Mustafa, on the grounds that it was not Turkish. As for his personal name, which seemed equally vulnerable on this criterion, an official communiqué maintained that it was not Kemal, a word meaning "perfection" in Arabic, but Kamâl, allegedly an old Turkish term meaning "fortification."[60] For a period he therefore signed documents as "Kamâl." All this created such major obstacles to communication that Mustafa Kemal decided to slow down the mobilization and reintroduce some of the purged vocabulary; but the process of Turkification continued nonetheless.

It was in 1935, when this pandemonium was at its height, that Mustafa Kemal and his linguists decided to launch an innovative language thesis that would support the Turkish history thesis in its ostentatious assertion of the Turkic origins of world civilization. They commissioned an obscure but maverick Viennese scholar, Hermann Feodor Kvergić, to produce a grandiose theory based on psychoethnology. As insinuated in the title of the brief, typewritten essay *La psychologie de quelques éléments des langues turques* that he submitted to Mustafa Kemal, Kvergić was basing his linguistic views on Sigmund Freud's psychological analysis, on fashionable Germanic theories about the symbolism of sounds, and on psychoethnology.[61] His thesis gained fame as the "sun-language

[59] See *Osmanlıcadan Türkçeye Cep Kılavuzu* (Istanbul: Devlet Matbaası, 1935) and *Türkçeden Osmanlıcaya Cep Kılavuzu* (Istanbul: Devlet Basımevi, 1935). See also "Osmanlıcadan Türkçeye ve Türkçeden Osmanlıcaya Cep Kılavuzları," *Türk Dili* 3/16 (April 1936): 8–11.

[60] "Atatürkün Öz Adı: Arabca Kemal Değil Türkçe Kamâldır," *Akşam*, February 5, 1935.

[61] See Jens Peter Laut, "Noch einmal zu Dr. Kvergić," *Turkic Languages* 6 (2002): 124ff.; Jens Peter Laut, *Das Türkische als Ursprache? Sprachwissenschaftliche Theorien in der Zeit des erwachenden türkischen Nationalismus* (Wiesbaden, Germany: Otto Harrassowitz, 2000), 109, 116 ff; and İlker Aytürk, "Turkish Linguists against the West: The Origins of Linguistic Nationalism in Atatürk's Turkey," *Middle Eastern Studies* 40/6 (November 2004): 16.

theory"; it maintained that primitive humans started referring to objects with gestures—for example, identifying the most revered object, the sun, with the cry "Aa"—and it claimed that proto-Turkish was the first language in which such sounds, later to become words, were uttered. Under Mustafa Kemal's instructions, the theory was utilized to bolster the grandiose claim that Turkish was the original language of humankind and to provide a theoretical basis for accepting words borrowed from European languages, since these after all originally derived from ancient Turkish. Somewhat inconsistently, although the sun-language theory was also used to claim the Turkic origins of the Semitic languages, it was not used to justify retaining Arabic vocabulary in Turkish.[62] Kvergić became a well-known figure in Turkey thanks to the popularization of his theory, and the Turkish authorities hired him to carry out a comparison of Turkish and other major languages instead of working on a Turkic lexicon project. He rendered valuable services to the Turkish nationalist cause, but the republican regime took his ideas to extremes he had never imagined. Once again we see how a scholar who was marginal to the intellectual history of Europe could play a central role in that of the Late Ottoman Empire and modern Turkey.

The sun-language theory was mainly employed to reinforce the claims of the Turkish history thesis that Turks had established the first civilization in human history, and that the remains left by ancient peoples testified to the spread of this Turkish civilization.[63] The anthropologists proved it with skull measurement; the archaeologists, by discovering remains from ancient civilizations;[64]

[62] See, for example, Naim Hâzım Onat, "Türk Dilinin Samî Dillerle Münasebeti," *Türk Dili* 3/14 (December 1935): 1–103.

[63] Ş. Günaltay and H. R. Tankut, "Dil ve Tarih Tezlerimiz Üzerine Bazı İzahlar," *Türk Dili* 5/29–30 (June 1938): 1–67.

[64] Çiğdem Atakuman, "Cradle or Crucible: Anatolia and Archeology in the Early Years of the Turkish Republic, 1923–1938," *Journal of Social Archeology*

the historians, by reinterpreting ancient texts; and now the philologists substantiated it through the pretentious claim that proto-Turkish had been the *Ursprache* of humankind.[65]

The sun-language theory and the Turkish history thesis were further confirmed when Mustafa Kemal received information regarding the work of James Churchward, a British-born American adventurer, mystic, and occultist who produced works of "psychic archaeology" about the lost continent of Mu, where, he claimed, a civilization called Lemuria had once flourished. According to Churchward, the people who had escaped from Mu were the mound builders of Mexico and other parts of the world. It was the Turkish chargé d'affaires in Mexico who brought all this to Mustafa Kemal's attention. The president immediately ordered translations of Churchward's major essays—*The Lost Continent of Mu*, *The Children of Mu*, *Cosmic Forces as They Were Taught in Mu*, and *The Sacred Symbols of Mu*—for his personal use. Mustafa Kemal seems to have doubted Churchward's claim that the first human lived on the continent of Mu, for he made a note in the margins asking, "How do you know this?"[66] However, the remarks about the Uighur origin of prehistoric languages and the alleged similarities between ancient Turkic runes and the symbols used in Naacal tablets, which Churchward claimed to have discovered in India, and Niven tablets, which William Niven had found in Mexico, led him to believe that the Turks had brought civilization to the Americas as well as to the Old World continents.[67] Likewise, Mustafa Kemal's careful ex-

8/2 (2008): 214–35; Klaus Kreiser, *Atatürk: eine Biographie* (Munich: Verlag C. H. Beck, 2008), 280.

[65] Jens Peter Laut, *Das Türkische als Ursprache?*, 150ff.

[66] *Atatürk'ün Okuduğu Kitaplar*, ed. Recep Cengiz, vol. 10, 273; James Churchward, *The Lost Continent of Mu: The Motherland of Man* (New York: Ives Washburn, 1931), 5–6.

[67] *Atatürk'ün Okuduğu Kitaplar*, ed. Recep Cengiz, vol. 10, 265ff. James Churchward, *The Lost Continent of Mu*, 7–8, 17–21, 23, 28–32, 34, 44–48, 50–

amination of Brasseur de Bourbourg's study on Mayan languages convinced him that these tongues originated from proto-Turkish.[68] The Turkic origin of Amerindian civilizations and languages thus became another aspect of the Turkish history thesis, though it was not widely accepted.[69]

Despite its insubstantial scientific foundations, the sun-language theory maintained its importance in Turkey until Mustafa Kemal's death. Turkish scholars prepared textbooks based on the theory, and it was taught as a course at Ankara University starting in 1936.[70] In addition, the official newspaper *Ulus* (Nation) and other dailies attempted to teach the theory to the general

---

52, 57–39, 61–68, 70, 75–78, 80, 85, 88, 90, 93, 96, 100, 119–120, 123, 129–38, 141–47, 149–50, 152–53, 158; James Churchward, *Cosmic Forces as They Were Taught in Mu: The Ancient Tale that Religion and Science are Twin Sisters* (Mount Vernon, NY: Baker and Taylor, 1934), 13–16; James Churchward, *The Children of Mu* (New York: Ives Washburn, 1933), 16–17, 20, 53–55, 57, 60–63, 67–68, 70, 73, 75, 77, 82–84, 86–88, 90–101, 131, 133, 140, 155–56, 159, 171–74, 177, 180, 183, 188–89, 192–93, 205–207, 209, 212, 216–17, 221–22, 242; and James Churchward, *The Sacred Symbols Mu* (New York: Ives Washburn, 1933), 15, 25–29, 32–33, 57, 69–70, 74, 104, 118–19, 152, 161, 200, 209, 240–41. Mustafa Kemal buttressed this idea with Pittard's theses on the origins of the Mexican Indians. See *Atatürk'ün Okuduğu Kitaplar*, ed. Recep Cengiz, vol. 22, 471ff.; and Pittard, *Les races et l'histoire*, 546ff.

[68] *Atatürk'ün Okuduğu Kitaplar*, vol. 20, 135–201; M [Charles Étienne] Brasseur de Bourbourg, *Dictionnaire, grammaire et chrestomathie de la langue Maya: précédés d'une étude sur le système graphique des indigènes du Yucatan (Mexique)* (Paris: Maisonneuve, 1872), 46ff. Hasan Reşit Tankut, a parliamentary deputy, who used the same parts of Churchward's essays and E. K. Pekarskii's multivolume *Slovar' Iakutskago Iazyka* that Mustafa Kemal read with great interest (see *Atatürk'ün Okuduğu Kitaplar*, ed. Recep Cengiz, vol. 10, 1–152), maintained that the very words *Mu* and *Maya* were Turkish, and that they were people of Turkic origin. See H. R. Tankut, "Maya Alfabesi ve Mayaların Türk Orijini," *Türk Dili* 5/27–28 (February 1938): 18.

[69] See Tahsin Ömer, "Meksikada Müstamel Maya Dilindeki Türkçe Kelimeler Hakkında İzahat," *Türk Dili* 3/12 (August 1935): 89–94.

[70] Abdülkadir İnan, *Güneş-Dil Teorisi Ders Notları* (Istanbul: Devlet Basımevi, 1936).

public.[71] Although the sun-language theory was quickly abandoned after Mustafa Kemal's death, attempts at purifying Turkish continued—albeit at a relatively slower pace—and priority
shifted to promoting the use of the new words instead of invent-
ing still more. In general, the language reform bolstered the historical thesis of Turkish nationalism, which sought to supplant
Muslim Ottoman identity with a new Turkish one. In the memorable words of the late Geoffrey Lewis, the reform was "a catastrophic success."[72] It produced an almost totally new language,
which rendered subsequent generations virtually incapable of
understanding anything published prior to the reform—including the entirety of Ottoman literature and historiography. Even
the constitution of the republic had to be translated into the
new Turkish in 1945, while Mustafa Kemal's own magnum opus,
The Speech, had to be rendered into modern usage in 1963.

Mustafa Kemal's was the principal mind driving the development of the twin theses of Turkish history and language that un-
derpinned the new state ideology. They might even be called his
pet projects. In the words of one of the leading members of the
Turkish Historical Association, "the Turkish history thesis was
recovered from the darkness of many centuries by the peerless
Turkish genius,"[73] and, as stated by the general secretary of the
Turkish Language Association, the sun-language theory was "an
invention" of "our Great Leader's towering genius."[74] The fact
that, two months before his death, Atatürk willed a substantial
portion of his shares in a major Turkish bank to the Turkish His-

[71] "1936 Kışı Sonunda Kurumun Çalışmaları," *Türk Dili* 3/16 (April 1936):
1–2.

[72] Lewis, *The Turkish Language Reform,* 2–3.

[73] Şemsettin Günaltay, "Türk Tarih Tezi Hakkındaki İntikatların Mahiyeti
ve Tezin Kat'î Zaferi," 338.

[74] İlker Aytürk, "H. F. Kvergić and the Sun-Language Theory," *Zeitschrift der
deutschen morgenländischen Gesellschaft* 159/1 (2009): 35.

tory and Language associations attests to the importance he attached to these two projects.[75]

Mustafa Kemal hoped that the new Turkish nationalism grounded in scientism, history, and language would serve as the foundation of a new civic religion, a concept he adopted from Émile Durkheim's *moralité civique*. He may well also have had before him the model of Shintōism in Japan after the Meiji reforms, a cult that successfully inculcated in the Japanese the self-image of a unique, peerless people. Though secular, Turkish nationalism could be expected to further a brand of patriotism that placed a premium on the individual's full commitment to the state. In place of the old religious trappings of Ottoman imperial glory, a modern form of hero worship buttressed by consecrated nationalist symbols would underpin the legitimacy of the republic and help mould a new soul for the Turks. The final goal was for every Turk to stand up and proudly declare, "My Turkishness is my religion." To be sure, the iconoclastic secularism of the new republic stood in tension with the pretensions to sanctity of the new nationalism that lay at its foundation. Thus, while many foundational texts, including the constitution and the Republican People's Party program, defined Turkishness in terms of secular citizenship, they were couched in terms of sacred glory and racial superiority.[76] Even if the new nationalism had not been intensely secular, it would still have had a problematic relationship with Islam. For, like state Shintōism in Japan, which sought to monopolize the holy and therefore had a troubled relationship with Buddhism, this new Turkish nationalism made claims on the sacred that encroached on

[75] Mazhar Leventoğlu, *Atatürk'ün Vasiyeti* (Istanbul: Bahar Matbaası, 1968), 49, 101.
[76] Cemil Koçak, "Kemalist Milliyetçiliğin Bulanık Suları," in *Modern Türkiye'de Siyasi Düşünce*, vol. 4, *Milliyetçilik*, ed. Tanıl Bora and Murat Gültekingil (Istanbul: İletişim Yayınları, 2002), 37–43.

the territory traditionally occupied by Islam. Like Durkheim, Mustafa Kemal thought that nationalism, through which secular citizens practice a cult of the state, would perform the function of the sacred.[77]

So important was this new civic religion to Mustafa Kemal that between 1929 and 1933 he personally took the lead in providing the main ideas for a number of civics books that he himself edited and published under his adopted daughter's name. In his most important work, *Vatandaş İçin Medenî Bilgiler* (Civics for the Citizen), he described the Turkish nation as "the greatest, the most ancient, and the purest" in world history and repeated the nationalist theses on language and religion.[78] He also attempted to formulate a secular morality along the lines of Durkheim's "collective representations": "Turks have a shared morality. This high morality does not resemble that of any other nation. . . . When I say moral, I do not mean advice given in books on morals. . . . Morals are above individuals, and they can only be societal, national. . . . Some people say that religious unity can play a role in nation formation, but we see the opposite in the Turkish nation."[79] He hoped that the Turks, in embracing the republican idealism at the core of this new civic religion, would take Turkey to new heights.

Mustafa Kemal knew well that the introduction of a new civic religion could not transform Turkish society overnight, and would

---

[77] Durkheim is acknowledged to have influenced Atatürk indirectly. See Robert F. Spencer, "Culture Process and Intellectual Current: Durkheim and Atatürk," *American Anthropologist* 60/4 (1958): 640–57. There seems to be a direct influence as well; Atatürk read Durkheim's works *De la division du travail social* (1893); *L'éducation morale* (1925); *'L'Allemagne au-dessus de tout,' la mentalité allemande et la guerre* (1915); and *Le suicide: étude de sociologie* (1897) in the 1930s. See Şerafettin Turan, *Atatürk'ün Düşünce Yapısını Etkileyen Olaylar, Düşünürler, Kitaplar* (Ankara: Türk Tarih Kurumu Yayınları, 1982), 21.

[78] Afet [Âfet İnan], *Vatandaş İçin Medenî Bilgiler*, vol. 1 (Istanbul: Devlet Matbaası, 1931), 7, 8–12.

[79] Ibid., 12.

not anchor the legitimacy of the new regime in the short run. Thus, as mentioned above, he wished to support this new religion with a number of cults, both personal and institutional in nature. First came the cult of reason—modeled on those of the French and American revolutions, but defined in scientistic terms. This cult was necessary both for the launching of a Turkish renaissance and for the rejection of any religious interference with the work of enlightenment. Like Moses Mendelssohn, Mustafa Kemal viewed enlightenment as a process of education based on pure reason. But he believed his revolution—and the enlightenment that was sure to follow in its wake—to be superior to the one that had occurred in seventeenth-century Europe. This was because unlike his revolutionary predecessors, who had only Newton to go by, he would benefit from the advances of modern science and the findings of Darwin and Huxley. Going beyond Mendelssohn, Mustafa Kemal saw no problem in stretching the limits of reason to an extreme. He saw himself as bringing about a renaissance and an enlightenment (terms used by Kemalists since the 1930s to define his life's work)[80]— two historical developments that had regrettably passed the Turks by when they had taken place in Europe. He saw himself as a latter-day Frederick the Great, Joseph II, or Catherine the Great, but one who transcended their achievements by serving both as the bearer of enlightenment and as the intellectual force behind it.

Parallel to the cult of reason was the cult of the republic, loosely modeled on the French esprit républicain. The republic, Mustafa Kemal argued, was not merely a system of administration but also "the only tool to safeguard the Turkish nation's welfare, prosperity, and freedom in the present and the future."[81] As such, all citizens

[80] See, for example, Melâhat Özgü, "Atatürk Devrimleri, Sanat Alanında Bir Renaissance'dır," *Türk Dili* 17/194 (November 1967): 120–30; and Ahmet Taner Kışlalı, "Kemalist Devrim ve Türk Aydınlanması," in *Dünya ve Türkiye Açısından Atatürk*, ed. Suna Kili (Istanbul: Yapı Kredi Yayınları, 1996), 33–43.
[81] Afet [Âfet İnan], *Vatandaş İçin Medenî Bilgiler*, 43.

were duty-bound to serve it. In order to instill republican idealism in the populace, the new regime praised republicanism in the most idealistic terms and used the adjective "republican" to add value to new institutions and differentiate them from previous ones. For instance, the government was called "the republican government," while state prosecutors were dubbed "republican prosecutors." In 1924, Mustafa Kemal's own People's Party affixed the word "Republican" to its title. Sailors in the navy wore hats emblazoned with the initials T.C.B. (standing for Sailor of the Turkish Republic). Likewise the abbreviation T.C. (standing for Turkish Republic) replaced all imperial monograms on former Ottoman buildings.

A third institutional cult that Mustafa Kemal wished to establish was that of the party. As a former member of the CUP, he fully comprehended the power of institutional cults. Like many single-party leaders of the first half of the twentieth century, he viewed his party as an institution "representing the entire Turkish people ... and the general interests of the nation."[82] He believed that the party was rendering "great services to the nation" as the medium of representation and as the molder of national ideology and national education.[83] There was, however, an irresolvable tension between Mustafa Kemal's desire for a CUP-style party cult and the growth of a personality cult around his own person. The institutional cult of the CUP had rested on its system of collective leadership and its arcane and mysterious rituals. By contrast, the Republican People's Party was universally identified simply as Mustafa Kemal's party. Although its membership was extensive, the party could not compete with its charismatic leader.

Having come of age in the Hamidian era, Mustafa Kemal understood the power of a personality cult. He had witnessed the galvanizing effect of the Hamidian cult in an area stretching from

---

[82] Âfetinan [Ayşe Âfet İnan], *Medenî Bilgiler ve M. Kemal Atatürk'ün El Yazıları* (Ankara: Türk Tarih Kurumu Yayınları, 1969), 425.

[83] Ibid., 425–26.

Scutari in Albania to Basra. Abdülhamid II had adroitly crafted the image of a pious caliph, father, and savior of Muslims everywhere. Now Mustafa Kemal posed as father and savior of the Turks. In November 1934 the Turkish Grand National Assembly bestowed upon him the surname Atatürk—literally, "Father Turk."[84] It was by this name that he became most widely known. The naming of Atatürk epitomized the crystallization of a strong personality cult which, with the aid of modern technology, bound the populace to his leadership. The most obvious manifestations of the cult were visual. Unrestricted by the traditional Islamic aversion to representational images that had inhibited his Ottoman predecessors from portraying almost anything beyond their monograms, Mustafa Kemal distributed his image throughout the land, which enabled him to be present in virtually every home, institution, and place of business around the country. His statues and busts adorned public places, while his pictures hung in every government office.

In 1923, Mustafa Kemal dismissed the Islamic prohibition of sculpture as obsolete. In the present, he announced, the Turkish nation "would advance to the furthest limit in sculpting, which is one of the components of progress, and every corner of our country will commemorate its children's [achievements] by exquisite sculptures."[85] The first statue of Mustafa Kemal was erected in 1926 at Sarayburnu, just outside the gardens of the Topkapı Palace, depicting him looking toward Anatolia while turning his back on the former imperial palace.[86] Less than a month later, another

[84] "Kemal Öz Adlı Cümhur Reisimize Verilen Soy Adı Hakkında Kanun" (Law #2587, November 24, 1934), in *Düstûr*, III/16 (Ankara: Başvekâlet Matbaası, 1935), 4.

[85] "Bursa'da Şark Sinemasında Halkla Konuşma, 22.I. 1923," in *Atatürk'ün Söylev ve Demeçleri*, vol. 2, *1906–1938*, ed. Nimet Unan (Ankara: Türk İnkılâp Tarihi Enstitüsü Yayımları, 1952), 66.

[86] Gültekin Elibal, *Atatürk ve Resim Heykel* (Istanbul: İş Bankası Kültür Yayınları, 1973), 196–97.

statue was erected in Konya. These were followed in the larger cities by others depicting Mustafa Kemal and his major achievements. In addition to these sculptures, a number of "victory monuments" featuring him as the prime hero of the War of Independence were erected in different parts of Turkey, and busts and masks in various sizes were placed in many public institutions, schools, and parks.[87] The Austrian sculptor Heinrich Krippel and the Italian professor of arts Pietro Canonica made many of the early sculptures of Mustafa Kemal.[88] Likewise, Turkish artists produced an abundance of paintings depicting him as a commander, statesman, and leader, showing him as saving the nation from extinction, spearheading the Turkish revolution (often with a Turkish Marianne waving a Turkish flag), or accepting the gratitude of the people for his extraordinary services and leadership.[89] While original paintings were displayed in official buildings or major museums, the most popular among them were reproduced in enormous numbers and placed in schools, banks, coffeehouses, and other public buildings. Similarly, Mustafa Kemal's witticisms appeared in the public sphere in the form of placards or writings on walls. In 1924 the first stamps bearing his image were issued.[90] In 1927 banknotes with his portrait entered circulation.[91] By the late 1920s it would be safe to say that Mustafa Kemal was the sole figure rep-

[87] Ibid., 206ff.

[88] See Burcu Dogramaci, *Kulturtransfer und nationale Identität: deutschsprachige Architekten, Stadtplaner und Bildhauer in der Türkei nach 1927* (Berlin: Gebr. Mann Verlag, 2008), 266–75; and Semavi Eyice, *Atatürk ve Pietro Canonica: Eserleri ve Türkiye Seyahatnâmesi ile Atatürk'e Dair Hatıraları* (Istanbul: Eren Yayıncılık, 1986), 8–13.

[89] Elibal, *Atatürk ve Resim Heykel*, 59ff.

[90] *Pulhan Türk Pulları Kataloğu*, XII, ed. Ali Nusret Pulhan (Istanbul: Fen Fakültesi Basımevi, 1973), 278.

[91] Tanju Demir, "Cumhuriyet Dönemi Paralarında Siyaset ve İdeoloji, 1923–1950," in *75 Yılda Para'nın Serüveni*, ed. Mustafa Sönmez (Istanbul: Tarih Vakfı Yayınları, 1998), 15–23.

resented in the public sphere. Buildings in which he had stayed, places he had visited, and spots where he had delivered speeches became shrines, and objects that he had used acquired the status of sacred relics. A plethora of superlatives attached to his name—terms such as *Büyük* (Grand), *Dahi* (Genius), *Eşsiz* (Peerless), *Halâskâr* (Savior), *Münci* (Deliverer), *Ulu* (Great), *Yaratıcı* (Creator), *Yüce* (Exalted), and *Beşeriyet Harikası* (Wonder of Humankind)—strengthened the quasi-religious aura around him.

Notwithstanding the tremendous amount of effort Mustafa Kemal invested in promoting his ideas within Turkish society, he was reluctant to develop his program into a full-fledged ideology. One reason for this hesitation was the pragmatic nature of the program and the fear that it would become dogma—something he despised. In addition, there was no major thinker or library of books on hand to serve as the basis of an elaborate ideology supported by sophisticated philosophical arguments. Although Mustafa Kemal's followers attempted to turn his magnum opus, *The Speech*, into such a foundational text, they were unsuccessful, since the book was basically a detailed description of the Turkish War of Independence and its aftermath from the vantage point of the new leader of Turkey. The resulting volume—which includes hundreds of documents reproduced to support the narrative—resembles a hybrid of historical monograph and memoir.[92] With the exception of the final peroration, in which Mustafa Kemal entrusted the future of the new republic to the Turkish youth,[93] it is virtually impossible to find a mise en abyme in this dry and unadorned text.

Over the years Turkish intellectuals and statesmen have nevertheless attempted to construct an ideology out of Mustafa Kemal's

[92] *Nutuk: Gazi Mustafa Kemal Tarafından* (Ankara: n.p., 1927), 543 pp.; and *Nutuk Muhteviyâtına Aid Vesâik: Gazi Mustafa Kemal Tarafından* (Ankara: n.p., 1927), 303 pp.
[93] *Nutuk*, 542–43.

Figure 13. The title page of Mustafa Kemal's magnum opus *Nutuk* (1927).

ideas on "the Turkish revolution." The first efforts were undertaken in the 1930s, while he was still alive. In 1932, a group of left-wing intellectuals began publishing a journal called *Kadro* (Cadre) that strove to interpret the Turkish revolution through a loosely Marxist, historical materialist theoretical prism. They also took many cues from the anti-imperialist, authoritarian, and neo-mercantilist nationalism of the journal *Die Tat* edited by Hans Zehrer.[94] In the words of Şevket Süreyya (Aydemir), one of the group's leading intellectuals, their aim was "to transform our revo-

[94] "Kadro ve Die Tat," *Kadro* 1/6 (June 1932): 5. Like the *Tatkreis* movement, the leading columnists of *Kadro* praised autarky and proposed that it would become the economic system of the future. See Şevket Süreyya, *İnkılâp ve Kadro: İnkılâbın İdeolojisi* (Ankara: Muallim Ahmet Halit Kitaphanesi, 1932), 16–17.

lution ... into one based on a chain of thought [and] ... by turning [this] chain of thought into an ideology, have it serve as the foundation of the revolution."[95] They conceded that the Turkish revolution was not the product of an ideology, but claimed that it was nonetheless a natural response to the expansion of capitalism (as well as to its inevitable consequence, colonialism), and that it represented a decisive victory against these evils.[96] For this reason, "the Turkish revolutionary state could not be a bourgeois state as produced by the French Revolution or a proletarian state as generated by the communist revolution, but was the first example of the liberation of a technologically backward semicolony."[97]

The authors of *Kadro* further maintained that all national liberation movements resembled each other, and that the Turkish revolution should serve as a model for the colonized peoples of Asia and Africa.[98] The pedagogical need to formalize the lessons of the Turkish experience required the construction of an ideology that might serve all oppressed peoples.[99] According to these intellectuals, Turkey, unlike the divided societies of the West, was a classless society. In such a situation, it fell to intellectuals under the leadership of Mustafa Kemal to drive the state-sponsored engine of revolutionary change.[100] Although the president initially per-

[95] Ibid., 46.

[96] Ahmet Hamdi, "Kapitalizm (Emperyalizm) ile Millet İktisat Rejimi ve Ferdiyetçilik ile Devletçiliğin Manaları," *Kadro* 2/18 (June 1933): 45.

[97] Vedat Nedim, "Devletin Yapıcılık ve İdarecilik Kudretine İnanmak Gerekir," *Kadro* 2/15 (March 1933): 13.

[98] Şevket Süreyya, "Millî Kurtuluş Hareketleri Hakkında Bizim Tezimiz," *Kadro* 1/12 (December 1932): 43.

[99] See, for example, "Çin ve Hindistan," *Kadro* 1/1 (January 1932): 46; and "Kadro," *Kadro* 1/5 (May 1932): 4.

[100] See Vedat Nedim, "Sınıflaşmamak ve İktisat Siyaseti," *Kadro* 1/11 (November 1932): 17–21; Vedat Nedim, "Mefhum Teşkilâtı Değil Madde Teşkilâtı," *Kadro* 1/8 (August 1932): 13–17; and "Türk İnkılâbında Gazi ve Bizim Bir İnanımız," *Kadro* 2/24 (December 1933): 3–4.

mitted publication of this journal, he disliked its attempt to craft an ideology out of his work and was appalled at the Marxist underpinnings of their arguments. In 1935, he lost patience with the *Kadro* group and ordered the closure of the journal.[101]

During the same period, another journal published by the People's Houses, the main agent of indoctrination of the new regime, represented an attempt to forge a right-wing Kemalist ideology. The statesmen and intellectuals who launched the journal *Ülkü* (Ideal) in 1933 wished to produce an ideology modeled on German national socialism and Italian fascism. Although their attitude toward Bolshevism was one of visceral hatred, they borrowed from Soviet methods of ideology diffusion. The movement's main ideologue, Mehmet Recep (Peker), a former officer and the general secretary of the country's sole political party, was deeply impressed by Germany's *Nazionalsozialistiche Deutsche Arbeiterpartei* and Italy's *Partito Nazionale Fascista*. Although he recognized that the Turkish case was unique (echoing Mustafa Kemal's maxim "We can only be likened to ourselves"),[102] he wished to model the Republican People's Party on these organizations. In 1934, he started lecturing at the first Turkish Revolution Institute, and prepared a textbook to serve as the basis of Kemalism.[103] Although he wished to have Mustafa Kemal as the spiritual guide of the movement, there was little doubt that he himself aspired to exploit the opportunity to become a party secretary similar to Stalin in the All-Union Communist Party.[104] However, Atatürk prevented him

[101] İlhan Tekeli-Selim İlkin, *Bir Cumhuriyet Öyküsü: Kadrocuları ve Kadro'yu Anlamak* (Istanbul: Tarih Vakfı Yurt Yayınları, 2003), 420–24.

[102] "Bakanlar Kurulunun Görev ve Yetkisini Belirten Kanun Teklifi Münasebetiyle, December 1, 1921," in *Atatürk'ün Söylev ve Demeçleri*, vol. 1, *T.B.M. Meclisinde ve C.H.P. Kurultaylarında, 1919–1938* (Istanbul: Türk İnkılâp Tarihi Enstitüsü Yayımları, 1945), 191.

[103] [Recep Peker], *Recep Peker'in İnkılab Dersleri Notları* (Ankara: Ulus Basımevi, 1935).

[104] He further proposed an all-out war against liberalism and strict party

from proposing this idea to the party congress in 1935, and dismissed him from his post the following year.[105] Undaunted, he and his comrades continued their work on a scientistic, corporatist, étatist, and solidaristic ideology expressed as a personality cult surrounding the figure of Atatürk.

The solidarism of Alfred Fouillée and Léon Bourgeois also exerted a strong influence in early republican intellectual circles.[106] According to one of the leaders of this right-wing variant of Kemalism, "one of the greatest duties of the Turkish intellectual [is] to invent the science of Kemalism . . . through scientific methods and to turn it into social engineering."[107] In the words of Şevket Kansu, the leading physical anthropologist of the period, "This pure, masculine, and robust ideology that can be called National Kemalism" should use biosociology and even eugenics to shape the new solidaristic society.[108] Members of this school believed that the greatest characteristic of the Turkish revolution was "its expression in a real genius and not . . . in a prophet who was the product of concealed psychological illnesses"—an unflattering reference to the Prophet Muḥammad.[109] Mustafa Kemal was "the first great guide to find cures for social ills."[110] To their way of thinking, it was appropriate for the ideology inspired by "the first

---

domination in all aspects of political life. See *C.H.P. Genel Sekreteri R. Peker'in Söylevleri* (Ankara: n.p., 1935), 3ff.

[105] Hasan Rıza Soyak, *Atatürk'ten Hatıralar*, vol. 1 (Ankara: Yapı ve Kredi Bankası Yayınları, n.d. [1973]), 58.

[106] Ertan Aydın, "Peculiarities of Turkish Revolutionary Ideology in the 1930s: The *Ülkü* Version of Kemalism," *Middle Eastern Studies* 40/5 (September 2004): 66–67. See also the "Solidarité" section in Afet [Âfet İnan], *Vatandaş İçin Medenî Bilgiler*, vol. 1, 98–101.

[107] Nusret Köymen, "Kemalizm ve Politika Bilgisi," *Ülkü* 7/41 (July 1936): 323–24.

[108] Şevket Aziz, "Biyososyoloji," *Ülkü* 3/16 (June 1934): 253–62.

[109] "İnkılâp Ülkülerini Yayma Yolunda," *Ülkü* 2/7 (August 1933): 25.

[110] Şevket Aziz, "Türk Topraklarının Adamı," *Ülkü* 4/20 (October 1934): 81–82.

genius who manifests both the soul of a societal guide and the mind of an intellectual" to be solidaristic and corporatist,[111] while rejecting individualism, liberalism, and socialism.[112]

These ideas amounted to a Turkish version of totalitarianism, which owed much to the analogous ideologies prevalent in Europe and elsewhere at that time. They were to prove more lasting than other interpretations of Kemalism, even though Mustafa Kemal himself remained aloof. When he died in 1938, this interpretation established a virtual monopoly. Despite the more accommodating attitude toward the left-wing Kemalists that characterized Atatürk's successor, İsmet İnönü, right-wing Kemalism formed the backbone of the official version that was strenuously promoted between 1938 and 1950. In general, this Kemalism advocated social transformation and authoritarian developmentalism under a single-party regime. It revolved around a scientistic weltanschauung, a new interpretation of Turkish nationalism based mainly on racial anthropology, and a robust personality cult.

By the time of his death, Mustafa Kemal had unintentionally, though not accidentally, become the revered founder of a new religion, Kemalism. In the eyes of many educated young Turks, he was a new prophet with a new teaching of salvation. As one school inspector told the visiting Grace Ellison, "Our prophet is our Ghazi: we have finished with that *individual* from Arabia. The religion of Mohamet was all very well for Arabia, but it is not for us." When Ellison posed the question, "But have you no belief?" he replied, "Yes . . . in the Ghazi, science, the future of my country,

---

[111] Nusret Köymen, "Kemalizmin Hususiyetleri," *Ülkü* 7/42 (August 1936): 417.

[112] Fikret Adanır, "Kemalist Authoritarianism and Fascist Trends in Turkey during the Interwar Period," in *Fascism Outside Europe: The European Impulse against Domestic Conditions in the Diffusion of Global Fascism*, ed. Stein Ugelvik Larsen (New York: Boulder, 2001), 335ff.

and myself."[113] In other words, regardless of his intentions, Mustafa Kemal had become not just an ideologue but a twentieth-century prophet preaching the new combination of scientism and nationalism, the twin pillars of a new religion—Kemalism. In a book titled "Kamâlism" (1936), parliamentarian Şeref Aykut called it "a religion for living."[114] As late as 1945, the Turkish lexicon prepared by the Turkish Language Association provided the following definition in its entry on the metaphorical meaning of religion: "A strongly held idea or ideal. Kemalism is the religion of the Turk."[115] Likewise, literary works elevated the personality cult to a quasi-religion. Behçet Kemal Çağlar's *Mevlid* eulogized Mustafa Kemal as a prophet, imitating the famous example of this genre composed by Süleyman Çelebi (d. 1422) in honor of the Prophet Muḥammad.[116] A poem by the Republican People's Party deputy Kemalettin Kamu ran,

> Çankaya [Mustafa Kemal's presidential residence]—here
>   Moses reached spiritual perfection
> Here Jesus ascended
> . . . .
> Neither miracle nor sorcery
> Let the Arab possess the Ka'ba
> Çankaya is sufficient for us.[117]

[113] Grace Ellison, *Turkey To-Day,* 187.

[114] Şeref Aykut, *Kamâlizm: C.H. Partisi Programının İzahı* (Istanbul: Muallim Ahmet Halit Kitap Evi, 1936), 3.

[115] *T.D.K. Türkçe Sözlük: Türk Dil Kurumu Lûgat Kolu Çalışmalariyle Hazırlanmıştır* (Istanbul: Cumhuriyet Basımevi, 1945), 153.

[116] Osman Ergin, *Türkiye Maarif Tarihi,* vol. 5 (Istanbul: Osmanbey Matbaası, 1943), 1532–34. Çağlar also produced poetry in this genre; see "Bizim Mevlût," *Yücel* 13/76 (June 1941): 168: "O god who landed in Samsun, greetings / . . . The real birthday of every Turk is May 19."

[117] *Kemâlettin Kâmi Kamu: Hayatı, San'atı ve Şiirleri,* ed. Gültekin Sâmanoğlu (Ankara: Kültür ve Turizm Bakanlığı Yayınları, 1986), 77.

Figure 14. President Mustafa Kemal engaged in study at his private library at Çankaya (1931). Source: http://www.tccb.gov.tr/sayfa/ata_ozel/fotograf/, picture no. 58.

In retrospect it can be said that Mustafa Kemal attempted one of the greatest societal transformations of modern times. Not only as a statesman, but also as a self-made thinker, he invested tremendous energy in preparing the intellectual groundwork for this momentous project. As an omnivorous autodidact unsystematically synthesizing ideas from a variety of sources, he worked on subjects and concepts such as history, language, nation, race, religion, and science, reaching certain conclusions and then discussing them with his intellectual comrades, often over lengthy dinners lasting well into the night. Since he was both studying and teaching simultaneously, his dilettante intellectualism is perhaps best captured by the dictum *Qui docet discit*. But the manner in which in the end his avant-garde opinions invariably prevailed calls to mind another maxim: *Rex non potest peccare*. The finality of Mustafa Kemal's pronouncements was such that in 1933, on the pretext of reforming the university, the regime dismissed scores of professors who had dared to articulate oblique criticisms of the leader's ideas or had simply not supported them enthusiastically enough.[118]

After Mustafa Kemal's death, the intellectual proponents of Kemalism gradually revised many of the outlandish historical and linguistic theories associated with the movement, and finally abandoned them. However, the brand of Turkish nationalism founded on these concepts continued to flourish in modern Turkey and was embraced as the main component of identity by a substantial portion of the population. Today, very few people recall the passionate debates on Hittites, brachycephalic skull formations, Turkish blood types, the Turkic origins of the Tlaskaltek dialects, or the global civilizing mission of the proto-Turks in the Neolithic age. It was not so much that these theories came to be recognized as unscientific but that it proved virtually impossible to convey them to the average person. Naming major institutions after the Sumerians and Hittites (the Turkish banks Sümerbank and Etibank were established in 1933 and 1935, respectively) was not sufficient to create an emotional relationship with these ancient civilizations. Compared to the Ottomans, whom the Kemalists wished to expunge from history, the proto-Turks who allegedly spoke the first language of humankind were just too remote. Less than a year after Mustafa Kemal's death in 1938, the regime decided to commemorate the centennial of the famous Ottoman-era reforms known as the Tanzimat; this signaled the establishment's desire to reintroduce the Ottoman past into Turkish history.[119] At the Third Turkish History Congress held in 1943, a substantial number of the presentations dealt with topics in Ottoman history.[120] Gradually, the regime in-

[118] Ali Arslan, *Darülfünun'dan Üniversite'ye* (Istanbul: Kitabevi, 1995), 331–53.

[119] *Tanzimat* I (Istanbul: Maarif Vekâleti, 1940), v–vii.

[120] See *III. Türk Tarih Kongresi, Ankara 15–20 Kasım 1943: Kongreye Sunulan Tebliğler* (Ankara: Türk Tarih Kurumu Yayınları, 1948), 124–30; 229–68; 367–79; 441–518; 556–62; 590–98; 648–88; 700–703.

corporated early Ottoman history into the glorious past of the Turks and accepted the Late Ottoman reforms as antecedents of the republican reforms—just as many contemporary historians now see them. Although such an approach represented a sharp deviation from the ideas of Mustafa Kemal, it actually reinforced among ordinary citizens the idea that the Turks had played a leading role in bringing civilization to other peoples, and that Turkishness was the proper basis of identity in Turkey.

After Mustafa Kemal's death, a similar diminution took place in the hostility of the state toward Islam and in the racial undertones of Turkish nationalism. In 1944, a number of leading Turkish racists were put on trial. After 1950, the regime increasingly sought to mend its relationship with Islam. In 1983, the Turkish establishment went so far as to adopt a new cultural policy that sought to reconcile Turkish nationalism and Islam, and to reconstitute the two ideologies as the twin pillars of Turkish national culture.[121] Not surprisingly, a countermovement to resuscitate the original tenets of Kemalism emerged in the late 1990s; this ultrasecularist, xenophobic nationalism became known as *Ulusalcılık*. Although this movement gained considerable traction in official circles, it did not penetrate deeply into Turkish society. The ongoing struggle over the official seal of the city of Ankara is characteristic of the enduring conflict over the implementation of Kemalism.[122] In 1973, a mayor supportive of early republican nationalism made the Hittite sun disk the emblem of the city. Then, in 1995, one of his conservative successors replaced it with a mosque. A subsequent lawsuit resulted in a 2008 court decision annulling the

[121] *Milli Kültür Özel İhtisas Komisyonu Raporu* (Ankara: Başbakanlık Devlet Planlama Teşkilatı, 1983), 26–27, 140–43, 517–23.

[122] Wendy Shaw, "The Rise of the Hittite Sun: A Deconstruction of Western Civilization from the Margin," in *Selective Remembrances: Archaeology in the Construction, Commemoration, and Consecration of National Pasts*, ed. Philip L. Kohl, Mara Kozelsky, and Nachman Ben-Yehuda (Chicago: University of Chicago Press, 2007), 163ff.

change and, with explicit reference to Mustafa Kemal's legacy, restoring the sun disk.[123]

Except for one brief interlude, the personality cult around Mustafa Kemal has remained strong. In December 1938 Atatürk's successor, İsmet İnönü, declared the deceased founder of the state the "Eternal Chief,"[124] and—perhaps consciously emulating the precedent set by the designation of Lenin as the "Leader of the Revolution" and Stalin as the "Leader of Progressive Humanity"—labeled himself "National Chief." For a while, the new president's image replaced that of Mustafa Kemal on banknotes and stamps. Over time, however, the personality cult surrounding Atatürk made a strong comeback. In the words of the third president, Celâl Bayar, whose party defeated the Republican People's Party in the elections of 1950, "To love Atatürk is a national cult."[125] Atatürk's image was restored on banknotes and stamps, and a law of 1951 made insulting Atatürk's memory a punishable offense.[126] Kemalism also served as the ideological basis for the military coups and interventions that occurred in 1960, 1971, 1980, and 1997. The architects of the 1980 coup attempted to restore the full-fledged hero worship of 1930s.

Despite Mustafa Kemal's lack of enthusiasm for dogma, Kemalism as a belief system has become the most resilient legacy of the founder of the republic. Today military schools in Turkey teach

[123] "Hitit Güneşi Manevrası Yargıdan Döndü," April 11, 2008; accessed June 17, 2008 at http://www.yapi.com.tr/Haberler/haber_Detay_60927.html.

[124] İnönü'nün Söylev ve Demeçleri, vol. 1, T.B.M. Meclisinde ve C.H.P Kurultaylarında, 1919–1946 (Istanbul: Türk Devrim Tarihi Enstitüsü Yayımları, 1946), 331; Cemil Koçak, "Tek Parti Yönetimi, Kemalizm ve Şeflik Sistemi: Ebedî Şef/Millî Şef," in Modern Türkiye'de Siyasî Düşünce, vol. 2, Kemalizm, ed. Ahmet İnsel (Istanbul: İletişim Yayınları, 2001), 119–37.

[125] Celâl Bayar'ın Söylev ve Demeçleri, vol. 1, 1921–1938, Ekonomik Konulara Dair, ed. Özel Şahingiray (Ankara: Doğuş Ltd. Ortaklığı, 1955), 241.

[126] "Atatürk Aleyhine İşlenen Suçlar Hakkında Kanun" (Law #5816, July 31, 1951), in Türkiye Cumhuriyeti Sicilli Kavanini, vol. 32 (Istanbul: Cihan Kitaphanesi, 1951), 240.

mandatory courses on the "Atatürkist System of Thought," which the officer corps considers to be the soul of military education. Likewise, all university seniors, regardless of their fields of specialization, are obliged before receiving their diplomas to pass an examination on the history of the Turkish revolution and Atatürk's principles. The president of the republic and the parliamentary deputies are sworn into office with a pledge to "remain faithful to Atatürk's principles and reforms."[127] The unalterable second article of the current Turkish constitution, promulgated in 1982, marshals the "nationalism of Atatürk" as one of the prime tenets of the republic, and its forty-second article specifies that "education and teaching should be carried out in accordance with the principles and reforms of Atatürk."[128] However, with the passage of time the legacy of the Eternal Chief has tended to lose much of its determinate character. Today Kemalism may rather be seen as an attempt on the part of the Turkish establishment to interpret current conditions through reference to Atatürk's sayings and doings, and everyone gives substance to this elusive concept in a different way. Thus, depending on the context and speaker, Kemalism may be invoked in support of ideas that are étatist or liberal, nationalist or socialist, religious or scientistic, elitist or populist.

[127] Articles 103 and 81, respectively; see *T. C. 1982 Anayasası: 1993 Değişiklikleriyle*, ed. A. Şeref Gözübüyük (Ankara: Turhan Yayınevi, n.d. [1993]), 88, 71.
[128] Articles 2 and 42; ibid., 23, 47.

8

Turkey and the West

To many in the West, the Muslim Ottoman had long represented the quintessential "Other." Despite this perception, the country of the Ottomans was largely a European one. Even the empire's detractors labeled it "the Sick Man of Europe."[1] Arguably the most important component of the realm had always been not Anatolia but Rumelia. What Westerners often referred to as "European Turkey" included some of the most densely populated and cosmopolitan centers of the region, such as Mustafa Kemal's hometown of Salonica and the cities of Durrës, Edirne, Iōánina, Monastir, Scutari in Albania, and Skopje. As late as 1878, it was the River Danube that divided the Ottoman realm from the rest of Europe. After the Berlin Congress of that year, which significantly reduced the empire's European possessions, the Ottomans were still left in control of a sizable territory in southeastern Europe. Despite suffering extensive territorial losses since the end of the seventeenth century, the Ottomans continued to adhere to their conception of the empire as made up of two core realms, Rumelia and Anatolia, flanking Istanbul, the jewel in the crown, with the Arab periphery looming in the background. In 1908, when the Great Powers were deliberating a new set of reforms for Macedonia, the Committee of Union and Progress (CUP) leaders explained their decision to

---

[1] The phrase (in the form *un homme malade*) was originally coined by Tsar Nicholas I during a conversation with the British ambassador Sir George Hamilton Seymour in January 1853.

launch a revolution on the grounds that "Macedonia's independence would mean the loss of half of the Ottoman Empire and,
therefore, its complete annihilation. . . . Without Macedonia in
between, Albania would naturally be lost. Since our border would
have to retreat to the gates of Istanbul, the capital could not remain in Istanbul. The removal of our capital from Europe to Asia
would exclude us from the European powers and turn us into a
second or third class Asiatic state. If, Heaven forfend, we lose Rumelia, then . . . Ottoman sovereignty will be reduced to the level of
Iranian power."[2] This prophetic analysis precisely identified the
drastic change that would occur in the wake of the Balkan Wars of
1912–13.

After the "Balkan catastrophe," as these wars were termed in
Ottoman parlance, the sole European territory left to the empire—namely, southeastern Thrace—was not significant enough
to justify continued use of the term European Turkey. As seen
from the West, the Ottoman Empire had retreated eastward to its
origins and become an Asiatic country—much to the dismay of its
ruling classes. To reach the Adriatic—the prewar Ottoman natural
border—from Istanbul, one now had to go through two or three
foreign countries, depending on the choice of route. Of the empire's major European cities, only Adrianople and Istanbul itself
remained in Ottoman hands.

In 1913–14, on the advice of its German military advisers, the
government briefly considered moving the capital to Konya in
central Anatolia or even to Damascus.[3] Although this radical idea
was not realized during the Great War, it was precisely what Mustafa Kemal set out to do in the aftermath of the Turkish War of

[2] M. Şükrü Hanioğlu, *Preparation for a Revolution: The Young Turks, 1902–
1908* (New York: Oxford University Press, 2001), 236.

[3] Tarık Zafer Tunaya, *Türkiye'de Siyasal Partiler*, vol. 3, *İttihat ve Terakki, Bir
Çağın, Bir Kuşağın, Bir Partinin Tarihi* (Istanbul: Hürriyet Vakfı Yayınları,
1989), 480–83.

Independence. Given that Turkey's European territory scarcely provided space for the letter T on maps of the new republic, it made good sense to move the capital to Ankara. With its capital in Asia, and a predominantly Muslim population no longer containing sizable Christian and Jewish minorities, Turkey, as seen from Europe, had become an ordinary Near Eastern country on the southeastern fringes of Europe.

Mustafa Kemal nevertheless held strongly to the old CUP belief that maintaining the state's European character was crucial for its survival. He, too, believed that becoming an Asiatic power like Iran meant the end of Turkey. Yet, what could be done in the face of geography? For Mustafa Kemal, Turkey's essential Europeanness remained unchanged; it simply had to be expressed in cultural rather than geographical terms. This attitude resembles the modern Israeli sense of belonging to the West despite residing in the East. Not unlike the Ashkenazi Jews of Israel, who championed the idea of belonging to Western civilization,[4] Mustafa Kemal—a native of European Turkey—was determined to shape the Turkish state and society in the cultural mold of Europe. His attempts in this regard constitute one of the greatest projects of intellectual and social transformation of the early twentieth century. His initiatives in Westernization surpassed even the most avant-garde projects of the radical Ottoman Westernizers of the Second Constitutional Period.

The Late Ottoman Empire had had fleeting successes in its quest for integration with Europe—such as the diplomatic recognition of the empire as a party to the European Balance of Power

[4] See Amnon Raz-Krakotzkin, "The Zionist Return to the West and the Mizrahi Jewish Perspective," in *Orientalism and Jews*, ed. Ivan Davidson Kalmar and Derek J. Penslar (Waltham, MA: Brandeis University Press, 2005), 162–81; and Sammy Smooha, "Jewish Ethnicity in Israel: Symbolic or Real?" in *Jews in Israel: Contemporary Social and Cultural Patterns*, ed. Uzi Rebhun and Chaim I. Waxman (Hanover, NH: Brandeis University Press, 2004), 47–80.

through the Paris Treaty of 1856. Even in Egypt, by now an autonomous province of the empire, the Khedive Ismā'īl had the
self-assurance to declare at the opening of the Suez Canal in 1869
that Egypt "had detached [itself] from the continent of Africa and
united [with] that of Europe."[5] Yet such moments only went to
prove that for Turkey to become an integral part of the West,
wholesale cultural and societal transformation was necessary. Accordingly, the Westernization project embarked upon by Mustafa
Kemal had two ambitious aims: first, to convince the Turkish populace that Turkey was part of Europe; and second, to persuade
Western public opinion that the West shared the same culture as
the Turks. His project had two main aspects, one ideological and
political, the other cultural and social.

At the ideological level, Mustafa Kemal sought to minimize everything that marked Turkey as non-European. Clearly, Islam was
the major obstacle in this regard. In fact, most of the various Westernizing movements in the Ottoman Empire since the mid-nineteenth century had constructed ideologies that would enable them
to bridge the enormous religious gulf separating the Muslims of
the Ottoman Empire from the Christians of Europe. For instance,
Ottoman positivists of the nineteenth century, like many Turkish
socialists of the twentieth century, viewed their ideology as a tool
to obliterate the barrier of religion and reach out to the West. Scientism, to which Mustafa Kemal passionately subscribed, was less
helpful in this regard, since internationally its proponents were
not as organized as the positivists or socialists. In part the new
Turkish history thesis, which posited Turks as the founders of
world civilization, was designed to create a cultural bond with Europe. A shared culture going back thousands of years to a time before the advent of Christianity or Islam could, it was thought, bol-

---

[5] Arthur Silva White, *The Expansion of Egypt under Anglo-Egyptian Condominium* (New York: New Amsterdam, 1900), 63.

ster claims of closeness based on common cultural origins. In Wellsian terms, what happened during the Neolithic age turned out to be more important than the teachings of Jesus or the Islamic conquests. Whether such ideas held out much hope for entrenching a European identity among Turkey's Muslim citizens is highly doubtful; to think that such dubious theories would have had an impact on European perceptions of Turkey seems in retrospect preposterous. Indeed, with few exceptions, Western scholarship paid no heed to the highly politicized, pseudoscientific theories advanced by the republican regime.

While Mustafa Kemal's Westernization efforts failed as an instrument of foreign policy, they met with surprising success domestically. A large segment of the Turkish elite did in fact develop a sense of belonging to the West in the course of his rule. Thus, although the republican history and language theses could fairly be seen as gross scientific errors; they accomplished their most important objective: to persuade the educated classes of the new society to embrace a new identity, rejecting any ties with the Orient and wholeheartedly espousing the Occident.

Still, convincing the Turks that they belonged to European culture was not enough to make Turkey a part of the West. For this it was necessary for Turkey to embrace Western civilization and thus appear to be an indissoluble part of Europe. In this respect, Mustafa Kemal stood out among twentieth-century Muslim leaders. Mahathir bin Muhammad of Malaysia, for example, championed "Asian Values," a concept resembling the German notion of *Zivilisationkritik*, and advanced a strongly anti-Western, authoritarian industrial developmentalism that promoted an allegedly superior culture and despised universal civilization.[6] For Mustafa Kemal, human "civilization" subsumed all cultures,[7]

[6] Mark R. Thompson, "The Survival of 'Asian Values' as 'Zivilisationkritik,'" *Theory and Society* 29/5 (2000): 651–86.
[7] "Kültür Hakkında, 29.X.1923," in *Atatürk'ün Söylev ve Demeçleri*, vol. 3,

but it was shaped by the most advanced European ones. His new Turkish nationalism glorified Turkish culture as a primary source of modern European civilization and not as something clashing with it. Like those Late Ottoman Westernizers who promoted wholesale Westernization on the grounds that "[t]here is no other civilization—civilization is European civilization,"[8] he adopted the idea that civilization was unitary. He believed that any aspects of a local non-Western culture that clashed with universal civilization should be eliminated. As a natural consequence of this train of thought, he also rejected the very possibility of a non-Western modernity, despite having lived in one of the major examples of such an environment, the Late Ottoman Empire. For Mustafa Kemal, adopting European civilization meant eradicating local cultural elements that clashed with the Western conception of modernity. Among these elements were many traditions associated with Islam.

In the Muslim world, Mustafa Kemal was not alone in his endeavors to Westernize his country through social and cultural change. But he enjoyed one significant advantage over other contemporary Muslim leaders, such as the Iranian Reza Shah Pahlavi and the Afghan ruler Amanullah Khan, who also attempted noteworthy cultural transformations in their societies: he could build on the foundations established by the reformers of the Late Ottoman Empire over the previous century and a half. By the turn of the twentieth century, the Ottoman reformers had succeeded in fashioning a particular brand of modernity that, if it did not succeed in penetrating the lower social strata, was accepted by the elites; they had devised a hybrid legal system that combined Western legal principles with Islamic jurisprudence; they had created a

---

1918–1937, ed. Nimet Unan (Ankara: Türk İnkilâp Tarihi Enstitüsü Yayımları, 1954), 67.

[8] Abdullah Cevdet, "Şime-i Muhabbet,"*İctihad* 89 (January 29, 1914): 1984.

European-style bureaucracy; and they had facilitated the emergence of private companies, a sizable socialist movement, trade unions, materialist journals, suffragettes, a school of fine arts, lotteries, cinemas, theaters, and newspapers featuring advertisements for women's corsets. The last caliph was known to paint nude women and compose concertos. Many of these changes, to be sure, affected only the elite—and the Ottoman elite was much smaller than its counterparts in the West—but they were real enough.

Although Mustafa Kemal's modernist vision was shared by his comrades, who had spent most of their lives in European Turkey, the acceptance of his ideas in the very different land of Anatolia, much eulogized by the new Turkish nationalism as the cradle of Turkish civilization, was far from assured. In fact, Mustafa Kemal did not set foot in Anatolia until he was in his thirties, having completed his entire socialization in European Turkey and the imperial capital. His service in Syria and Cyrenaica created and reinforced the false impression that the Turkish heartland of the empire must be much more developed and modern than these Arab provinces. His eventual encounter, as ruler of Turkey, with a far more conservative and less modern part of the fatherland came as something of a shock.

In 1918, Mustafa Kemal had written that once he seized power he "would like to carry out the social revolution in our social life in the form of a sudden coup."[9] This was exactly how he proceeded after gaining power, implementing a radical program designed to quickly complete this transformation. Once he had accomplished his mission, he thought, Turkey would irrevocably become an integral part of the West regardless of its geographical location. Like the Westernizers of the Second Constitutional Period, he thought that the Western way of life was not a result of the socioeconomic

[9] *M. Kemal Atatürk'ün Karlsbad Hatıraları*, ed. Ayşe Afetinan (Ankara: Türk Tarih Kurumu Yayınları, 1983), 43.

dynamics prevalent in certain societies, but rather was itself a de-
terminant of those dynamics. According to this thesis, adopting
Western ways would bring about a transformation in social and
cultural life which went far beyond cosmetic changes. It is only
with this in mind that one can understand the sudden prolifera-
tion in the late 1920s of books purporting to instruct Turks on
how to look, behave, and live like Westerners. For example, in
1927 the leading wholesale Westernist, Abdullah Cevdet, published a Turkish rendition of Gaston Jollivet and Marie-Anne
L'Heureux's *Pour bien connaître les usages mondains*, teaching
Turks how to kiss the hand of a lady, make home visits, celebrate
the new year, serve Médoc after the second course of a meal, keep
women fit with exercise, and manage interfaith marriages.[10] The
illustrated propaganda journal *La Turquie kemaliste* (*kamâliste*),
which started publication in 1934 and continued after Atatürk's
death, demonstrated in pictures how Turkish women and villages
had allegedly begun to resemble European ones. Mihri İffet Pektaş,
one of the first women parliamentary deputies, depicted this period of change, from her vantage point, as a process of enlightenment.[11] However, for most villages the "progressive village" pic-
tured in this propaganda journal was in many ways foreign.[12] The
theory held that once all Turkish women and villages looked like
these "enlightened," "modern," and "progressive" role models, the
country as a whole would become an authentic part of the West.
The leaders of the regime thought that those who could not adopt

[10] Gaston Jollivet, Marie-Anne L'Heureux, *Mükemmel ve Resimli Âdâb-ı
Muʿaşeret Rehberi*, trans. Abdullah Cevdet (Istanbul: Yeni Matbaa, 1927), 115–
16; 147–95; 316–18; 241; 367; and Gaston Jollivet, Marie-Anne L'Heureux,
Muhtelit İzdivaclar, trans. Abdullah Cevdet ([Istanbul]: n.p., 1928), 1–4.

[11] Mihri Pektaş, "Turkish Woman," *La Turquie Kemaliste* 32–40 (August
1939–December 1940): 10–14.

[12] See Nusret Köymen, "Forward Progressive Village," *La Turquie Kemaliste*
32–40 (August 1939–December 1940):15–20. See also "La question de l'éducation au village," *La Turquie Kamâliste* 20 (August 1937): 22–26.

the new modernity in toto could not survive in Turkey. As time has shown, however, this *aut dice aut discede* approach was not productive. Most of the civilizing reforms imposed by the government were viewed by the Turkish masses as hostile attempts to displace long-standing Muslim traditions. To the utter dismay of the Kemalists, they refused the wholesale adoption of the version of modernity unilaterally imposed on them, and quietly persevered in their traditional ways.

Reforms aimed at keeping up with international civilization, as Mustafa Kemal conceptualized it, gained particular momentum after the emergence of the full-fledged single party monopoly over politics in 1925. In the course of a domestic trip in the summer of that year, Mustafa Kemal made a point of donning a Panama hat. In a public statement, he contended that the hat constituted an inseparable part of civilized and international dress, that it was not un-Islamic, and that it was preferable to wearing a fez, an originally Greek head cover.[13] Sultan Mahmud II (r. 1808–39) had in fact resorted to force in his attempts to make the fez the official male headgear of the empire. However, in the intervening years, the fez had acquired a religious connotation and become a symbol differentiating Muslims from non-Muslim Westerners. In a society governed for centuries by strictly enforced sartorial codes, for a Muslim man to wear a Western hat was tantamount to apostasy. The "hat reform" of 1925 required state employees to don hats as "one of the visible symbols of the struggle against fanaticism and ignorance" and as a means to achieving "entry into the family of world civilization."[14] This reform prompted a stronger reaction than the

[13] "İnebolu'da Bir Konuşma, 28. VIII. 1925," in *Atatürk'ün Söylev ve Demeçleri*, vol. 2, *1906–1938*, ed. Nimet Unan (Ankara: Türk İnkılâp Tarhi Enstitüsü Yayımları, 1952), 213.

[14] Şerafettin Turan, *Kendine Özgü Bir Yaşam ve Kişilik: Mustafa Kemal Atatürk* (Istanbul: Bilgi Yayınevi, 2004), 473; and "Şapka İktisası Hakkında Kanun" (Law #671, November 25, 1925), in *Türkiye Cumhuriyeti Sicill-i Kavânini*, ed. Karakoç Sarkiz, vol. 2 (Istanbul: Cihan Matbaası, 1926), 15.

abolition of the caliphate a little more than a year before.[15] Conservatives were not swayed by the various favorable explanations offered by the Turkish religious authorities, such as the reiteration of Muḥammad ʿAbduh's reasoning in his famous Transvaal fatwā of 1903,[16] which maintained that wearing a hat did not violate Islam unless it was done with the intention of imitating the religious habits of non-Muslims. In an extraordinary effort to quash resistance to the reform, Independence Courts tried scores of its opponents and even ordered the execution of many leaders of the agitation against the hat reform.[17] The ban on the fez was enforced so strictly that, notwithstanding considerable popular resentment, it swiftly disappeared from the scene. To Mustafa Kemal, this visible accomplishment represented a victory over those who rejected the blessings of civilization. In 1932 he provoked a diplomatic crisis by asking the Egyptian ambassador not to wear his tarboosh at a banquet on the anniversary of the proclamation of the republic.[18]

The status and appearance of women was yet another major concern of Mustafa Kemal. As early as 1916, while in one of the most underdeveloped parts of Anatolia, he had expressed support for the emancipation of women and the abolition of the veil.[19] Although he was merely echoing some of the main contentions of the antiveiling campaign that had been waged by the Westernizers,

[15] Mete Tunçay, *T.C.'nde Tek Parti Yönetimi'nin Kurulması* (Istanbul: Cem Yayınevi, 1989), 152–59.

[16] Charles C. Adams, "Muḥammad ʿAbduh and the Transvaal Fatwā," in *MacDonald Presentation Volume* (Princeton, NJ: Princeton University Press, 1933), 16–17.

[17] Ergün Aybars, *İstiklâl Mahkemeleri, 1920–1927*, vol. 2 (İzmir: Dokuz Eylül Üniversitesi Yayınları, 1988), 406–18.

[18] Bilâl N. Şimşir, *Doğunun Kahramanı Atatürk* (Istanbul: Bilgi Yayınevi, 1999), 112ff.

[19] *Atatürk'ün Hatıra Defteri*, ed. Şükrü Tezer (Ankara: Türk Tarih Kurumu Yayınları, 1972), 75.

who had entered into a long-lasting debate with the Islamists on this sensitive subject,[20] he seems to have decided to act on these ideas when the time was right. But on this issue, unlike the hat reform, he proceeded with caution, initiating a gradualist program over the course of many years.

First came the adoption of a modified Swiss Civil Code, granting extensive rights to women, in 1926. This was followed by other legal initiatives making women equal in various aspects of life. The regime accorded women the right to vote and stand for election at the municipal level in 1930, and at the national level in 1934—long before many Western countries. Alongside these legal measures, the regime promoted an image of the new "republican woman": she was educated, nationalist, dressed in a civilized fashion, professional, secular, and had fully internalized *l'esprit républicain*. Most conspicuously, piety the paramount virtue of the ideal Ottoman woman—was left out. Yet no effort was made to enforce the outward transformation of Turkish women. Notably, despite Mustafa Kemal's ridiculing of traditional women's dress, which, according to him, rendered Turks a laughingstock in the eyes of Europeans, he made no attempt to abolish the veil.[21] When in 1935 some radicals in the Republican People's Party proposed a law prohibiting traditional female dress, Mustafa Kemal withheld his support.[22] His prudence proves that he understood the extreme

[20] See, for example, Abdullah Cevdet, "Tesettür Mes'elesi," *Mehtab* 4 (August 14, 1911): 29–31; Selâhaddin Âsım, "Tesettür ve Mahiyeti," *İctihad* 100 (April 16, 1914): 2255–58; "Tesettür Mes'elesine Cevab," *Sırat-ı Mustakim* 6/156 (August 31, 1911): 413–17; Mehmed Fahreddin, "Medeniyet-i İslâmiye'den Bir Sahife yahud Tesettür-i Nisvân," *Sırat-ı Mustakim* 6/141 (May 18, 1911): 164–65ff.

[21] "Konya Kadınları ile Konuşma, 21.III.1923," 149–50, and "Kastamonu'da İkinci Bir Konuşma, 30.VIII.1925," 219–20, in *Atatürk'ün Söylev ve Demeçleri*, vol. 2.

[22] *C.H.P. Dördüncü Büyük Kurultayı Görüşmeleri Tutulgası, 9–16 Mayıs 1935* (Ankara: Ulus Basımevi, 1935), 144–48, 151–52, and 154–55.

sensitivity of the issue; it remains a major bone of contention between conservatives and Kemalists in Turkey today.

The republican regime promoted as female role models not those pursuing a feminist agenda or making gender-related demands but those women serving the republican ideology or, in Mustafa Kemal's own words, acting like "mothers of the nation." [23] Emblematic of this approach was the early republic's extensive use of a Turkish Marianne figure to symbolize Turkey or the republic. Thus, the republican women's movement had far less marked feminist undertones than the Late Ottoman women's movement of 1908–14. In 1913, the Ottoman feminist leader Belkıs Şevket had flown aboard a military plane in traditional Muslim dress to prove that "Oriental women will not accept a position that falls behind that of their Western sisters."[24] By contrast, the republican role model in 1937 was combat pilot Sabiha Gökçen, one of the adopted daughters of Mustafa Kemal; she bombarded Kurdish rebels from the air wearing a Turkish military uniform. Gökçen was apparently far ahead of her Western peers as a republican role model and a Western woman, but not as a feminist.[25] Just as the Hamidian regime had attempted to create a new type of Muslim woman, who shopped at Muslim stores and raised pious children, through its mouthpiece *Hanımlara Mahsus Gazete* (Ladies' Gazette),[26] so also did the republic try to promote the image of a modern "republican woman" through a media under its absolute control. In a related effort to promote this ideal type, Mustafa Kemal adopted a number of girls as his daughters in addition to Sabiha Gökçen. They served as more

[23] "Konya Kadınları ile Konuşma, 21.III. 1923," in *Atatürk'ün Söylev ve Demeçleri*, vol. 2, 153.

[24] Belkıs Şevket, "Tayarân Ederken," in *Nevsâl-i Millî*, ed. T. Z. (Istanbul: Artin Asadoryan, 1330 [1914]), 438–40.

[25] See Sabiha Gökçen, *Atatürk'le Bir Ömür*, ed. Oktay Verel (Istanbul: Altın Kitaplar Yayınevi, 1994), 135ff.

[26] Elizabeth B. Frierson, "Unimagined Communities: Women and Education in the Late-Ottoman Empire, 1876–1909," *Critical Matrix* 9/2 (1995): 70–81.

Figure 15. Sabiha Gökçen, one of the adopted daughters of Mustafa Kemal, in aviator uniform (1938). Source: *La Turquie Kemaliste* 30 (April 1939): 29.

accessible role models for the public than the Western-educated, elegant first lady Latife (Uşşaki) to whom Mustafa Kemal was married for a brief period between January 1923 and August 1925, since most of the important reforms were instigated later.

The Miss Turkey pageants, first organized in 1929 by the semi-official newspaper *Cumhuriyet* (Republic), produced role models for appearance. A striking example was beauty queen Keriman Halis, who went on to win the Miss World contest in Belgium in 1932. As an exemplar of "the exquisitely preserved beauty of the Turkish race," as Mustafa Kemal put it,[27] Keriman Halis—later given the family name "Ece," from an ancient Turkic word meaning "queen," by the president—not only presented the new Western face of Turkey to the "civilized world" but also embodied the truth of the official version of Turkish history.

Another feminine role model and adopted daughter of Mustafa Kemal was history teacher (later professor) Âfet İnan. She became one of the staunchest defenders of the Turkish history thesis through her research and lectures. At the First Turkish History Congress she censured eminent professors who dared to express doubts regarding the official history thesis, doing this not as a feminist but as a republican role model for educated women in state service.[28] Similarly, all seventeen women deputies handpicked by Atatürk in 1935 represented the regime's ideal type of the politically engaged woman committed to defending the interests of the republic. These women were neither feminists nor genuine politicians. In fact, in 1923 Mustafa Kemal had persuaded some feminist-oriented women not to form a political party.[29] Nonetheless,

[27] "Gazi Hz.nin Beyanatı: Reisicumhur Hz. Evvelki Akşam Başmuharririmizi Kabul Buyurdular," *Cumhuriyet*, August 3, 1932.

[28] *Birinci Türk Tarih Kongresi: Konferanslar Müzakere Zabıtları* (Ankara: Maarif Vekâleti, 1932), 50–51.

[29] Yaprak Zihnioğlu, *Kadınsız İnkılap: Nezihe Muhiddin, Kadınlar Halk Fırkası, Kadın Birliği* (Istanbul: Metis Yayınları, 2003), 147–49.

women in 1935 made up 4.5% of the membership of the Turkish Grand National Assembly,[30] a figure not surpassed until 2007.

The regime supported the women's movement in Turkey insofar as it embraced the republican ideology and served the state without criticism. For instance, the Turkish Women's Union, the main national women's organization established in 1924, hosted the Twelfth Congress of the International Alliance of Women for its first meeting outside of Western Europe in 1935. In so doing, the union rendered an important service to the regime, demonstrating that Turkey belonged to the West.[31] However, the regime, annoyed by the slightly feminist speeches of some members of the organization, proceeded to close down the union a mere two weeks after the adjournment of the congress. The director of the union, no doubt seeking to find favor with the regime, explained that since Turkish women had received all imaginable legal and political rights, there was no longer a need for a women's organization.[32]

In retrospect, it can be said that the leaders of the Late Ottoman women's movement, despite wearing traditional garb, advanced modern ideas and made substantial gender-related demands. The republican women pioneers, who looked very Western with their two-piece dresses and with their fashionable hats, expressed modernity in a different way, however. Because of the cultural sensitivity of the question, the regime opted to disseminate its ideal type in society by means of role models rather than legal measures that were liable to arouse opposition. Although the regime succeeded to a certain degree in expanding the ranks of edu-

[30] Nermin Abadan-Unat, "Social Change and Turkish Women," in *Women in Turkish Society*, ed. Nermin Abadan-Unat (Leiden, Netherlands: Brill, 1981), 19.

[31] Leila J. Rupp, "Challenging Imperialism in International Women's Organization, 1888–1945," in *Identity Politics in the Women's Movement*, ed. Barbara Ryan (New York: New York University Press, 2001), 249.

[32] Zihnioğlu, *Kadınsız İnkılap*, 258.

cated, European-style women, those who came to embody the republican ideal never amounted to a majority of the female population of Turkey. A large segment of the populace remained thoroughly traditional.

In a further attempt to transform the social character of modern Turks, Mustafa Kemal asked them to adopt new familial identities. As in many Muslim societies, the Ottomans did not have surnames. Instead, people were known by a bewildering array of appellations: by their personal names, by a combination of their birth names and personal names, by a combination of an adjective indicating place of birth and a personal name, by a combination of birth name and father's birth name, or by a combination of a patronymic indicating family genealogy and a personal name. Not surprisingly, this elaborate system often led to confusion, especially when two individuals bore identical names. The Surname Law issued in June 1934 served both to put an end to such confusion and to provide Western-style identities for Turks. The ruling coincided with the peak of the influence of the Turkish language and history theses, inspiring many people to adopt new names evoking the ancient Turkish past.

Mustafa Kemal also set in motion a number of cultural changes designed to make Turkey look more Western. His decision to adopt a modified Latin alphabet in place of the centuries-old Arabo-Persian script, demonstrated his desire to eliminate yet another religiously loaded symbol of the past. Turkic peoples had adopted the Arabo-Persian alphabet long before the Ottomans, who merely continued its use without questioning its suitability for Turkish—a language with a far richer set of vowels than Arabic or Persian. It was only with the increase in literacy and with the emergence of a journalistic language for the new Ottoman press during the Tanzimat era that a serious discussion was launched concerning the suitability of the Arabo-Persian alphabet for Turkish. In the 1860s, Ottoman, Azerbaijani, and Iranian intellectuals developed a number of alphabet revision projects, but these suggestions did not result in any significant change.[33] At the time of the Great War, Enver Pasha led the development of a new form of the alphabet eliminating the distinctive initial, medial, and final forms of the letters of the Arabo-Persian script, and writing each letter separately with additional vowels. This set of characters saw limited use for a while, but was soon abandoned because it too was impractical.[34] During the Second Constitutional Period, leading Westernizers had proposed a more radical solution: the adoption of a new alphabet based on the Latin one. The CUP strongly opposed this because it had been adopted by nationalist Albanians as a way to unify their kinsmen of different faiths. The committee received support from some pious Muslim Albanians as well as from the Ottoman religious authorities, who issued a fatwā in 1910 declaring that for a Muslim using another alphabet was a sin.[35] When in 1914 Westernizers suggested a similar change for the entire empire and challenged religious opinion by maintaining that there was no relationship between the script and religion, the CUP leaders prohibited the publication of their articles.[36] Despite their strong modernist proclivities, the CUP leaders felt that the Islamic character of the alphabet was too important to be challenged.

While in Jerusalem on his way to Beirut in 1907, Mustafa Kemal apparently discussed the issue with Eliezer Ben-Yehuda, a leading figure in the revival of Hebrew as a modern spoken language. On that occasion, he allegedly vowed that if he should occupy a position of authority in the future, he would impose the

[33] Agâh Sırrı Levend, *Türk Dilinde Gelişme ve Sadeleşme Evreleri* (Ankara: Türk Dil Kurumu Yayınları, 1960), 153–58.

[34] Ibid., 360.

[35] Ibid., 363–64.

[36] See "Latin Harfleri," *Hürriyet-i Fikriye* 7 (April 2, 1914): 15–16ff.; and Kılıçzâde Hakkı, "İzmir İktisad Kongresi'nde Harfler Mes'elesi," *İctihad* 154 (June 1, 1923): 1375.

Figure 16. Mustafa Kemal teaching the new alphabet in Kayseri (1928).
Source: *Fotoğrafla Atatürk* (Istanbul: Cumhuriyet, 1939) [picture 101].

Latin alphabet instead of going for piecemeal, technical reform.[37] In fact, when the discussion of the alphabet issue resurfaced following the establishment of the republic, Mustafa Kemal sided with those proposing the adoption of a Latin-based alphabet, dismissing conservative opposition with the statement, "The Arabic alphabet had not been revealed by [the angel] Gabriel."[38]

In the summer of 1928, Mustafa Kemal cut short debate on the subject in a landmark speech in Istanbul, deriding the Arabo-Persian alphabet as a collection of "incomprehensible signs that we cannot understand and that squeeze our minds in an iron frame."[39] Despite requests for an extended period of transition, he enjoined an abrupt switch and a widespread mobilization to teach the new alphabet to the masses. To symbolize the transition, he ordered that all ship names be repainted immediately in Latin characters. Two months later the Turkish Grand National Assembly adopted a law ordering an immediate switch to "international" letters.[40] As a result, Turkey—which was surrounded by countries that continued to employ non-Latin alphabets—drifted farther away from the Muslim world and closer to Europe.

An ostensibly minor change in the national calendar represented yet another significant cultural transformation undertaken at Mustafa Kemal's behest. In December 1925, Turkey switched officially

---

[37] Nuyan Yiğit, *Atatürk'le 30 Yıl: İbrahim Süreyya Yiğit'in Öyküsü* (Istanbul: Remzi Kitabevi, 2004), 20–21; Uluğ İğdemir, *Atatürk'ün Yaşamı*, vol. 1, *1881–1918* (Ankara: Türk Tarih Kurumu Yayınları, 1980), 23–25. Ben-Yehuda's son provides a different account of this exchange; see Jacob M. Landau, *Jews, Arabs, Turks: Selected Essays* (Jerusalem: Magnes Press, 1993), 197–98.

[38] Levend, *Türk Dilinde Gelişme*, 397.

[39] "Türk Yazı İnkılâbı Hakkında Konuşma, 8.VIII.1928," in *Atatürk'ün Söylev ve Demeçleri*, vol. 2, 254.

[40] "Türk Harfleri Kanunu" (Law #1353, November 3, 1928), in *Türkiye Cumhuriyeti Sicilli Kavanini*, ed. Karakoç Sarkiz, vol. 5 (Istanbul: Cihan Matbaası, 1930), 3–4.

to the Gregorian calendar,[41] which calculates years from the time of the birth of Jesus, and abandoned the two traditional Muslim calendars that had been in use during the Ottoman era: the Hijrī calendar, which uses the traditional Arab lunar months and counts years from the Prophet Muḥammad's flight from Mecca to Medina in 622, and the Rūmī calendar, which combines the solar months of the Julian calendar with a divergent numbering of the years according to the Hijrī era. Although newspapers and journals in the Late Ottoman Period had begun to provide Gregorian dates in addition to traditional dates, and the Ottoman foreign ministry had been using the Gregorian calendar in most of its correspondence since the second half of the nineteenth century, a full switch to the Christian calendar produced a new concept of time devoid of any connection to Islam. This development also produced confusion in the field of cultural memory, since the new generations could no longer understand certain folk terms coined for important events, such as "the War of 93," a reference to the Rūmī year 1293, in which the Russo-Ottoman War of 1877–78 began; "the Revolution of 1324"—the Young Turk Revolution of 1908, which took place in Rūmī 1324; or "the fifteeners"—the Ottoman soldiers who were born in Hijrī 1315 (1897–98) and drafted during the mobilization immediately prior to the Great War. The acceptance of the Western way of reckoning the time of day, instead of *Ezanî* time, which was related to the times of Muslim prayers and reckoned from sunset, added further to the de-Islamization of time.[42] The final blow came in May 1935 when the weekly holiday was switched from the Muslim Friday to the Christian Sunday.[43]

[41] "Takvimde Tarih-i Mebde'nin Tebdili Hakkında Kanun" (Law #698, December 26, 1925), in Karakoç, ed., *Sicill-i Kavânin*, vol. 2, 27.

[42] "Günün 24 Saate Taksimine Dair Kanun" (Law #697, December 26, 1925); ibid., 27.

[43] "Ulusal Bayram ve Genel Tatiller Hakkında Kanun" (Law #2739, May 27, 1935), in *Düstûr*, III/16 (Ankara: Başvekâlet Matbaası, 1935), 1171.

As these examples illustrate, Mustafa Kemal wished the Turks to internalize "international" culture and values in every aspect of their lives. To use a concept coined by Jürgen Habermas,[44] he wished to inculcate "aesthetic modernity" as well as social modernity, two concepts he believed to be causally linked. This is why he passionately advocated transformation in both architecture and the arts. Thus, for example, in addition to promoting Western fine arts such as sculpture and painting, the regime also adopted a new reform program to encourage Turks to listen to and enjoy homophonic music produced in Western styles.

In 1914, while serving as Ottoman military attaché in Sofia, Mustafa Kemal attended a performance of Georges Bizet's opera *Carmen*. Both the performance and the newly completed neo-Byzantine opera building impressed him deeply. It was not that a taste for Western music was anything new in Late Ottoman society. Sultan Abdülhamid II, for instance, loved opera and invited stars like the Belgian coloratura soprano Blanche Arral to perform for him in the privacy of his palace;[45] but he had no desire to disseminate Western music to the wider public. By contrast, Mustafa Kemal, who enjoyed traditional Turkish songs and knew only a handful of arias, such as "Recondita Armonia" from Giacomo Puccini's *Tosca*, aspired to make Western music the average Turk's music of choice.[46] For him this was not a matter of individual taste but a matter of progress. He is said to have remarked that after attending the opera in Sofia he understood

---

[44] Jürgen Habermas, "Modernity versus Postmodernity," trans. Seyla Ben-Habib, *New German Critique* 9/22 (1981): 9ff.

[45] Blanche Arral, *The Extraordinary Operatic Adventures of Blanche Arral*, ed. Ira Glackens and William R. Moran (Portland, OR: Amadeus Press, 2002), 200–203.

[46] Osman Ergin, *Türkiye Maarif Tarihi*, vol. 5 (Istanbul: Osmanbey Matbaası, 1943), 1520ff.; Gönül Paçacı, "Cumhuriyet'in Sesli Serüveni," in *Cumhuriyet'in Sesleri*, ed. Gönül Paçacı (Istanbul: Tarih Vakfı, 1999), 25.

how the Bulgarians had defeated the Ottomans the previous year.[47]

Accordingly, shortly after the establishment of the republic, Mustafa Kemal initiated a music reform program. In 1924 he transferred the Imperial Band (later the Presidential Symphony Orchestra) to Ankara. In the same year, a school for educating music teachers was established in the new capital. The Ottoman Darü'l-elhân (House of Melodies) became the Istanbul Conservatory, and its Oriental music branch was closed in 1926. The closure of the *tekye*s of the Şūfīs in 1925 had already dealt a tremendous blow to the production and performance of traditional music. In 1928, while listening to the famous Egyptian singer, Munīra al-Mahdiyya, Mustafa Kemal decided on a more radical measure. "This Oriental music . . . this primitive music is not sufficient to express the Turk's spirit and intense feelings," as he put it.[48] The regime then started sending numerous talented young musicians to Europe for training. Starting in the late 1920s, a leading Turkish composer, Cemal Reşit (Rey), composed Western-style orchestral pieces on Turkish themes, including his "Turkish Panoramas."[49]

In June 1934 a major musical event was staged linking the music reform initiative to the Turkish history thesis. Mustafa Kemal commissioned from composer Adnan Saygun a Turkish opera named *Özsoy* (Genuine Ancestor) to be composed and performed during the visit of the Shah of Iran to Turkey that summer. He himself edited the libretto, which, based partly on Firdawsī's *Shāhnāme* and partly on Turkic mythology, advanced the thesis that Turks and Iranians were true brothers sharing the same lin-

---

[47] Turan, *Kendine Özgü Bir Yaşam*, 126.

[48] "Türk Yazı İnkılâbı Hakkında Konuşma, 8.VIII.1928," in *Atatürk'ün Söylev ve Demeçleri*, vol. 2, 255.

[49] Yılmaz Aydın, *Türkiye'nin Avrupa ile Müzik İlişkileri Işığında Türk Beşleri* (Ankara: Müzik Ansiklopedisi Yayınları, 2003), 25ff.

eage. A few months later, in a speech delivered at the beginning of the new legislative year, Atatürk gave the signal for a more drastic reform. Stridently criticizing *Alla Turca* (traditional) music, he urged the authorities to upgrade "Turkish national music" to make it part of "international music."[50] The Ministry of the Interior responded two days later in an official communiqué: "Taking inspiration from the enlightenment regarding traditional music provided by His Excellency the Gazi, the Ministry of the Interior has instructed all relevant parties that, starting this evening, *Alla Turca* music will be removed altogether from radio programs and that only those national music compositions using Western musical techniques and played by musicians familiar with Western practices may be performed."[51] Likewise, local and municipal authorities issued strict prohibitions of any performance of Turkish monophonic music, and even briefly considered banning records of traditional music. They also barred those who attempted to perform monophonic music under deceptive rubrics such as "modern Alla Turca music." Meanwhile Atatürk invited the celebrated German music theorist and composer Paul Hindemith, who had a troubled relationship with the Nazi regime, to visit Turkey and reform Turkish music through new institutions.[52] On Hindemith's recommendation, the Ankara Conservatory opened its doors in 1936. Despite all these efforts, the general public showed little interest in music reform, and abandoned Turkish radio stations for Radio Cairo. Although the authorities lifted the absolute ban on broadcasting traditional Turkish music in September 1936, much

[50] "Reisicumhur Gazi Hazretlerinin T.B.M. Meclisinin IVüncü Devre Dördüncü Toplantı Yılını Açış Nutku," in *Atatürk'ün T.B.M.M. Açık ve Gizli Oturumlarındaki Konuşmaları*, vol. 2, ed. Kâzım Öztürk (Ankara: Kültür Bakanlığı Yayınları, 1992), 1096–97.

[51] *Atatürk ile Küğ: Belgeler ve Veriler*, ed. Gültekin Oransay (İzmir: Küğ Yayını, 1985), 49. See also "Alaturka Musikiye Paydos!" *Vakit*, November 2, 1934.

[52] Michael H. Kater, *Composers of the Nazi Era: Eight Portraits* (New York: Oxford University Press, 2000), 31ff.

of the programming continued to be devoted to Western music, or to the new Turkish homophonic imitations of it. The use of Western-style music for state propaganda was attempted with Necil Kâzım Akses's opera *Bay Önder* (Mr. Leader), the libretto of which was again edited by Atatürk in 1934. However, little benefit accrued to the regime from these initiatives, and the whole project was gradually dropped.[53] Music reform was an attempt to promote Western music through state sponsorship and to increase the number of citizens enjoying this international art form. It did not target any particular religious icon or concept, but like many other cultural projects of the Kemalist era, it expressed a strong desire to make Turkey a part of the West.

All these efforts at social engineering, many of which appear quixotic in hindsight, stemmed from a strong ideological commitment to forcing Turkey to absorb "civilization" and in the process become an integral part of the "civilized world." The far-reaching reforms instigated by Mustafa Kemal encompassed the totality of life: from speech to writing, from modes of dress to art, from conceptions of history to the very definition of time, and from the inculcation of a sense of belonging to the construction of identity. It would be simplistic to dismiss these reforms as superficial changes that stood no chance of penetrating society below the level of the elite. Despite their more limited effect on the masses, they changed Turkish society dramatically while molding a new elite with a new weltanschauung. A European visiting Ankara in 1938 would have found the city much more Western than the highly cosmopolitan capital of the Ottoman Empire in 1918. The new, modern section of Ankara with its cubical, functional architecture resembled a medium-sized European town.[54] Its population—mostly bureaucrats—dressed,

[53] Füsun Üstel, "1920'li ve 30'lu Yıllarda 'Millî Musiki' ve 'Musiki İnkılabı,'" in *Cumhuriyet'in Sesleri*, 48.

[54] Sibel Bozdoğan, *Modernism and Nation Building: Turkish Architectural*

lived, and entertained like Europeans. Nevzat Tandoğan, who had become the governor of the province in 1929, did not allow shabbily dressed or traditionally garbed people enter the new, sanitized section of the city.[55] A European visitor would have been able to decipher some signs written in the modified Latin alphabet, such as "telefon," to do business on a Friday, and to make sense of the date.

One could argue that Ankara was not representative of the rest of Turkey. Like Reza Shah Pahlavi's ban on photographs of aspects of Iran that did not look Western,[56] Mustafa Kemal's dramatic edicts did not have much of an impact outside the capital. To be sure, even though it monopolized the tools of propaganda, the Turkish republican regime could not transform society as a whole. Its agents, such as the People's Houses and People's Chambers, were too weak to indoctrinate a predominantly rural population, a significant portion of which was still illiterate and deeply attached to tradition.[57] However, Mustafa Kemal's reforms went well beyond the mainly "cosmetic" measures adopted by the Shah of Iran, and their influence extended far beyond isolated "green zones."[58] A large section of the elite internalized the new modernism and indeed considered it the only possible form of modernity. Although this segment of the population had few links to the "traditional" elements of society, it was quite large compared to its counterparts in Iran or Afghanistan. And over time, the new state-sponsored modernity has compelled

---

Culture in the Early Republic (Seattle: University of Washington Press, 2001), 223–25.

[55] L. Funda Şenol Cantek, *"Yaban"lar ve Yerliler: Başkent Olma Sürecinde Ankara* (Istanbul: İletişim Yayınları, 2003), 218–24.

[56] Vincent Monteil, *Iran: 'Petite Planète'* (Paris: Éditions du Seul, 1957), 13.

[57] Sefa Şimşek, *Bir İdeolojik Seferberlik Deneyimi: Halkevleri, 1932–1951* (Istanbul: Boğaziçi Üniversitesi Yayınevi, 2002), 224–25.

[58] For a stimulating comparison between the two cases, see Touraj Atabaki and Erik J. Zürcher, *Men of Order: Authoritarian Modernization under Atatürk and Reza Shah* (London: I. B. Tauris, 2004).

even the proponents of tradition to respond. The importance of the emergence of a new elite, and of the urban upper and middle classes enthusiastically supportive of the new ideology, should not be underestimated. These segments of society, and the ideology they espouse, have ruled modern Turkey since the inception of the republic.

Although the regime's Westernizing reforms contributed to de-Islamization, they did not achieve a completely non-Islamic society. The reforms affected those strongly committed to Islam as well as other conservatives along with everyone else. In Clifford Geertz's analysis,[59] a strikingly different Turkish Islam emerged in the wake of Mustafa Kemal's reform program. In the early stages of the reform period, the Egyptian sheikh Muḥammad al-Ghunaymī al-Taftāzānī expressed the fear that the Qur'ān would soon be seen in Turkey only in museums.[60] Events proved him wrong. Instead of disappearing from Turkey, Turkish Islam redefined its relationship with modernity. During the early republican transformation, few could have envisaged an Islamist party leading Turkey on the path to membership in the European Union.

Thus, while Mustafa Kemal's vision of making Turkey a part of the West was not fully realized, it was far from being a complete failure. Although a small number of people in Turkey today pay much attention to the Turkish history thesis of the 1930s, a majority of the Turkish population views Turkey as a genuinely European country. The notion of Turkey as an Asiatic country is an alien if not insulting one for many Turks. Thus when the Union of European Football Associations did not accept Turkey's membership applications between 1954 and 1962, and instead recommended membership in the Asian Football Confederation, the

[59] Clifford Geertz, *Islam Observed: Religious Development in Morocco and Indonesia* (Chicago: University of Chicago Press, 1971), 1ff.

[60] Gotthard Jäschke, "Der Islam in der neuen Türkei: eine Rechtsgeschichtliche Untersuchung," *Die Welt des Islams* 1/1–2 (1951): 168–69.

Turkish authorities rejected the idea in the strongest terms, with the claim that Turkey was not and had never been an Asiatic country. More recently, French President Nicolas Sarkozy's remark "I do not think Turkey has a right to join the European Union because it is not European"[61] provoked a public outcry in Turkey and was condemned by politicians and intellectuals from across the political spectrum. A great majority of Turks maintain that any challenge to the European character of Turkey stems from ignorance and deep-seated prejudice. Yet as Turkey's EU accession process has also shown, the majority of Europeans do not view Turkey as part of the West. Thus, while Mustafa Kemal succeeded in his prime objective of creating a new sense of belonging to Europe among large segments of the Turkish population, he failed to persuade Europeans to embrace Turkey as a society sharing their culture and values.

[61] "Making France a Power for the Future-I," *National Interest Online*, April 17, 2007, accessed January 9, 2009 at http://www.nationalinterest.org/Article .aspx?id=14044.

Conclusion

This study has shown that while Mustafa Kemal Atatürk played a momentous role in the transition from the Ottoman order to modern Turkey, his work cannot be considered that of a sagelike dispenser of wisdom who came to the scene with novel ideas and an original program.

First, Atatürk was no thinker of the order of Auguste Comte, Karl Marx, or Vladimir Il'ich Lenin. He was not a philosopher who produced a systematic theory attempting to encompass all aspects of life and society. He was not even a devout disciple of an ideology, nor did he try to reinterpret and implement a philosophy within a society, as Brazilian leaders did when they made positivism the official ideology of their state. Indeed, a scholar of political theory might find Atatürk's ideas extremely pragmatic and thin on content. Rather, he was a down-to-earth leader who strove to realize a vision not by depending on any one ideology but by utilizing a range of sources—some with dubious intellectual pedigrees—without paying much attention to contradictions among them. The magnitude of Mustafa Kemal's achievements should not blind us to the fact that he was not even the initiator of this vision. The Westernizers of the Second Constitutional Period had envisaged a Mannheimian utopia in which a scientistic society categorically rejected tradition and wholeheartedly embraced a modernity within the parameters of an "international civilization." Mustafa Kemal, as an "authoritarian savior," brought this utopia to fruition; thus, his role was that of an interpreter and executor. More precisely, he was the individual who transformed an intellectual utopia envisaged by a marginal group into a political program and then proceeded to implement it vigorously as head of state.

Consequently, despite the radical changes that it brought about, the Turkish transformation led by Atatürk was not a rupture with the Late Ottoman past but, in important respects, its continuation. The ideas he espoused had been widely discussed in detail long before the republican reforms, and were not novelties originated by the founder of the republic. Had the Great War not occurred, the normal evolution of Ottoman society would not, in all likelihood, have brought about the triumph of these ideas in the 1920s. Fundamental political and societal changes prompted by the Great War and the subsequent Ottoman collapse provided an unforeseen impetus to this process. These events also weakened existing structures that might otherwise have been better able to oppose radical reforms. Mustafa Kemal's rise to power coincided with and was made possible by the breakdown of the empire, the War of Independence, and the process of state-building that followed.

The predicament of the Ottoman Empire in the years following the Armistice of Mudros required a determined and innovative leadership to resist the implementation of the settlement the Allies sought to impose, to create a new political order, to organize an exceedingly difficult military campaign, and then to transform the heartland of the empire into a nation-state. Mustafa Kemal's remarkable achievements as a soldier and national leader who fought and won a war against apparently insurmountable odds undoubtedly helped him capture the unchallengeable aura of infallibility that came to pervade his leadership. Although it has been overlooked by Western historiography as a minor postwar affair in the Near East, the struggle he led and unexpectedly brought to a triumphant conclusion marked the first challenge to the new world order unilaterally imposed by the seemingly invincible victors. Only a leader with such an astounding record had the power to implement a utopia of the kind envisaged by Mustafa Kemal. Here Robert Tucker's concept of "situationism,"[1] according to which societal conditions largely predetermine the characteristics of the individual that will emerge as the leader, is a far better explanatory device for Atatürk's career than the "great man theory" most commonly associated with the founder of modern Turkey. The key to Atatürk's success, in other words, lay not in the originality of his ideas but in the singularity of the opportunity he seized.

An amalgam of scientism, materialism, social Darwinism, positivism, Turkism, and other popular theories provided Mustafa Kemal with a grand utopian framework for understanding the past and anticipating the future. He was not a Marxist, but he developed a similarly unlimited confidence in his beliefs regarding where the world was going and where his own society had its place in this evolutionary process. An unwavering scientistic faith in the alleged rules of human evolution provided the certainty needed to transcendentalize the vision and implement it as an imperative imposed by modernity. Atatürk truly believed that this supreme ideal was not just the best one, but also the essential one for Turkish society. Like other utopians, he did not let minor details, discomfiting realities, or latent contradictions stand in the way of realizing the grandeur of his vision. To understand and interpret modernity, the main pillar of his vision, he took inspiration from numerous intellectual and political trends of fin-de-siècle and early-twentieth-century Europe and the Ottoman world, such as German vulgar materialism; Thomas Henry Huxley's moral Darwinism; H. G. Wells's cosmological juxtaposition of time, space, and the human in history; Gustave Le Bon's elitism; nationalism;

---

[1] Robert C. Tucker, "Personality and Political Leadership," *Political Science Quarterly* 92/3 (1977): 383–93.

racial anthropology; and early-twentieth-century authoritarian-ism, as well as the ideas of the Enlightenment. These helped him to quickly construct a visionary framework that stood in substantial contradiction to the reality in which he lived. He acquired most of his ideas from Western and Ottoman popularizers of grand theo-ries. For instance, he learned scientism and social Darwinism from Ludwig Büchner and H. G. Wells, elitism from Gustave Le Bon, nationalism from Ottoman journals, and solidarism from Ziya Gökalp. In many cases he came to know about these European ideas from intellectual discussions that took place in the Ottoman Empire, in the course of which Ottoman intellectuals tried to apply these concepts in a domestic context. In addition, in order to advance his theses, he did not hesitate to use theories developed by obscure scholars such as Kvergić or even occult writers such as James Churchward. The quality of these substantiating theses was of little importance since Atatürk's principal aim was to realize a broad vision. The various ideas he collected tended to be tools for the implementation of his grand project, not goals in and of them-selves. Consequently, his intellectual reach knew no limits; as a visionary, he took anything that seemed useful from any source in order to further his political program and realize his utopia.

Atatürk was a product of the social realities of his time. The environment in which he lived compelled him to pick and choose certain pieces to complete his vision. His Salonican background, his education at nonreligious and military schools, his service in the army, his participation in the Young Turk movement, and his membership in the Committee of Union and Progress (CUP)—all these played substantial roles in shaping his views and forming his concept of utopia. Thus, not surprisingly, his leanings as a lit-eratus reflected the tension between the traditional and the mod-ern evident in Ottoman society since the Tanzimat. Typical of this background were the unflinching scientism that viewed reli-gion as the major obstacle to human progress, the perception of a single modernity to the exclusion of other possibilities, and an authoritarian organization monopolizing politics for the lofty aim of serving the public good. Not everyone who had gone through the same processes would embrace an identical vision, and some Westernizers who envisaged a somewhat similar utopia had different backgrounds; but the stages of his evolution from a Salonican Muslim boy to the leader of the Turkish nationalist movement undoubtedly molded Atatürk's vision and his capacity to implement it.

In this new utopian state, it was nationalism sanctified by science that would reign supreme as the new religion. This was not something that the Westernizers of the Second Constitutional Period had ever proposed; Atatürk's conception of utopia as Turkish nationalist in character was bold and original. Yet in the final analysis, he was a product of the age of nationalism. Like many literati of his generation influenced by Émile Durkheim's theses, he assumed that while science would triumph over religion, it was the role of nationalism to provide new identities to replace religious ones. In his view, a secular nation-state in which religion played a minimum role and gradually faded away was the perfect form of political community. In his own terms, the principles on which such a community would be based should not be confused with "the dogmas of books thought to have descended from the heavens"; they were not inspired by clues from "the heavens or the invisible world, but directly from life."[2] Naturally, this scientistic-nationalist vision overtly conflicted with Islam. It was in that sense that Atatürk was one of the most important shapers of the modern Muslim world. He faced dilemmas quite similar to those confronting the Muslim modernists of his day. But his vantage point was

---

[2] "Reisicumhur Kemal Atatürk'ün T.B.M. Meclisinin Vinci Devre Üçüncü Toplantı Yılını Açış Nutku," in *Atatürk'ün T.B.M.M. Açık ve Gizli Oturumlarındaki Konuşmaları*, vol. 2, ed. Kâzım Öztürk (Ankara: Kültür Bakanlığı Yayınları, 1992), 1135.

exactly the opposite. Whereas Muḥammad ʿAbduh worried about how to reconcile modern Western headgear with Islam, Mustafa Kemal was bent on reconciling Islam with the practice of wearing a hat. In his view, only an Islam open to modernity—indeed enthusiastically promoting it—would help convince the masses of the need to embrace it. His attempts at Islamic reformation, which went back to the original sources in search of arguments to justify modernity, differed dramatically from other Islamic movements of the early twentieth century; Salafism, for example, proposed a similar return to the sources, but for the purpose of recovering a pure, premodern Islam. Atatürk did not attempt to provide Islamic responses to the challenges of modernity but tried to transform Islam into a system fully embracing it.

It was nevertheless his view that even a thoroughly reformed Islam ought not to play a determining role in society. The republic he founded embraced a version of *laïcité* more radical than that of the French republic on which it was modeled, and it maintained strict control of organized religion. This was a wrenching program for a predominantly Muslim society of the early twentieth century. And yet Atatürk's emulators in the second half of the twentieth century, such as Ḥabīb Būrqība of Tunisia, scored fewer successes. In part this was due to the differences between the Turkish heartland of the Ottoman Empire and the more traditionally inclined Arab world. Indeed, many Ottoman practices had been judged idolatrous within the empire's Arab provinces long before Atatürk's modernizing reforms. Nevertheless, although the Ottoman center after the Great War was ripe for change, the transformation that took place during Atatürk's lifetime was an unusually drastic one by the standards of the period.

The radicalism of Atatürk's program led to the authoritarian character of his politics. Like many other transformative state builders, he harbored little tolerance for dissent or criticism. He regarded the Republican People's Party as his main agent of reform and insisted on its hegemony. Like the CUP leaders who had abandoned democratic politics when it jeopardized their program, Mustafa Kemal resorted to single-party rule in order to execute his agenda without compromise. Since, in his eyes, the mission was historically preordained, all measures were permissible to assure its success.

Having implemented a substantial portion of his program, Mustafa Kemal Atatürk died on November 10, 1938, at the age of fifty-seven. His legacy has lived on in Turkey and, to a lesser degree, in the Muslim world. His intellectual contribution did not amount to a coherent ideology, but various interpretations of his work have developed under the title Kemalism and, more recently, Atatürkism. Although the Turkish establishment invested considerable effort in developing Kemalism as an official ideology, especially after 1960, it is often difficult to relate the evolving state doctrine of Kemalism to Atatürk's own legacy. None of this is to underestimate the dramatic transformation that he led or to belittle its present-day ramifications. In his single-minded efforts to realize his utopia, Mustafa Kemal Atatürk brought about a drastic reshaping of Turkish state and society. Neither Turkey nor the Muslim world will ever be the same again.

BIBLIOGRAPHY

Official Publications

C.II.P. Dördüncü Büyük Kurultayı Görüşmeleri Tutulgası, 9–16 Mayıs 1935. Ankara: Ulus Basımevi, 1935.

Cümhuriyet Halk Fırkası Nizamnamesi ve Programı. Ankara: T.B.M.M. Matbaası, 1931.

Düstûr, I/2. Istanbul: Matbaa-i Âmire, 1289 (1872).

Düstûr, II/1. Istanbul: Matbaa i Osmaniye, 1329 (1911).

Düstûr, II/9. Istanbul: Evkaf Matbaası, 1928.

Düstûr, II/11. Istanbul: Evkaf Matbaası, 1928.

Düstûr, II/12. Istanbul: Evkaf Matbaası, 1927.

Düstûr, III/16. Ankara: Başvekâlet Matbaası, 1935.

Guerre Européenne: Documents 1918: Conventions d'armistice passées avec la Turquie, la Bulgarie, l'Autriche-Hongrie et l'Allemagne par les puissances Alliées et associées. Paris: Ministère des Affaires Étrangères, 1919.

T.B.M.M. Gizli Celse Zabıtları, vol. 2 (17 Mart 1337 [1921]–25 Şubat 1337 [1922]); vol. 3 (6 Mart 1338 [1922]–27 Şubat 1338 [1923]); vol. 4 (2 Mart 1339 [1923]–25 Teşrin-i evvel 1939). Ankara: T. İş Bankası Kültür Yayınları, 1985.

T. C. 1982 Anayasası: 1993 Değişiklikleriyle, ed. A. Şeref Gözübüyük. Ankara: Turhan Yayınevi, (1993).

Türkiye Büyük Millet Meclisi Kavânin Mecmuası, vol.1. Ankara: Büyük Millet Meclisi Matbaası, 1925.

Türkiye Cumhuriyeti Sicill-i Kavânini, ed. Karakoç Sarkiz, vols. 1–2. Istanbul: Cihan Matbaası, 1926.

Türkiye Cumhuriyeti Sicill-i Kavânini, ed. Karakoç Sarkiz, vol. 4. Istanbul: Cihan Matbaası, 1928.

Türkiye Cumhuriyeti Sicilli Kavanini, ed. Karakoç Sarkiz, vol. 5. Istanbul: Cihan Matbaası, 1930.

Türkiye Cumhuriyeti Sicilli Kavanini, ed. Sarkiz Karakoç, vol. 18 (Istanbul: Cihan Kitaphanesi, 1938).

Türkiye Cumhuriyeti Sicilli Kavanini, vol. 32. Istanbul: Cihan Kitaphanesi, 1951.

Primary Sources and Biographies of Atatürk

Âfetinan [İnan, Ayşe Âfet]. *Atatürk Hakkında Hâtıralar ve Belgeler.* Ankara: Türkiye İş Bankası Yayınları, 1959.

———. *Medenî Bilgiler ve M. Kemal Atatürk'ün El Yazıları.* Ankara: Türk Tarih Kurumu Yayınları, 1969.

Akyol, Taha. *Ama Hangi Atatürk.* Istanbul: Doğan Kitap, 2008.

Atatürk, Mustafa Kemal. *Anafartalar Muharebatı'na Ait Tarihçe,* ed. Uluğ İğdemir. Ankara: Türk Tarih Kurumu Yayınları, 1962.

———. *Arıburnu Muharebeleri Raporu,* ed. Uluğ İğdemir. Ankara: Türk Tarih Kurumu Yayınları, 1968.

———. *Atatürk'ten Düşünceler,* ed. Enver Ziya Karal. Ankara: Türkiye İş Bankası Kültür Yayınları, 1956.

———. *Atatürk'ün Anıları: "Büyük Gazimizin Büyük Hayatından Hatıralar,"* ed. İsmet Görgülü. Ankara: Bilgi Yayınevi 1997.

———. *Atatürk'ün Bütün Eserleri,* vol. 1, *1903–1915.* Istanbul: Kaynak Yayınları, 1998.

———. *Atatürk'ün Bütün Eserleri,* vol. 2, *1915–1919.* Istanbul: Kaynak Yayınları, 1999.

———. *Atatürk'ün Bütün Eserleri,* vol. 9, *1920.* Istanbul: Kaynak Yayınları, 2002.

———. *Atatürk'ün Bütün Eserleri,* vol. 10, *1920–1921.* Istanbul: Kaynak Yayınları, 2003.

———. *Atatürk'ün Bütün Eserleri,* vol. 13, *1922.* Istanbul: Kaynak Yayınları, 2004.

————. *Atatürk'ün Bütün Eserleri*, vol. 15, *1923*. Istanbul: Kaynak Yayınları, 2005.

————. *Atatürk'ün Bütün Eserleri*, vol. 16, *1924*. Istanbul: Kaynak Yayınları, 2005.

————. *Atatürk'ün Bütün Eserleri*, vol. 24, *1930–1931*. Istanbul: Kaynak Yayınları, 2008.

————. *Atatürk'ün Hatıra Defteri*, ed. Şükrü Tezer. Ankara: Türk Tarih Kurumu Yayınları, 1972, 65–92.

————. *Atatürk'ün Not Defterleri*, vol. 2, *Harp Akademisi Öğrencisi Mustafa Kemal'in Not Defteri*. Ankara: Genelkurmay ATASE Yayınları, 2004.

————. *Atatürk'ün Söylev ve Demeçleri*, vol. 1, *T.B.M. Meclisinde ve C.H.P. Kurultaylarında, 1919–1938*. Istanbul: Türk İnkılâp Tarihi Enstitüsü Yayımları, 1945.

————. *Atatürk'ün Söylev ve Demeçleri*, vol. 2, *1906–1938*, ed. Nimet Unan. Ankara: Türk İnkılâp Tarihi Enstitüsü Yayımları, 1952.

————. *Atatürk'ün Söylev ve Demeçleri*, vol. 3, *1918–1937*, ed. Nimet Unan. Ankara: Türk İnkılâp Tarihi Enstitüsü Yayımları, 1954.

————. *Atatürk'ün Söylev ve Demeçleri*, vol. 4, *Atatürk'ün Tamim, Telgraf ve Beyannâmeleri, 1917–1938*, ed. Nimet Arsan. Ankara: Türk İnkılâp Tarihi Enstitüsü Yayımları, 1964.

————. *Atatürk'ün Söylev ve Demeçleri*, vol. 5, *Atatürk'ün Söylev ve Demeçleri Tamim ve Telgrafları*, ed. Sadi Borak and Utkan Kocatürk. Ankara: Türk İnkılâp Tarihi Enstitüsü Yayınları, 1972.

————. *Atatürk'ün T.B.M.M. Açık ve Gizli Oturumlarındaki Konuşmaları*, vol. 2, ed. Kâzım Öztürk. Ankara: Kültür Bakanlığı Yayınları, 1992.

————. *Gazi Mustafa Kemal Atatürk'ün 1923 Eskişehir- İzmit Konuşmaları*, ed. Arı İnan. Ankara: Türk Tarih Kurumu Yayınları, 1982.

————. *Gazi Mustafa Kemal Paşa Hazretleri'nin Bir Hitabesi: Halkçılık, Halk Hükûmeti, Hakimiyet Bilâ Kayd ü Şart Milletindir*. Ankara: Hakimiyet-i Milliye Matbaası, 1338 (1922).

————. *Hilâfet ve Saltanat Mes'elesi Hakkında Türkiye Büyük Millet Meclisi Re'isi Gazi Mustafa Kemal Paşa Hazretleri'nin Nutuk-*

ları. Ankara: Türkiya Büyük Millet Meclisi Matbaası, 1341/1338 (1922).

Atatürk, Mustafa Kemal. *M. Kemal Atatürk'ün Karlsbad Hatıraları,* ed. Ayşe Afetinan. Ankara: Türk Tarih Kurumu Yayınları, 1983, 29–61.

———. *Nutuk: Gazi Mustafa Kemal Tarafından.* Ankara: n.p., 1927.

———. *Sofya Askerî Ataşesi Mustafa Kemal'in Raporları (Kasım 1913–Kasım 1914),* ed. Ahmet Tetik. Ankara: Genelkurmay ATASE Yayınları, 2007.

Atatürk ile İlgili Arşiv Belgeleri, 1911–1921. Ankara: Başbakanlık Osmanlı Arşivi Daire Başkanlığı, 1982.

Atatürk'ün Okuduğu Kitaplar: Altını Çizdiği Satırları, Özel İşaretleri, Uyarıları, Düştüğü Notlar ve Kitap İçerisindeki Özel Yazıları İle, vols. 2–3, 5–10, 12, 16–24, ed. Recep Cengiz. Ankara: Anıtkabir Derneği Yayınları, 2001.

Atatürk'ün Okuduğu Kitaplar: Özel İşaretleri, Uyarıları ve Düştüğü Notlar İle, ed. D. Gürbüz Tüfekçi. Ankara: Türkiye İş Bankası Kültür Yayınları, 1983.

Atatürk'ün Özel Kütüphanesinin Kataloğu: Anıtkabir ve Çankaya Bölümleri. Ankara: Başbakanlık Kültür Müsteşarlığı, 1973.

Atay, Falih Rıfkı. *Çankaya: Atatürk'ün Doğumundan Ölümüne Kadar.* Istanbul: Sena Matbaası, 1960.

Aydemir, Şevket Süreyya. *Tek Adam: Mustafa Kemal,* vols. 1, 3. Istanbul: Remzi Kitabevi, 1981.

Bayur, Yusuf Hikmet. *Atatürk: Hayatı ve Eseri,* vol. 1, *Doğumundan Samsun'a Çıkışına Kadar.* Ankara: Güven Basımevi, 1963.

Bozok, Salih, and Bozok, Cemil S. *Hep Atatürk'ün Yanında: Baba Oğul Bozok'lardan Anılar.* Istanbul: Çağdaş Yayınları, 1985.

Cebesoy, Ali Fuat. *Sınıf Arkadaşım Atatürk: Okul ve Genç Subaylık Hâtıraları.* Istanbul: İnkılâp ve Aka, 1967.

[Ertuna, Hamdi]. *1911–1912 Osmanlı-İtalyan Harbi ve Kolağası Mustafa Kemal.* Ankara: Kültür Bakanlığı Yayınları, 1985.

İğdemir, Uluğ. *Atatürk'ün Yaşamı,* vol. 1, *1881–1918.* Ankara: Türk Tarih Kurumu Yayınları, 1980.

Kinross, Lord [Patrick]. *Ataturk: A Biography of Mustafa Kemal, Father of Modern Turkey.* New York: William Morrow, 1978.

Kreiser, Klaus. *Atatürk: eine Biographie*. Munich: Verlag C. H. Beck, 2008.

Leventoğlu, Mazhar. *Atatürk'ün Vasiyeti*. Istanbul: Bahar Matbaası, 1968.

Mango, Andrew. *Atatürk*. London: John Murray, 1999.

Mustafa Kemal Atatürk'ün İlk Gazetesi Minber: Açıklamalı Çevirisi, ed. Erol Kaya. Ankara: Ebabil Yayıncılık, 2007.

Ruşen Eşref. *Anafartalar Kumandanı Mustafa Kemal ile Mülâkat*. Istanbul: Hamit Matbaası, 1930.

Soyak, Hasan Rıza. *Atatürk'ten Hatıralar*, vol. 1. Ankara: Yapı ve Kredi Bankası Yayınları, n.d. [1973].

Turan, Şerafettin. *Atatürk'ün Düşünce Yapısını Etkileyen Olaylar, Düşünürler, Kitaplar*. Ankara: Türk Tarih Kurumu Yayınları, 1982.

———. *Mustafa Kemal Atatürk: Kendine Özgü Bir Yaşam ve Kişilik*. Istanbul: Bilgi Yayınevi, 2004.

Secondary Sources

Abadan-Unat, Nermin. "Social Change and Turkish Women." In *Women in Turkish Society*, ed. Nermin Abadan-Unat, 5–31. Leiden, Netherlands: Brill, 1981.

Adams, Charles C. "Muḥammad 'Abduh and the Transvaal Fatwā." In *The MacDonald Presentation Volume*. Princeton, NJ: Princeton University Press, 1933, 13-29.

Adanır, Fikret. "Kemalist Authoritarianism and Fascist Trends in Turkey during the Interwar Period." In *Fascism Outside Europe: The European Impulse against Domestic Conditions in the Diffusion of Global Fascism*, ed. Stein Ugelvik Larsen, 313–61. New York: Boulder, 2001.

Aksakal, Mustafa. *The Ottoman Road to War in 1914: The Ottoman Empire and the First World War*. Cambridge: Cambridge University Press, 2008.

'Alī 'Abd al-Rāziq. *Al-Islām wa-uṣūl al-ḥukm: baḥth fī al-Khilāfah wa-al-ḥukūmah fī al-Islām*. Cairo: Maṭba'at Miṣr, 1925.

Ali, Souad T. *A Religion Not a State: Ali 'Abd al-Raziq's Islamic Jus-*

tification of Political Secularism. Salt Lake City: University of Utah Press, 2009.

Alp, [Munis] Tekin [Moiz Kohen]. *Kemalizm*. Istanbul: Cumhuriyet Matbaası, 1936.

Anastassiadou, Meropi. *Salonique: 1830–1912: Une ville ottomane à l'âge des Réformes*. Leiden, Netherlands: Brill, 1997.

Apak, Rahmi. *Yetmişlik Bir Subayın Hatıraları*. Ankara: Türk Tarih Kurumu Yayınları, 1988.

Ardıç, Nureddin. *Antakya-İskenderun Etrafındaki Türk Davasının Tarihî Esasları*. Istanbul: Tecelli Matbaası, 1937.

Arnold, Thomas W. *The Caliphate*. New York: Barnes and Noble, 1967.

Arral, Blanche. *The Extraordinary Operatic Adventures of Blanche Arral*, ed. Ira Glackens and William R. Moran. Portland, OR: Amadeus Press, 2002.

Arslan, Ali. *Darülfünun'dan Üniversite'ye*. Istanbul: Kitabevi, 1995.

Atabaki, Touraj-Zürcher, Erik J. *Men of Order: Authoritarian Modernization under Atatürk and Reza Shah*. London: I. B. Tauris, 2004.

Atakuman, Çiğdem, "Cradle or Crucible: Anatolia and Archeology in the Early Years of the Turkish Republic, 1923–1938." *Journal of Social Archeology* 8/2 (2008): 214–35.

Atatürk ile Küğ: Belgeler ve Veriler, ed. Gültekin Oransay. İzmir: Küğ Yayını, 1985.

Avetian, A[ndrei] S[ergeevich]. *Germaniskii imperialism na blizhnem vostoke: kolonial'naia politika germanskogo imperializma i missia Limana fon Sandersa*. Moscow: Mezhdunarodnye otnosheniia, 1966.

Aybars, Ergün. *İstiklâl Mahkemeleri, 1920–1927*, vol. 2. İzmir: Dokuz Eylül Üniversitesi Yayınları, 1988.

Aydemir, Şevket Süreyya. *İkinci Adam*, vol. 2, *1938–1950*. Istanbul: Remzi Kitabevi, 1979.

Aydın, Ertan. "Peculiarities of Turkish Revolutionary Ideology in the 1930s: The *Ülkü* Version of Kemalism." *Middle Eastern Studies* 40/5 (September 2004): 55–82.

Aydın, Yılmaz. *Türkiye'nin Avrupa ile Müzik İlişkileri Işığında Türk Beşleri*. Ankara: Müzik Ansiklopedisi Yayınları, 2003.

Aykut, Şeref. *Kamâlizm: C.H. Partisi Programının İzahı.* Istanbul: Muallim Ahmet Halit Kitap Evi, 1936.

Aytürk, İlker. "H. F. Kvergić and the Sun-Language Theory." *Zeitschrift der deutschen morgenländischen Gesellschaft* 159/1 (2009): 23–44.

———. "Turkish Linguists against the West: The Origins of Linguistic Nationalism in Atatürk's Turkey." *Middle Eastern Studies* 40/6 (2004): 1–25.

Baer, Marc David. *The Dönme: Jewish Converts, Muslim Revolutionaries, and Secular Turks.* Stanford, CA: Stanford University Press, 2010.

Bali, Rıfat N. *New Documents on Atatürk: Atatürk as Viewed through the Eyes of American Diplomats.* Istanbul: Isis Press, 2007.

Barenton, Hilaire de. *L'origine des langues*, vols. 1–2. Paris: Maisonneuve, 1932.

Bartlett, Ellis Ashmead. *With the Turks in Thrace.* New York: G. H. Doran, 1913.

Bayar, Celâl. *Ben de Yazdım: Millî Mücadeleye Giriş*, vol. 2. Istanbul: Baha Matbaası, Istanbul, 1966.

———. *Celâl Bayar'ın Söylev ve Demeçleri*, vol. 1, *1921–1938, Ekonomik Konulara Dair*, ed. Özel Şahingiray. Ankara: Doğuş Ltd. Ortaklığı, 1955.

Ben Na'eh, Yaron. "Hebrew Printing Houses in the Ottoman Empire." In *Jewish Journalism and Printing Houses in the Ottoman Empire and Modern Turkey*, ed. Gad Nassi, 73–96. Istanbul: Isis Press, 2001.

Bennigsen, Alexandre, and Lemercier-Quelquejay, Chantal. *Sultan Galiev, le père de la révolution tiers-mondiste.* Paris: Fayard, 1986.

Birinci Türk Dili Kurultayı: Tezler Müzakere Zabıtları. Istanbul: Devlet Matbaası, 1933.

Birinci Türk Tarih Kongresi: Konferanslar Müzakere Zabıtları. Ankara: Maarif Vekâleti, 1932.

Bourbourg, M. [Charles Étienne] Brasseur de. *Dictionnaire, grammaire et chrestomathie de la langue Maya: précédés d'une étude sur le système graphique des indigènes du Yucatan (Mexique).* Paris: Maisonneuve, 1872.

Bozdoğan, Sibel. *Modernism and Nation Building: Turkish Architectural Culture in the Early Republic*. Seattle: University of Washington Press, 2001.

Bozkurt, Mahmut Esat. *Atatürk İhtilâli: Türk İnkılâbı Tarihi Enstitüsü Derslerinden*. Istanbul: İstanbul Üniversitesi Yayınları, 1940.

A Brief Record of the Advance of the Egyptian Expeditionary Force under the Command of General Sir Edmund H. H. Allenby, G.C.B., G.C.M.G., July 1917 to October 1918. London: His Majesty's Stationary Office, 1919.

Büchner, Ludwig. *Kraft und Stoff oder Grundzüge der natürlichen Weltordnung*, 16th ed. Leipzig, Germany: Verlag von Theodor Thomas, 1888.

Caetani, Leone. *Annali dell'Islām*, vol. 1. Milan: Ulrico Hoepli, 1905.

Cahun, Léon. *Fransa'da Arî Dillere Takaddüm Etmiş Olan Lehçenin Turanî Menşei*, trans. Ruşen Eşref. Istanbul: Cumhuriyet Matbaası, 1930.

———. *Introduction à l'histoire de l'Asie: Turcs et Mongoles des origines à 1405*. Paris: A. Colin, 1896.

Cantek, L. Funda Şenol. *"Yaban"lar ve Yerliler: Başkent Olma Sürecinde Ankara*. Istanbul: İletişim Yayınları, 2003.

Çelebi, Mevlüt. *Milli Mücadele Döneminde Türk-İtalyan İlişkileri*. Ankara: Dışişleri Bakanlığı, SAM, 1999.

Chatterton, E. Keble. *Dardanelles Dilemma: The Story of the Naval Operations*. London: Rich and Cowan, 1935.

Churchill, Winston S. *The World Crisis, 1918–1928: The Aftermath*. New York: Charles Scribner's Sons, 1929.

Churchward, James. *The Children of Mu*. New York: Ives Washburn, 1933.

———. *Cosmic Forces as They Were Taught in Mu: The Ancient Tale That Religion and Science Are Twin Sisters*. Mount Vernon, NY: Baker and Taylor, 1934.

———. *The Lost Continent of Mu: The Motherland of Man*. New York: Ives Washburn, 1931.

———. *The Sacred Symbols of Mu*. New York: Ives Washburn, 1933.

Congress of the Peoples of the East, Baku, September 1920: Stenographic Report, trans. Brian Pearce. London: New Park, 1977.

Cumhuriyet'in Sesleri, ed. Gönül Paçacı. Istanbul: Tarih Vakfı, 1999.

Cündioğlu, Dücane. *Bir Siyasî Proje Olarak Türkçe İbadet*, vol. 1, *Türkçe Namaz, 1923–1950*. Istanbul: Kitabevi, 1999.

———. *Türkçe Kur'an ve Cumhuriyet İdeolojisi*. Istanbul: Kitabevi, 1998.

Daddis, Gregory A. *Armageddon's Lost Lessons: Combined Arms Operations in Allenby's Palestine Campaign*. Air Command and Staff College Wright Flyer Paper 20. Maxwell Air Force Base, Alabama: Air University Press, 2005.

Dakin, Douglas. *The Greek Struggle in Macedonia, 1897–1913*. Thessaloniki, Greece: Institute for Balkan Studies, 1966.

Davison, Roderic H. *Reform in the Ottoman Empire, 1856–1876*. Princeton, NJ: Princeton University Press, 1963.

Demir, Tanju. "Cumhuriyet Dönemi Paralarında Siyaset ve İdeoloji, 1923–1950." In *75 Yılda Para'nın Serüveni*, ed. Mustafa Sönmez, 11–28. Istanbul: Tarih Vakfı Yayınları, 1998.

Demirel, Ahmet. *Birinci Meclis'te Muhalefet: İkinci Grup*. Istanbul: İletişim Yayınları, 1994.

Demirhan, Pertev. *Generalfeldmarschall Colmar Freiherr von der Goltz: das Lebensbild eines großen Soldaten: aus meinen persönlichen Erinnerungen*. Göttingen, Germany: Göttingen Verlagsanstalt, 1960.

Djelaleddin, Moustapha. *Les Turcs anciens et modernes*. Paris: Libraire Internationale, 1870.

Dogramaci, Burcu. *Kulturtransfer und nationale Identität: deutschsprachige Architekten, Stadtplaner und Bildhauer in der Türkei nach 1927*. Berlin: Gebr. Mann Verlag, 2008.

Dozy, Reinhart. *Essai sur l'histoire de l'Islamisme*, trans. Victor Chauvin. Paris: Maisonneuve, 1879.

Elibal, Gültekin. *Atatürk ve Resim Heykel*. Istanbul: Türkiye İş Bankası Kültür Yayınları, 1973.

Ellison, Grace. *Turkey To-Day*. London: Hutchinson, n.d. [1928].

Engin, M. Saffet. *Kemalizm İnkilâbının Prensipleri: Büyük Türk Mede-*

niyetinin Tarihî ve Sosyolojik Tetkikine Methal, vol. 1. Istanbul: Cumhuriyet Matbaası, 1938.

Erdem, Sami. "Cumhuriyet'e Geçiş Sürecinde Hilafet Teorisine Alternatif Yaklaşımlar: Seyyid Bey Örneği, 1922–1924." *Dîvân* 1/2 (1996): 119–46.

Ergin, Osman. *Türkiye Maarif Tarihi*, vol. 2, *Tanzimat Devri Mektepleri*. Istanbul: Osmanbey Matbaası, 1940.

———. *Türkiye Maarif Tarihi*, vol. 5. Istanbul: Osmanbey Matbaası, 1943.

[Eşref Edib]. *Hilâfet-i İslâmiye ve Büyük Millet Meclisi*. Ankara: Ali Şükrü Matbaası, 1339 (1923).

Eyice, Semavi. *Atatürk ve Pietro Canonica: Eserleri ve Türkiye Seyahatnâmesi ile Atatürk'e Dair Hatıraları*. Istanbul: Eren Yayıncılık, 1986.

Fouillée, Alfred. *Psychologie du peuple Français*. Paris: Félix Alcan, 1898.

Frierson, Elizabeth B. "Unimagined Communities: Women and Education in the Late-Ottoman Empire, 1876–1909." *Critical Matrix* 9/2 (1995): 55–90.

Geertz, Clifford. *Islam Observed: Religious Development in Morocco and Indonesia*. Chicago: University of Chicago Press, 1971.

Gerasimov, M[ikhail] M[ikhailovich]. "Portret Tamerlana: opyt skul'pturnogo vosproizvedeniya na kraniologicheskoi osnove." *Kratkie soobshcheniia istorii material'noi kul'tury* 17 (1947): 14–21.

Gladstone, W[illiam] E[wart]. *Bulgarian Horrors and the Question of the East*. London: John Murray, 1876.

Gökbilgin, M. Tayyib. *Rumeli'de Yürükler, Tatarlar ve Evlâd-ı Fâtihan*. Istanbul: Edebiyat Fakültesi Yayınları, 1957.

Gökçen, Sabiha. *Atatürk'le Bir Ömür*, ed. Oktay Verel. Istanbul: Altın Kitaplar Yayınevi, 1994.

Goltz, Colmar von der. *Denkwürdigkeiten*. Berlin: E. S. Mittler und sohn, 1929.

———. *Millet-i Müsellaha: Asrımızın Usûl ve Ahvâl-i Askeriyesi*, tr. Mehmed Tahir. Istanbul: Matbaa-i Ebüzziya, 1301(1886).

———. *The Nation in Arms: A Treatise on Modern Military Systems and the Conduct of War*, trans. Philip A. Ashworth. London: Hodder and Stoughton, 1914.

Graebner, Fritz. *Das Weltbild der primitiven; eine Untersuchung der Ur-formen weltanschaulichen Denkens bei Naturvölkern*. Munich: Verlag Ernst Reinhardt, 1924.

Gregory, Frederic. *Scientific Materialism in Nineteenth Century Germany*. Dordrecht, Netherlands: D. Reidel, 1977.

Grigg, John. *Lloyd George: From Peace to War, 1912–1916*. Berkeley and Los Angeles: University of California Press, 1985.

Grunwald, Kurt. *Türkenhirsch; A Study of Baron Maurice de Hirsch, Entrepreneur and Philanthropist*. Jerusalem: Israel Program for Scientific Translations, 1966.

Güneş, İhsan. *Türkiye Büyük Millet Meclisi'nin Düşünsel Yapısı, 1920–1923*. Eskişehir: Anadolu Üniversitesi Yayınları, 1985.

Habermas, Jürgen. "Modernity versus Postmodernity," trans. Seyla Ben-Habib. *New German Critique* 9/22 (1981): 3–14.

Haddon, Alfred C. *The Races of Man and Their Distribution*. Cambridge: Cambridge University Press, 1924.

[Halide Edib]. *The Turkish Ordeal: Being the Further Memoirs of Halidé Edib*. New York: Century, 1928.

Hanioğlu, M. Şükrü. *Bir Siyasal Düşünür Olarak Doktor Abdullah Cevdet ve Dönemi*. Istanbul: Üçdal Neşriyat, 1981.

———. "Blueprints for a Future Society: Late Ottoman Materialists on Science, Religion, and Art." In *Late Ottoman Society: The Intellectual Legacy*, ed. Elisabeth Özdalga, 28–116. London: RoutledgeCurzon, 2005.

———. "Garbcılar: Their Attitudes toward Religion and Their Impact on the Official Ideology of the Turkish Republic." *Studia Islamica* 86/2 (August 1997): 133–58.

———. *Preparation for a Revolution: The Young Turks, 1902–1908*. New York: Oxford University Press, 2001.

———. *The Young Turks in Opposition*. New York: Oxford University Press, 1995.

Harington, Charles. *Tim Harington Looks Back*. London: John Murray, 1940.

Hatipoğlu, Süleyman. *Filistin Cephesi'nden Adana'ya Mustafa Kemal Paşa*. Istanbul: Yeditepe, 2009.

Hayes, Carlton J[oseph] H[untley]. *A Generation of Materialism, 1871–1900*. London: Harper and Brothers, 1941.

Helmreich, Paul C. *From Paris to Sèvres: The Partition of the Ottoman Empire at the Peace Conference of 1919–1920*. Columbus: Ohio State University Press, n.d. [1974].

Henderson, Nevile. *Water under the Bridges*. London: Hodder and Stoughton, 1945.

Holbach, Paul–Henri Dietrich d'. *Le bon sens du curé Meslier, suivi de son testament*. Paris: Au Palais des Thermes de Julien, 1802.

Howard, Harry N. *The Partition of Turkey: A Diplomatic History, 1913–1923*. Norman: Oklahoma University Press, 1931.

İkinci Türk Tarih Kongresi: Kongrenin Çalışmaları, Kongreye Sunulan Tebliğler. Istanbul: Kenan Matbaası, 1943.

İnan, Abdülkadir. *Güneş-Dil Teorisi Ders Notları*. Istanbul: Devlet Basımevi, 1936.

[İnan], Afet. *L'Anatolie, le pays de la "Race" turque: Recherches sur les caractères anthropologiques des populations de la Turquie: Enquête sur 64.000 individus*. Geneva: Imprimerie Albert Kundig, 1939.

———. *Vatandaş İçin Medenî Bilgiler*, vol. 1. Istanbul: Devlet Matbaası, 1931.

[İnönü, İsmet]. *İnönü'nün Söylev ve Demeçleri*, vol. 1, *T.B.M. Meclisinde ve C.H.P Kurultaylarında, 1919–1946*. Istanbul: Türk Devrim Tarihi Enstitüsü Yayımları, 1946.

———. *İsmet İnönü: Lozan Barış Konferansı Konuşma, Demeç, Makale, Mesaj, Anı ve Söyleşileri*, ed. İlhan Turan. Ankara: Atatürk Araştırma Merkezi, 2003.

[İsmail Enver]. *Kendi Mektuplarında Enver Paşa*, ed. M. Şükrü Hanioğlu. Istanbul: Der Yayınları, 1989.

[İsmail] Hakkı Hafız. *Bozgun*. Istanbul: Matbaa-i Hayriye ve Şürekâsı, 1334 (1914).

Jäschke, Gotthard. "Der Islam in der neuen Türkei: Eine Rechtsgeschichtliche Untersuchung." *Die Welt des Islams* 1/1–2 (1951): 1–174.

Jollivet, Gaston, and L'Heureux, Marie-Anne. *Muhtelit İzdivaclar*, trans. Abdullah Cevdet. Istanbul: n.p., 1928.

————. *Mükemmel ve Resimli Âdâb-ı Mu'aşeret Rehberi*, trans. Abdullah Cevdet. Istanbul: Yeni Matbaa, 1927.

Kansu, Şevket Aziz. *Türk Antropoloji Enstitüsü Tarihçesi*. Istanbul: Maarif Matbaası, 1940.

Karabekir, Kâzım. *İstiklâl Harbimiz*. Istanbul: Merk Yayıncılık, 1988.

Kater, Michael H. *Composers of the Nazi Era: Eight Portraits*. New York: Oxford University Press, 2000.

Kathīr, Ismā'īl ibn 'Umar ibn. *Al-Bidāyah wa-al-nihāyah fī al-Tarīkh*, vol. 13. Cairo: Maṭbaʿat al-Saʿadah, n.d. [1939].

Kemâlettin Kâmi Kamu: Hayatı, San'atı ve Şiirleri, ed. Gültekin Sâmanoğlu. Ankara: Kültür ve Turizm Bakanlığı Yayınları, 1986.

Khan, Qamaruddin. *Al-Mawardi's Theory of the State*. Lahore, Pakistan: Islamic Book Foundation, 1983.

Kieser, Hans-Lukas. "Türkische Nationalrevolution, anthropologisch gekrönt: Kemal Atatürk und Eugène Pittard." *Historische Anthropologie* 14/1 (2006): 105–18.

Kışlalı, Ahmet Taner. "Kemalist Devrim ve Türk Aydınlanması." *Dünya ve Türkiye Açısından Atatürk*, ed. Suna Kili, 33–43. Istanbul: Yapı Kredi Yayınları, 1996.

Koçak, Cemil. "Atatürk Hakkında Bazı Belgeler: Ali Rıza Bey, Anıtkabir, MacArtur ile Mülakat." *Toplumsal Tarih* 10/119 (2003): 22–27.

————. "Kemalist Milliyetçiliğin Bulanık Suları." *Modern Türkiye'de Siyasi Düşünce*, vol. 4, *Milliyetçilik*, ed. Tanıl Bora and Murat Gültekingil, 37–43. Istanbul: İletişim Yayınları, 2002.

————. "Tek Parti Yönetimi, Kemalizm ve Şeflik Sistemi: Ebedî Şef/Millî Şef." *Modern Türkiye'de Siyasî Düşünce*, vol. 2, *Kemalizm*, ed. Ahmet İnsel, 119–37. Istanbul: İletişim Yayınları, 2001.

Köksal, M. Âsım. *Müsteşrık Caetani'nin Yazdığı İslâm Tarihi'ndeki İsnad ve İftiralara Reddiye*. Ankara: Balkanoğlu Matbaacılık, 1961.

Korsun, N[ikolai] G[eorgievich]. *Kavkazskii front Pervoi mirovoi voiny*. Moscow: Izdatel'stvo Tranzitkniga, 2004.

Kurtuluş Savaşı'nın İdeolojisi: Hakimiyeti Milliye Yazıları, ed. Hadiye Bolluk. Istanbul: Kaynak Yayınları, 2003.

Landau, Jacob M. *Jews, Arabs, Turks: Selected Essays.* Jerusalem: Magnes Press, 1993.

Łątka, Jerzy S. *Pasza z Lechistanu: Mustafa Dzëlaleddin (Konstanty Borzęcki)* Kraków: Społeczny Instytut Historii i Kultury Turcji, 1993.

Laut, Jens Peter. "Noch einmal zu Dr. Kvergić." *Turkic Languages* 6 (2002): 120–33.

———. *Das Türkische als Ursprache? Sprachwissenschaftliche Theorien in der Zeit des erwachenden türkischen Nationalismus.* Wiesbaden, Germany: Otto Harrassowitz, 2000.

Le Bon, Gustave. *Hier et demain: pensées brèves.* Paris: Ernest Flammarion, 1918.

———. *Les incertitudes de l'heure présente.* Paris: Ernest Flammarion, 1923.

———. *La révolution française et la psychologie des révolutions.* Paris: E. Flammarion, 1912.

Levend, Agâh Sırrı. *Türk Dilinde Gelişme ve Sadeleşme Evreleri.* Ankara: Türk Dil Kurumu Yayınları, 1960.

Lewis, Geoffrey. *The Turkish Language Reform: A Catastrophic Success.* New York: Oxford University Press, 1999.

Lloyd George, David. *Through Terror to Triumph: Speeches and Pronouncements of the Right Hon. David Lloyd George, M.P., since the Beginning of the War,* ed. F. L. Stevenson. London: Hodder and Stoughton, 1915.

———. *War Memoirs of David Lloyd George,* vol. 4, *1917.* Boston: Little, Brown, 1934.

Ludendorff, Erich. *Kriegführung und Politik.* Berlin: Verlag von E. S. Mittler und sohn, 1922.

Mardin, Şerif. "Super Westernization in Urban Life in the Ottoman Empire in the Last Quarter of the Nineteenth Century." In *Turkey: Geographic and Social Perspectives,* ed. Peter Benedict, Erol Tümertekin, and Fatma Mansur, 403–46. Leiden, Netherlands: Brill, 1974.

Markova, Zina. *Bŭlgarskata ekzarhia, 1870–1879.* Sofia, Bulgaria: Bŭlgarska Akademia na Naukite, 1989.

Mazower, Mark. *Salonica, City of Ghosts: Christians, Muslims and Jews, 1430–1950*. London: HarperCollins, 2004.

Mehmed Emin. *Türkçe Şiirler*. Istanbul: Matbaa-i Ahmed İhsan ve Şürekâsı, 1334 (1916).

Mehmed Es'ad. *Mir'at-ı Mekteb-i Harbiye*. Istanbul: Artin Asadoryan, 1310 [1892–93].

[Mehmed Seyyid, Çelebizâde]. *Hilâfet ve Hakimiyet-i Milliye*. Ankara: n.p., 1923.

———. *Türkiye Büyük Millet Meclisi'nin 3 Mart 1340 Tarihinde Mün'akid İkinci İctima'ında Hilâfet'in Mahiyet-i Şer'iyyesi Hakkında Adliye Vekili Seyyid Bey Tarafından İrâd Olunan Nutuk*. Ankara: Türkiye Büyük Millet Meclisi Matbaası, n.d. [1924].

Meserve, Margaret. *Empires of Islam in Renaissance Historical Thought*. Cambridge, MA: Harvard University Press, 2008.

Military Operations: Gallipoli, vol. 1, *Inception of the Campaign to May 1915*, ed. C. F. Aspinall-Oglander. London: William Heinemann, 1929.

Mill, John Stuart. *On Liberty*. London: Longmans, 1921.

Milli Kültür Özel İhtisas Komisyonu Raporu. Ankara: Başbakanlık Devlet Planlama Teşkilatı, 1983.

Montadon, George. *L'ethnie française*. Paris: Payot, 1935.

———. *La race les races: mise au point d'ethnologie somatique*. Paris: Payot, 1933.

Monteil, Vincent. *Iran: "Petite Planète."* Paris: Éditions du Seul, 1957.

Müderrisoğlu, Alptekin. *Kurtuluş Savaşının Malî Kaynakları*. Ankara: Atatürk Kültür, Dil ve Tarih Yüksek Kurumu, 1990.

Nevsâl-ı Millî, ed. T. Z. Istanbul: Artin Asadoryan, 1330 [1914].

Okay, Orhan. *Beşir Fuad: İlk Türk Pozitivist ve Natüralisti*. Istanbul: Dergâh Yayınları, 2008.

Öksüz, Yusuf Ziya. *Türkçenin Sadeleşme Tarihi: Genç Kalemler ve Yeni Lisan Hareketi*. Ankara: Türk Dil Kurumu Yayınları, 1995.

Okyar, Ali Fethi. *Serbest Cumhuriyet Fırkası Nasıl Doğdu, Nasıl Fesh Edildi?* Istanbul: n.p. [1987].

Osmanlıcadan Türkçeye Cep Kılavuzu. Istanbul: Devlet Matbaası, 1935.

The Ottoman Domination. London: T. Fisher Unwin, 1917.

Özdemir, Yavuz. *Bir Savaşın Bilinmeyen Öyküsü: Sarıkamış Harekâtı.* Erzurum: Erzurum Kalkınma Vakfı Yayınları, 2003.

Pakalın, Mehmet Zeki. *Osmanlı Tarih Deyimleri ve Terimleri Sözlüğü,* vol. 1. Istanbul: Millî Eğitim Basımevi, 1983.

Parlak, Türkmen. *Yeni Asır'ın Selânik Yılları: Evlâd-ı Fatihan Diyarları.* İzmir: Yeni Asır, 1986.

[Peker, Recep]. *C.H.P. Genel Sekreteri R. Peker'in Söylevleri.* Ankara: n.p. [1935].

———. *Recep Peker'in İnkılab Dersleri Notları.* Ankara: Ulus Basımevi, 1935.

Perinçek, Mehmet. *Atatürk'ün Sovyetler'le Görüşmeleri: Sovyet Arşiv Belgeleriyle.* Istanbul: Kaynak Yayınları, 2005.

Perry, Duncan M. *The Politics of Terror: The Macedonian Liberation Movements, 1893–1903.* Durham, NC: Duke University Press, 1988.

Pittard, Eugène. "Comparaison de quelques caractères somatologiques chez les Turcs et les Grecs." *Revue Anthropologique* 25 (1915): 447–54.

———. *Les peuples des Balkans: esquisses anthropologiques.* Paris: Attinger Frères, n.d. [1916].

———. "Quelques nouveaux crânes Grisons de la Valée du Rhin." *Bulletin de la Société d'anthropologie de Lyon* 21 (1902): 249–68.

———. *Race and History: An Ethnological Introduction to History.* New York: Alfred A. Knopf, 1926.

———. *Les races et l'histoire.* Paris: La Renaissance du Livre, 1924.

Pulhan Türk Pulları Kataloğu, vol. 12, ed. Ali Nusret Pulhan. Istanbul: Fen Fakültesi Basımevi, 1973.

Qureshi, M. Naem. *Pan-Islam in British Indian Politics: A Study of the Khilafat Movement, 1918–1924.* Leiden, Netherlands: Brill, 1999.

Rahman, Fazlur. *Islam.* Chicago: University of Chicago Press, 1979.

Rashīd Riḍā. *Al-Khilāfa aw al-imāma al-ʿuẓmā.* Cairo: Maṭbaʿat al-Manār, 1341 (1923).

Raz-Krakotzkin, Amnon. "The Zionist Return to the West and the Mizrahi Jewish Perspective." In *Orientalism and Jews,* ed. Ivan Davidson Kalmar and Derek J. Penslar, 162–81. Waltham, MA: Brandeis University Press, 2005.

Resolutions of the All India Muslim League from October 1937 to December 1938, ed. Liaquat Ali Khan. Delhi: Muslim League Printing Press, n.d. [1944].

Rousseau, J[ean]-J[acques]. *Du Contrat sociale ou principes du droit politique*. Amsterdam: Mark Michel Rey, 1762.

Rouvier, Catherine. *Les idées politiques de Gustave Le Bon*. Paris: Presses Universitaires de France, 1986.

Rudenno, Victor. *Gallipoli: Attack from the Sea*. New Haven, CT: Yale University Press, 2008.

Rupp, Leila J. "Challenging Imperialism in International Women's Organization, 1888–1945." In *Identity Politics in the Women's Movement*, ed. Barbara Ryan, 245–60. New York: New York University Press, 2001.

Sadri Maksudi. *Türk Dili İçin: Türk Dilindeki Sözleri Toplama, Dizme, Türk Dilini Ayırtlama, Türkçe Köklerden Bilgi Sözleri Yaratma İşi Üzerinde Düşünceler*. İstanbul. Türk Ocakları İlim ve Sanat Heyeti Neşriyatı, 1930.

Sagadaev, A[rtur] V[ladimirovitch]. *Mirsait Sultan-Galiev i ideologinatsional'no-osvoboditel'nogo dvizheniiaa: Nauchno-analiticheskii obzor*. Moscow: Akademiia nauk, 1990.

Sanhoury, A[hmad]. *Le Califat: son évolution vers une société des nations orientale*. Paris: P. Geuthner, 1926.

Scholem, Gershom. *Sabbatai Şevi: The Mystical Messiah, 1626–1676*. Princeton, NJ: Princeton University Press, 1973.

Şevket Süreyya. *İnkılâp ve Kadro: İnkılâbın İdeolojisi*. Ankara: Muallim Halit Kitaphanesi, 1932.

Shaw, Wendy. "The Rise of the Hittite Sun: A Deconstruction of Western Civilization from the Margin." In *Selective Remembrances: Archaeology in the Construction, Commemoration, and Consecration of National Pasts*, ed. Philip L. Kohl, Mara Kozelsky, and Nachman Ben-Yehuda, 163–88. Chicago: University of Chicago Press, 2007.

Sherrill, Charles H. *A Year's Embassy to Mustafa Kemal*. New York: Charles Scribner's Sons, 1934.

Şimşek, Sefa. *Bir İdeolojik Seferberlik Deneyimi: Halkevleri, 1932–1951*. Istanbul: Boğaziçi Üniversitesi Yayınevi, 2002.

Şimşir, Bilâl N. *Doğunun Kahramanı Atatürk.* Istanbul: Bilgi Yayınevi, 1999.

[Sinan, Mimar]. *Sâî Mustafa Çelebi, Yapılar Kitabı: Tezkiretü'l-Bünyan ve Tezkiretü'l-Ebniye (Mimar Sinan'ın Anıları)*, ed. Hayati Develi. Istanbul: K Kitaplığı, 2003.

Sivas Kongresi Tutanakları, ed. Uluğ İğdemir. Ankara: Türk Tarih Kurumu Yayınları, 1969.

Smooha, Sammy. "Jewish Ethnicity in Israel: Symbolic or Real?" In *Jews in Israel: Contemporary Social and Cultural Patterns*, ed. Uzi Rebhun and Chaim I. Waxman, 47–80. Hanover, NH: Brandeis University Press, 2004.

Snegarov, Iv[an]. *Solun v bŭlgarskata dukhovna kultura: istoricheski ocherk i dokumenti.* Sofia, Bulgaria: Pridvorna Petchatnitsa, 1937.

Sökmen, Tayfur. *Hatay'ın Kurtuluşu İçin Harcanan Çabalar.* Ankara: Türk Tarih Kurumu Yayınları, Ankara 1978.

Spencer, Robert F. "Culture Process and Intellectual Current: Durkheim and Atatürk." *American Anthropologist* 60/4 (1958): 640–57.

Stewart, Desmond. *The Middle East: Temple of Janus.* Garden City, NY: Doubleday, 1971.

Subkī, Tāj al-Dīn ʿAbd al-Wahhāb ibn ʿAlī. *Ṭabaqāt al-Shāfiʿīyah al-kubrā*, vol. 3. Cairo: Maṭbaʿat ʿĪsā al-Bābī al-Ḥalabī wa shurakāʾ, n.d., [1964].

Sulaymān Musā. *Al-Ḥusayn ibn ʿAlī waʾl-thawra al-ʿArabīya al-kubrā.* Amman, Jordan: Lajnat Tārīkh al-Urdunn, 1992.

Taghrī-Birdī, Yūsuf ibn. *Al-Nujūm al-zāhirah fī mulūk Miṣr wa-al-Qāhirah*, vol. 7. Cairo: Maṭbaʿat Dār al-Kutub al-Miṣriyya, 1938.

Tanör, Bülent. *Türkiye'de Kongre İktidarları, 1918–1920.* Istanbul: Yapı ve Kredi Bankası Yayınları, 1998.

Tanzimat, I. Istanbul: Maarif Vekâleti, 1940.

Tarih, I: *Tarihtenevvelki Zamanlar ve Eski Zamanlar*; II: *Ortazamanlar*; III: *Yeni ve Yakın Zamanlarda Osmanlı-Türk Tarihi*; IV: *Türkiye Cümhuriyeti.* Istanbul: Devlet Matbaası, 1931.

Tarihçeleri ve Açıklamaları ile Birlikte Türkiye'nin Siyasal Andlaşmaları, vol. 1, *1920–1945*, ed. İsmail Soysal. Ankara: Türk Tarih Kurumu Yayınları, 1983.

T.D.K. Türkçe Sözlük: Türk Dil Kurumu Lûgat Kolu Çalışmalariyle Hazırlanmıştır. Istanbul: Cumhuriyet Basımevi, 1945.

Tekeli, İlhan-İlkin, Selim. *Bir Cumhuriyet Öyküsü: Kadrocuları ve Kadro'yu Anlamak.* Istanbul: Tarih Vakfı Yurt Yayınları, 2003.

Temo, Ibrahim. *Atatürkü N'için Severim?* Medgidia, Romania: n.p., 1937.

Tevetoğlu, Fethi. *Ömer Naci.* Ankara: Kültür ve Turizm Bakanlığı Yayınları, 1987.

Thompson, Mark R. "The Survival of 'Asian Values' as 'Zivilisationkritik.'" *Theory and Society* 29/5 (2000): 651–86.

Toynbee, Arnold J. *Survey of International Affairs, 1925,* vol. 1. Oxford: Oxford University Press, 1927.

Tucker, Robert C. "Personality and Political Leadership." *Political Science Quarterly* 92/3 (1977): 383–93.

Tunaya, Tarık Zafer. *Devrim Hareketleri İçinde Atatürk ve Atatürkçülük.* Istanbul: Turhan Kitabevi, 1981.

———. *Türkiye'de Siyasal Partiler,* vol. 2, *Mütareke Dönemi, 1918–1922.* Istanbul: Hürriyet Vakfı Yayınları, 1986.

———. *Türkiye'de Siyasal Partiler,* vol. 3, *İttihat ve Terakki, Bir Çağın, Bir Kuşağın, Bir Partinin Tarihi.* Istanbul: Hürriyet Vakfı Yayınları, 1989.

Tunçay, Mete. "Atatürk'e Nasıl Bakmak." *Toplum ve Bilim,* 1/4 (1977): 86–92.

———. "İkinci Meclis Tutanaklarında İlginç Bir Montaj Olayı." *Toplumsal Tarih* 10/105 (2002): 24–25.

———. *T.C.'nde Tek Parti Yönetimi'nin Kurulması, 1923–1931.* Istanbul: Cem Yayınevi, 1989.

———. *Türkiye'de Sol Akımlar, I, 1908–1925,* vol. 1. Istanbul: BDS Yayınları, 1991.

III. Türk Tarih Kongresi: Kongreye Sunulan Tebliğler. Ankara: Türk Tarih Kurumu Yayınları, 1948.

Türkçeden Osmanlıcaya Cep Kılavuzu. Istanbul: Devlet Basımevi, 1935.

Türk Tarihinin Ana Hatları, ed. Afet et al. Istanbul: Devlet Matbaası, 1930.

Turner, Bryan S. "Islam, Capitalism and the Weber Theses." *British Journal of Sociology* 25/2 (June 1974): 230–43.

'Ubayd Allāh [al]-Afghānī. *Kavm-i Cedîd: Kitabü'l-Mevâiz*. Istanbul: Şems Matbaası, 1331 [1913].

Ünaydın, Ruşen Eşref. *Atatürk: Tarih ve Dil Kurumları Hâtıralar; VII. Türk Dil Kurultayında Söylenmiştir*. Ankara: T.D.K., 1954.

———. *Türk Dil Tetkik Cemiyeti'nin Kuruluşundan İlk Kurultaya Kadar Hâtıralar*. Ankara: Recep Ulusoğlu Basımevi, 1943.

Us, Hakkı Tarık. *Meclis-i Mebusan, 1293 =1877*, vol. 2. Istanbul: Vakit Kütüphanesi, 1954.

Vacalopoulos, Apostolos E. *A History of Thessaloniki*, trans. T. F. Carney, Thessaloniki, Greece: Institute for Balkan Studies, 1972.

Vishniak, M[ark] V[en'iaminovich]. *Vserossiiskoe uchreditel'noe sobranie*. Paris: Sovremennyia zapiski, 1932.

Vryonis, Speros, Jr. "The Ottoman Conquest of Thessaloniki in 1430." In *Continuity and Change in Late Byzantine and Early Ottoman Society*, ed. Anthony Bryer and Heath Lowry, 281–321. Washington, DC: Dumbarton Oaks Research Library and Collection, 1986.

Walder, David. *The Chanak Affair*. London: Hutchinson, 1969.

Wells, H[erbert] G[eorge]. *The Outline of History: Being a Plain History of Life and Mankind*, vols. 1, 4. New York: Review of Reviews, 1924.

White, Arthur Silva. *The Expansion of Egypt under Anglo-Egyptian Condominium*. New York: New Amsterdam, 1900.

Widenor, William C. *Henry Cabot Lodge and the Search for an American Foreign Policy*. Berkeley and Los Angeles: University of California Press, 1980.

Wittich, Dieter. *Vogt, Moleschott, Büchner; Schriften zum kleinbürgerlichen Materialismus in Deutschland*, vols. 1–2. Berlin: Akademie-Verlag, 1971.

Yerolympos, Alexandra, and Colonas, Vassilis. "Un urbanisme cosmopolite." In *Salonique, 1850–1918: La "ville des Juifs" et le réveil des Balkans*, ed. Gilles Veinstein, 158–76. Paris: Autrement, 1993.

Yiğit, Nuyan. *Atatürk'le 30 Yıl: İbrahim Süreyya Yiğit'in Öyküsü*. Istanbul: Remzi Kitabevi, 2004.

Zihnioğlu, Yaprak. *Kadınsız İnkılap: Nezihe Muhiddin, Kadınlar Halk Fırkası, Kadın Birliği*. Istanbul: Metis Yayınları, 2003.

Ziogou-Karastergiou, Sidiroula. "Education in Thessaloniki: The Ottoman Period, 1430–1912." In *Queen of the Worthy: Thessaloniki: History and Culture*, ed. I. K. Hassiotis, 351–67. Thessaloniki, Greece: Paratiritis, 1997.

Zürcher, Erik Jan. "Atatürk as a Young Turk." *New Perspectives on Turkey* 22/41(2009): 211–26.

———. *Political Opposition in the Early Turkish Republic: The Progressive Republican Party, 1924–1925*. Leiden, Netherlands: Brill, 1991.

———. *The Unionist Factor: The Rôle of the Committee of Union and Progress in the Turkish National Movement, 1905–1926*. Leiden, Netherlands: Brill, 1984.

———. "The Vocabulary of Muslim Nationalism." *International Journal of the Sociology of Science* 137 (1999): 81–92.

Journals and Newspapers

Akşam (Istanbul)
Asker (Istanbul)
Belgelerle Türk Tarihi Dergisi (Istanbul)
Belleten (Ankara)
Cumhuriyet (Istanbul)
Genc Kalemler (Salonica)
Hakimiyet-i Milliye (Ankara)
Harb Mecmuası (Istanbul)
Hürriyet (Istanbul)
Hürriyet-i Fikriye (Istanbul)
İctihad (Cairo and Istanbul; it also appeared as *İştihad*)
International Affairs (Moscow)
İslâm Mecmuası (Istanbul)
Kadro (Istanbul)
Al-Manār (Cairo)
Mehtab (Istanbul)

Mizan (Geneva)
Musavver Cihan (Istanbul)
Öz Dilimize Doğru (Istanbul)
Sırat-ı Mustakim (Istanbul)
Tarih Vesikaları (Ankara)
The Times (London)
Toplumsal Tarih (Istanbul)
Türk (Cairo)
Türk Antropoloji Mecmuası (Istanbul)
Türk Dili (Ankara)
La Turquie Kamâliste (*Kemaliste*) (Ankara)
Ülkü (Ankara)
Vakit (Istanbul)
Yirminci Asırda Zekâ (Istanbul)
Yücel (Istanbul)

Electronic Sources

"Making France a Power for the Future-I." *National Interest Online*, April 17, 2007. Accessed January 9, 2009 at http://www.national interest.org/Article.aspx?id=14044.

"Hitit Güneşi Manevrası Yargıdan Döndü." April 11, 2008. Accessed June 17, 2008 at http://www.yapi.com.tr/Haberler/haber_ Detay_60927.html.

Sevilay Yükselir. "O Söz Atatürk'e Ait Değil Ama Atatürk'çe Bir Söz!" February 26, 2008. Accessed February 27, 2008 at http://www.ga zeteport.com.tr/Yazarlar/News/Gp_162225.

INDEX

Muslim Ottomans did not normally have family names. An individual might be known by his personal name (e.g., "Mustafa"), by a combination of his birth name and personal name (e.g., "Ali Rıza"), by a combination of an adjective indicating his place of birth and his personal name (e.g., "Langazalı Hüseyin Ağa, born in Langaza"), by a combination of an honorific and his personal name (e.g., "Çakırcalı Mehmed"), or by combination of a patronymic indicating the geneaology of his family and his personal name (e.g., "Sofuzâde Feyzullah, descended from Sofu"). In this index Muslim Ottoman names are therefore alphabetized by personal name: "Ali Rıza" and not "Rıza, Ali"; "Hüseyin Ağa Langazalı" and not "Langazalı Hüseyin Ağa"; "Mehmed Çakırcalı" and not "Çakırcalı Mehmed"; and "Feyzullah Sofuzâde" rather than "Sofuzâde Feyzullah." An exception is made for those individuals who survived long enough into the Republican period to adopt family names in accordance with the Surname Law of June 21, 1934, which required all citizens of the Turkish Republic to adopt a family name by January 1, 1935. Such individuals are alphabetized by family name: "Kansu, Şevket Aziz" rather than "Şevket Aziz."

lower classes and Muslim clerics, 12–13
Ottoman Freedom Society, 64
Ottoman-Greek War (1897), 71
Ottoman Red Crescent, 93
Ottoman Union Committee, 51
Ottomanism, 26–27, 28, 133; proponents of, 94
Outline of History, The (Wells), 162
Özsoy (Genuine Ancestor [Saygun]), 220

Pahlavi, Reza Shah, 204, 223
Palestine, 81, 87
Papillault, Georges, 170
Paris Peace Conference (1919), 90
Paris Treaty (1856), 202
Partito Nazionale Fascista (Italy), 190
Peker, Mehmet Recep, 190–91; opposition of to liberalism, 190–91n104
Pektaş, Mihri İffet, 206
People's Chambers, 190
People's Group, 116
People's Houses, 190, 223
People's Party (later Republican People's Party), 143–44, 150, 158, 161, 190, 197, 209; identification of as Atatürk's party, 184, 231–32
Persians, 63, 87
Peter the Great, 11
Pittard, Eugène, 167–69, 167–68n26
Poincaré, Raymond, 121
Polish Constitution (1921), 157
Polklozic-Borzęcki, Konstanty. See Mustafa Celâleddin Pasha
polygamy, 62
populism, 109, 111–13
positivism, 51, 131, 226, 228
Pour bien connaître les usages mondains (L'Heureux), 206

Progressive Republican Party, 144
Protestant Reformation, 56
La psychologie de quelques éléments des langues turques (Kvergić), 176–77

Qur'ān, the, 131, 132, 224; modern interpretation of, 156; Turkish translation of, 154, 154n78

racism, 167–68, 196; ethnoracism, 167
Le Radical, 91
Rahman, Fazlur, 139
Ralliement, 154
Reform Group, 116
religion, 12–13, 61, 62, 154, 155, 160–61, 193; abandonment of, 157, 230; concept of civic religion, 181–83; control of, 159, marginalization of in Europe, 56; role of in society, 157; Turkification of, 63. See also Islam, as the "Arab religion"; Atatürk, Mustafa Kemal, and opinion of religion; religion, and science
religion, and science, 53–54, 55; triumph of science over religion, 51
"Religion According to a Turk" (Ziya Gökalp), 62
Republic of Turkey, 23, 62–63, 94, 141; abolishment of madrasahs, ṭarīqas, and dervish lodges in, 155; abolishment of the Sharī'a Courts in, 158; adoption of the Gregorian calendar, 159, 217–18; adoption of a modified 1881 Swiss Code of Obligations, 158; adoption of a modified 1912 Swiss Civil Code, 158, 209; elimination of Ṣūfī religious establishment, 156; emancipation of women in, 208–10, 212–